W9-ACJ-266

Fast Food, Stock Cars,
and Rock 'n' Roll

Fast Food, Stock Cars, and Rock 'n' Roll

Place and Space in American Pop Culture

Edited by
George O. Carney

ROWMAN & LITTLEFIELD PUBLISHERS, INC.

ROWMAN & LITTLEFIELD PUBLISHERS, INC.

Published in the United States of America
by Rowman & Littlefield Publishers, Inc.
4720 Boston Way, Lanham, Maryland 20706

3 Henrietta Street
London WC2E 8LU, England

Copyright © 1995 by Rowman & Littlefield Publishers, Inc.

All rights reserved. No part of this publication may be reproduced,
stored in a retrieval system, or transmitted in any form or by any
means, electronic, mechanical, photocopying, recording, or otherwise,
without the prior permisison of the publisher.

British Cataloging in Publication Information Available

Library of Congress Cataloging-in-Publication Data

Fast food, stock cars, and rock 'n' roll : place and space in American
pop culture / edited by George O. Carney.
p.   cm.
Includes bibliographical references and index.
1. Popular culture—United States—History—20th century.
2. United States—Social life and customs—20th century.
I. Carney, George O.
E169.02.F37   1995   306.4'097—dc20   95-22422   CIP

ISBN 0-8476-8079-7 (cloth: alk. paper)
ISBN 0-8476-8080-0 (pbk.: alk. paper)

Printed in the United States of America

 The paper used in this publication meets the minimum requirements of
American National Standard for Information Sciences—Permanence of
Printed Library Materials, ANSI Z39.48—1984.

To Janie, Brian, and Mark

Contents

Illustrations

Graphs

Tables

Preface

It may seem ironic that one who was reared in the folk culture environment of the Missouri Ozarks would edit an anthology on geography and popular culture. I spent roughly the first eighteen years of my life on a 360-acre farm experiencing the rural/agrarian lifestyle of milking cows, bucking baled hay, and cultivating corn and soybeans with my "B" Farmall tractor. I attended a one-room country school and a one-room country church. Since then, most of my adult life has been confined to the small-town university atmosphere of Stillwater, Oklahoma, a community of approximately twenty thousand people (not counting students)—certainly not what one could describe as a metroplex!

Scholars claim that popular culture is generally based on large, heterogeneous populations concentrated mainly in urban areas. Apparently, my lifetime experiences with popular culture ran contrary to this assumption. I was first influenced by popular culture in the isolated backwaters of Missouri through the process of cultural osmosis. Later, the younger set, primarily my children and students, affected my popular culture preferences via the cultural milieu (or my surroundings).

Unknowingly, two major popular media transformed my rural lifestyle—radio and television. Some insist that television was the principal catalyst for popular culture; I contend, however, that radio was the first electronic medium to affect farm folks.

I retain vivid memories of my mother turning the knob on our Philco table model radio, which sat alongside the kitchen table, to the radio "soaps." She was as much a fan as are those glued to *Days of Our Lives* in today's culture. Her favorites were *The Romance of Helen Trent* and *Portia Faces Life*. And I would listen and follow the daily dialogue while helping her stem green beans in preparation for the summer canning process.

My father also had his nightly favorites on the radio. He preferred the comedy shows such as *Fibber McGee and Molly* and *Amos 'n' Andy* or the mystery programs like *The Green Hornet*. Huddled in front of the radio, we enjoyed those rare opportunities for family time together because Mom and Dad worked from sunup to sundown—a typical schedule for farm families. And, of course, I had my own special radio programs that were listened to religiously each afternoon after my daily chore of milking "Old Daisy" was completed. There was *Bobby Benson and the B-B Riders*, *Sgt. Preston of the Yukon*, and *Skye King*. These adventure programs fueled the imagination of youngsters like me who sought heroes on the radio airwaves.

Radio also sparked my interest in sports, particularly baseball. When I was about six, my parents started taking me to the barbershop in Calhoun, the nearest town of 350 people. Rather than sport "crock" haircuts given by my mother (a crock was placed over my head and the hair was trimmed around the base), they decided I needed a more professional look.

Jimmy Martin was the only barber in Calhoun. He was a fanatic baseball fan, namely the St. Louis Cardinals. Their broadcasts were carried over radio station KDRO in Sedalia, which included Calhoun in its listening area. Nestled among the hair tonic bottles near the barber's chair was Jimmy's radio. He always had it tuned to the Cardinals broadcasts on Saturday afternoons when my haircut was scheduled. I became fascinated with the play-by-play announcing of Harry Caray, who made the game almost seem alive. The Redbirds became my team. Shortly thereafter, I subscribed to *The Sporting News* and closely followed the farm teams of the Cardinals from Class D to AAA.

In 1954, when I was twelve, the ultimate of my sports dreams came true. Accompanied by a friend and his uncle, I boarded the Missouri Pacific passenger train in Warrensburg for the ride to St. Louis, where I witnessed my first major-league game. It was the Cardinals versus the New York Giants at old Sportsman's Park. Harry Caray's play-by-play came to life as I watched Stan "The Man" Musial, Ray Jablonski, Rip Repulski, and Harvey Haddix, my Redbird heroes. And the Giants counted among their stars the "Say Hey" kid, Willie Mays. Another form of popular culture had become a part of my life—baseball. And it had been introduced to me via the radio.

Radio likewise opened my ears to two genres of popular music in the 1950s: rock 'n' roll and country. WHB (World's Happiest Broadcasters) in Kansas City was one of the first stations in the United States to initiate a Top 40 programming format. When Mom was not tuned into a soap opera, I had the dial set on WHB. It was through radio that I became familiar with Chuck Berry, Bo Diddley, Jerry Lee Lewis, and other pioneer artists of the rock 'n' roll era. On Saturday mornings, I listened avidly to the *Hillbilly Hit Parade* on KCMO, another Kansas City station. My favorites were Ernest Tubb ("I'm Walking the Floor Over You") and Hank Williams ("Your Cheatin' Heart").

My generation spanned the transition from radio to television in the post-World War II era. I still recall the day we purchased our first television set—a console Philco model. It had a special place in the northeast corner of our living room. As most farm boys are accustomed, I would rise early in the morning. The new television provided breakfast fare with Dave Garroway (replete with bow tie and horn-rimmed glasses); Jack Lescoulie, the weatherman; and J. Fredd Muggs, the lovable chimpanzee who waved to onlookers outside the NBC studio in Rockefeller Plaza. This morning television ritual was repeated upon my return from school in the afternoon. Howdy Doody, Buffalo Bob, and Clarabelle captured my attention in the "peanut gallery" of our family farmhouse. By 1954, *American Bandstand* was on in the afternoon. The venerable Dick Clark, sporting his Pepsodent smile, was the host. The young, skinny farm "hick" could now view the latest dance steps performed by the teenagers from South Philly.

For family time in front of the television, we immersed ourselves in the *Lawrence Welk Show* on Saturdays and the *Ed Sullivan Show* on Sundays. These programs were broadcast during "suppertime" (dinner hour). The television transformed our daily routine and dietary habits because Mom purchased "TV trays" so we could eat "TV dinners" while watching these programs. Additional segments of my lifestyle were undergoing transition because of popular culture.

Beyond the influence of radio and television in the home, I viewed further changes in our lifestyle. It was customary for farm families to make a weekly sojourn to the county seat for shopping. For the Carney family, the weekly routine was to Clinton (county seat of Henry County), a town of approximately five thousand people. One of the first stops was the A & P, then referred to as a "combination grocery store" from back East. It featured sliced loaf bread in a package ("Tastee" was our favorite brand), assorted fresh fruits and vegetables in the "produce" section, dairy products (bottled milk and packaged butter), and fresh meat prepared by a butcher on duty. This was a dramatic change because our family had produced all these items on the farm, but they could now be purchased in one store with little effort or time involved.

A second stop was at the J. C. Penney store, one of the first department store chains. Clinton was able to boast of such a store because Mr. Penney was a native Missourian. Here we bought ready-made clothing without my Mom having to sit for hours in front of the old Singer sewing machine. The culmination of our Saturday trip was a visit to the A & W Drive-In. Here we feasted on burgers, chili dogs, and a frosty mug of their famed root beer.

It was a time when I first experienced the "franchising" of the American retail industry.

As a high school teenager in the 1950s, I was subjected to the cultural innovations of that decade. Especially affected was music. It was the emerging era of rock 'n' roll, a time when the young generation claimed a music it could call its own. The period was marked by teenagers singing for teenagers, with emphasis on themes that focused on the teen lifestyle. "Teenager in Love," "Sweet Little Sixteen," and "Sixteen Candles," for example, reflected the home and school life of puppy love, soda shops, and study halls. Incidentally, both "Sweet Little Sixteen" and "Sixteen Candles" were recorded in 1958, when I turned sixteen. This new music genre constituted a major force in recasting American culture. A generational gap opened as teenagers disavowed the music of Frank Sinatra, Perry Como, and Jo Stafford, their parents' music, and embraced the likes of Bill Haley, Little Richard, and Elvis Presley.

Associated with the music were changes in teenage dress, vocabulary, dance, food, and cars. Even in our small high school of only forty students, the girls wore poodle skirts and tied their hair in pony tails, while the boys donned leather jackets and sported duck-tails and sideburns à la Elvis. Our high school "sock hops" featured 45-rpm records spun by one of the local boys who served as DJ (disc jockey), a new term of the 1950s. The latest dance steps included "The Stroll," "The Monkey," and "The Swim." "Cool Cat" was a new term of honor bestowed upon a popular male. The evening "at the hop" was topped off with a stop at the local soda fountain or drive-in, where we could partake of our favorite teenage food and drink such as Coca-Cola (Cokes), chocolate malts, burger and fries, or cherry limeades. Finally, we would pile in someone's '57 Chevy for the ride to "Blueberry Hill" for some "smoochin'."

I entered college the fall of 1960. The "sixties" was to be a decade of social and political ferment, although as an innocent freshman I was unaware of what was to happen. John Fitzgerald Kennedy had been elected president. Politically speaking, that was a momentous change in itself, for he was the first Roman Catholic to occupy the White House as well as the youngest (42) to hold the highest office in the land. His inaugural address outlining the "New Frontier" spoke of optimism and idealism. An emphasis on reaching the moon, the Peace Corps, and civil rights held promise for young Americans who sought heroes in the political realm.

But the American scene turned sour with the assassination of JFK in 1963 and the continued escalation of American involvement in Vietnam. These events spawned numerous changes in American culture, especially among my generation. "The War" turned many college-age youth off. They "tuned out" by seeking refuge in the "hippie" movement, which indulged in communal living, hallucinated with LSD, and "turned on" to the sounds of the acid/psychedelic rock of the Jefferson Airplane and the Grateful Dead.

As for me, I was drafted in 1965. After failing my physical, I entered graduate school and decided on a teaching career. Although I never "turned on" to the drug scene of the 1960s, the era affected me in other ways. My opposition to the Vietnam War resulted in participation in campus war moratoriums and political campaigning for Gene McCarthy for president in 1968. I took on some of the trappings associated with the sixties including shoulder-length hair, sideburns and moustache, bell-bottom pants, "love" beads, and the singing of "protest" songs.

By the time I finished graduate school with a Ph.D. in hand, Richard Nixon had withdrawn from Vietnam, civil rights legislation was in force, and the moon had been reached. And I was looking for both employment and a wife. During the latter stages of my Ph.D. study, I met a southern girl (Hapeville, Georgia). We dated for a couple of years and were married. About the same time, I was invited to join the newly created Department of Geography at Oklahoma State University. As was the case with most baby-boomers who had experienced the 1960s, I settled into married life, purchased a home, and produced two sons within the next five years.

With the new family lifestyle, I entered into a different arena of popular culture in the 1970s. Television once again played a key role during this period. Now I was viewing *Sesame Street, Mr. Rogers' Neighborhood,* and Saturday morning cartoons with my offspring. Dr. Seuss books became the primary reading material around the house and Fisher-Price toys (some of which we have in our attic) were the dominant playthings. Finally, Dr. Spock's books were the sources we consulted for guidance on child-rearing.

Popular culture continued to occupy a major portion of our family life-style as we moved into the 1980s. The boys began piano lessons, played Little League baseball, and participated in school activities. It was a busy time, with the primary focus on the children and the parents serving as chauffeurs.

My wife and I reverted to our country music roots. We started attending bluegrass music festivals in Oklahoma. My car radio dial was locked on "Big Country" KVOO out of Tulsa, while my wife preferred KEBC ("Keep Everybody Country") broadcast from Oklahoma City. We also began to observe more closely the cultural landscape of Oklahoma. Weekend jaunts took us to Tulsa for tours of the futuristic architecture on the Oral Roberts University campus and the extraordinary examples of Art Deco ("Okie Deco") found in the city's downtown buildings. Route 66 ("The Mother

Road of America") also attracted us on our peripatetic wanderings of the state as we traveled from Claremore (Will Rogers country) to Guthrie ("Williamsburg of the West"). The intact gas stations, motels, and drive-ins along Route 66 conveyed a sense of mobility that so heavily influenced popular culture in the twentieth century. Finally, our summer vacations with the children took us to the popular culture "fantasylands" including Disney World, Opryland, and Dollywood—theme parks that have become American icons.

As the boys grew into adolescence, teenage music pervaded our house-hold. Because of my abiding interest in popular music, I did not "tune it out." They listened to a variety of music and introduced me to the "head-banging" heavy metal of Metallica, the smooth harmony sound of Boys II Men, and the rap chants of LL Cool J.

In terms of fashion, my teenage sons kept me abreast with the latest jeans look (brands, hues, and fits), tennis shoes, and hats. Junk food became a part of our daily diet, from Snickers candy bars to Hostess Twinkies con-sumed in the home to a myriad of fast foods offered by Arby's, Hardee's, and McDonald's. Thus my children have been profound influences in the shaping of my popular culture preferences for more than twenty years.

College students have likewise greatly influenced my perspective on pop-ular culture. Each day of the week hundreds of them enter my classroom or office sporting the latest trends in contemporary culture. For the past ten years, I have conducted a student survey in my introductory cultural geogra-phy sections (approximately 150 students) to determine what is "in" and "out" in their lifestyle choices. Not unexpected from the results of this annual poll is the rapidity with which students change their cultural tastes, a key element in popular culture criteria. During the past decade, for exam-ple, potato bars, Michael Jackson, Coca-Cola shirts, kinky perms, twist bead necklaces, and bomber jackets have become passé.

As I write this preface (1995), the standard college "uniform" is jeans of some sort (color, brand, and fit vary), baseball caps (both men and women) labeled with a college or pro sports team logo, T-shirts (emblazoned with innumerable objects and phrases), and tennis shoes (styles, colors, and brands too numerous to mention). Mid-1990s leisure activities beyond the classroom include large-scale music concerts (Rolling Stones Voodoo Lounge Tour in Dallas, the Grateful Dead extravaganza in St. Louis, or the George Strait performance in Oklahoma City), watching favorite "soaps" and TV "sitcoms" (*Days of Our Lives* and *Cheers* are the most popular in these categories), and reading (Danielle Steel and Stephen King are the most preferred).

Young people are the principal innovators and carriers of popular culture.

They exude the latest, most contemporary trends in music, clothing, food, dance steps, television programming, film, and literature. Some criticize the emphasis on allowing the younger generation to set national trends; however, as a former member of the youth culture, father, and educator, it has been an exciting and dynamic ride through the past forty-five years of popular culture from the time I entered the halls of that one-room country school in Missouri to the present-day happenings in Office 301 in the Geography Building on the Oklahoma State campus.

In closing, let me remind you that popular culture varies from place to place across this vast landscape we call America. The popular culture traits and trends that I have described may not have happened in your locale. It is possible that an entirely different set of popular culture characteristics may have emerged in your area of the country. I suspect, however, that many of the traits described herein were experienced in your region because they were of such profound influence throughout America.

I now invite you to join me as we explore seven popular culture topics from a geographical viewpoint—music, clothing, food, religion, architecture, politics, and sports. This collection of readings was assembled and edited with no vested interests on my part—they are for your edification and gratification in hopes you will reach a fuller and richer understanding of popular culture and its geographic implications. It is a collection born out of my interest in popular culture and one that I wanted to share with college students. Thus, it is a labor of love with you in mind.

Acknowledgments

Editing a book is by no means an easy task. It is a time-consuming and demanding piece of work; yet, at the same time, an extremely challenging and rewarding experience. It is acknowledged that without the interest and cooperation of many individuals, *Fast Food, Stock Cars, and Rock 'n' Roll* would not have been possible. My debts to these people are many.

I wish to express my gratitude, first of all, to those authors who contributed articles to this anthology. Thirteen popular culture scholars graciously provided support and encouragement throughout the editorial process. Many of them furnished photographs and maps as well as responded to editorial inquiries.

Second, acknowledgment is in order to Jon Sisk, editor in chief of Rowman & Littlefield, who gave me the opportunity to put in print the best collection of readings on geography and popular culture. Much credit goes to Jon and his staff for the advancement of scholarship in the field of geography. I want to express my sincere appreciation to Jennifer Ruark, acquisitions editor, and Julie Kirsch, managing editor, for their constructive support during completion of the book.

Finally, the personnel in the Oklahoma State University Department of Geography is first class. Kimberly Cundiff, chief word processor, spent countless hours in preparation of the manuscript. Had it not been for Kimberly this project would never have been realized. A special note of thanks to Susan Shaull, department office supervisor, who keeps our operation running efficiently and smoothly. A note of gratitude is extended to Tom Wikle, my department head, who has lent positive support to my academic projects and provided a professional atmosphere for all of us.

Introduction

Culture: A Workable Definition

George O. Carney

To define culture is an elusive exercise. It has long enjoyed wide currency, and its meaning has changed over time. There is "culture" in the sense of tillage or cultivation when it refers to a skilled human activity such as agriculture or viticulture. It also connotes possession of standards of value and discrimination, and implies refinement and learning, as in a "cultured" person. Finally, it often indicates a collection of intellectual and artistic activities produced by a people of like spirit. However, as used in this anthology, culture has a broader, more all-encompassing definition.

One of the first to give culture a more all-inclusive interpretation was Paul Vidal de la Blache, the father of modern French geography. Almost a century ago, Vidal defined it as a concept that deals with a way of life (*genre de vie*). It refers to the inherited traits that members of a group learn. According to Vidal, culture included the complex set of institutions, attitudes, purposes, and technical skills of a people. Since that time, a wide range of definitions has been presented in the academic literature. After carefully scrutinizing a multitude of these, I have determined that six overriding characteristics appear to be common in all of them.

First, culture is what distinguishes humans from other living forms and sets us apart as a unique form of life. As "culture bearers," we are able to communicate our cumulative experiences, and we are the first species capable of consciously and deliberately altering the course of our own destinies.

Second, culture is learned behavior, not biological—in other words, it has nothing to do with our genes. It is transmitted within a society to succeeding generations by imitation, instruction, and example. We all learn something of the culture we are born into, our cultural milieu; however, we do

1

not learn all of it, because age, sex, occupation, and status may affect which parts of the whole we learn.

Third, culture embraces a set of learned phenomena (values, morals, habits, ideas, beliefs, attitudes, customs, livelihood, and language, to name a few) that a group of people hold in common and that binds them together through communication and interaction with one another.

Fourth, culture serves as a filter or lens into our society. It is that acquired knowledge called culture that we use to make sense of the events through which we live. We use it to interpret human experiences and to orient ourselves in a chaotic world.

Fifth, culture shapes human behavior to produce mentifacts (nonmaterial) and artifacts (material)—those intangible (e.g., religious beliefs and political ideologies) and tangible (e.g., clothing and buildings) components of culture.

Finally, it should be made clear that there is a distinction between culture as a collective body and cultures, the parts of the totality. The splitting and branching of human beings over the Earth gave rise to individual cultures. These "cultures"—the systems that developed as ways of life by many fragments of humankind—gradually came into existence via the unique experiences in space and time of various population groups.

For this anthology, a simple definition, which summarizes the aforementioned trademarks of culture, provides a workable definition for our purposes. It combines Vidal's nineteenth-century definition with a contemporary characterization by geographer Terry Jordan: *culture is the total way of life held in common by a group of people.*

In sum, culture is our everyday lifestyle, or what we do from the time we rise in the morning until we retire in the evening. This fulfills our objective of defining culture as a whole and gives us a framework into which we can incorporate popular culture and analyze its relationship to the total cultural mosaic.

Popular Culture: Definition and Rationale

Popular culture at the outset was defined as only those elements of culture that were associated with the electronic media—radio, television, and movies. Over time, popular culturalists have agreed that this early definition was too restrictive. Today, most would contend that popular culture embraces the everyday world around us—the mass media, music and dance, foodways, religion, clothing and adornment, recreation and entertainment, rituals, heroes and icons, and language. It is our current lifestyle—our total life picture—and it may or may not be disseminated by the mass media. Most important, the popular culture of America is the voice of the people, the lifeblood of existence. Some scholars say it represents the triumph of the "democratic aesthetic," or in layman's language, it is what makes America tick.

Ray Browne, whom most consider the founding father of popular culture studies, describes popular culture as culture of the people, by the people, and for the people. Others have explained it as the "common person's history," several have called it a look at "culture from the ground level," and some have been bold enough to label it the "New Humanities." M. Thomas Inge, editor of the six-volume *Handbook of Popular Culture*, says popular culture should be studied because "there is no more revealing index to the total character and nature of a society. . . . It is of necessity to understand the manner in which humans spend their leisure time." Popular culture serves as a mirror wherein society can see itself and better understand its own character and needs. Popular culture is what we do by choice to engage our minds and our bodies when we are not working or sleeping. This can be active (such as playing baseball or dancing) or passive (watching television or reading a book). Moreover, it can be creative, such as writing a short story or cooking a meal, or simply responsive, such as watching a play or listening to music.

The study of popular culture began in the 1960s when a group of academics began to reassess what they were studying and teaching because it was becoming irrelevant to the students they taught and the public they served. Academics had too long defined "culture" in its strictest sense, i.e., a promulgation of only the best of what was written and spoken in the world. The tendency in academe had been to rank culture on the basis of its supposed artistic quality as determined by a group who had decided what is "good" for students to study. Students had been forced to study this elitist-based curriculum—the so-called "classics" in literature, music, and art; they had been lectured that they must appreciate only the "good" in these fields. This elitist evaluation of culture was both philosophically unsound and educationally counterproductive.

This elitist and anachronistic definition of culture was then challenged by a core of cultural analysts who stated that all levels of culture must be examined. It was a clarion call to include "low" as well as "high" culture, "crude" as well as "fine" arts, and "populist" as well as "elitist" culture. The time had come, they concluded, that all facets of culture are worthy of study if we are to reach a fuller understanding and deeper appreciation of the meaning of culture.

The popular culture movement was formalized with the establishment of the *Journal of Popular Culture* in 1967 and the founding of the Popular Culture Association in 1969, which has held its own national convention annually since 1971. In addition, there are also a dozen regional and state associations that meet regularly. The Popular Culture Association now boasts of more than 3,500 members, including representation from a wide array of disciplines.

Over the past three decades, the field of popular culture has been severely criticized regarding its validity, its role, and its definition. The cultural elitists continued to verbalize their complaints against the "incurable disease" of popular culture. Robert Osborne described it as the "culture of foaming nonsense that now engulfs us," while Barbara Tuchman declared that "the tides of trash rise a little higher by the week." Finally, Norman Cousins issued the ultimate damnation: "A sleaziness has infected the national culture. . . . There seems to be a fierce competition . . . to find even lower rungs on the ladder of bad taste." Despite these naysayers, popular culture studies and the number of popular culture enthusiasts continue to grow.

A recent study on popular culture in higher education projected that nearly 20,000 courses are being offered in colleges and universities across the nation. More and more areas of academia are turning to popular culture as a broad field to help them understand human behavior—lituraturists, historians, anthropologists, sociologists, communicationists, journalists, and yes, geographers. At recent Modern Language Association annual meetings, up to 25 percent of the papers related to popular culture. The editor of the *Journal of American History* recently stated that popular culture is a "mainstream field in American history." Centers and departments devoted to the study of popular culture have sprung up across the country and the Popular Press, based at Bowling Green State University, continues to publish significant books on the subject, ranging from architecture to women in fiction.

As academicians, we are in the business of promoting tolerance, understanding, and open-mindedness. If a student prefers *The Lion King* over *King Lear* or blues over Beethoven, we should be tolerant of these preferences. An appreciation for eclectic tastes maximizes the possibilities for a liberalizing education and promotes a greater awareness for *all* cultural preferences and experiences. As we move toward 2001, the quantity of our leisure time increases. Assuredly, the range of cultural events and experiences will expand. An understanding of those sets of experiences will be made richer if we include research and teaching devoted to popular culture. Finally, American popular culture is known throughout the world and continues its diffusionary process as political boundaries are erased. It may be our most effective diplomat, serving as a silent ambassador to places where our government policies remain a mystery. For this reason alone, we need to know what popular culture says about us.

Popular Culture and Geography: Retrospect and Prospect

Cultural geographers were slow to accept popular culture as a field of study. Several reasons are possible for this reluctance. Perhaps it was because we are a more cautious, conservative lot—careful of jumping on the popular culture bandwagon as did sociologists and historians. It may have been that we were waiting to determine if it was just another academic fad or a blip in the academic monitor. It could be attributed to the fact that cultural geographers had historically focused on the agricultural and folk-oriented elements of American culture (e.g., house types, barns, and fences). Some would say this was due to the Carl Sauer legacy established at Berkeley in the 1920s. It is true that a host of Sauer's students fanned out into geography departments across the country, where they influenced a multitude of students in this direction (e.g., Andrew Clark at Wisconsin, Fred Kniffen at Louisiana State, and Leslie Hewes at Nebraska). There was also the elitist attitude to consider. This may have been at work from two different angles. First, cultural geographers so indoctrinated in the Sauer methodology and content matter had excluded more contemporary, urban-oriented aspects of American culture. Second, the scientific-quantitative geographers claimed that popular culture studies lacked a scientific rigor and were not based in any theoretical or conceptual framework. In both cases, cultural geographers who dabbled with popular culture were viewed as dilettantes.

When research on popular culture was launched in the 1960s and other academics initiated studies on rock music, fast-food franchises, televangelism, and numerous other topics, these were, if not dismissed outright by geographers, relegated to the periphery of the geographical enterprise. The handful of geographers who studied popular culture topics were forced to seek outlets for their research outside the traditional geography journals, as was the case in 1978 when Alvar Carlson assembled a collection of articles by geographers that was published in the *Journal of Popular Culture*.

Those of us who studied popular culture during that time remember all too well being mocked by many of our colleagues, who considered our interest in the alleged ephemera of popular culture quirky at best, irrelevant at worst. An example of this attitude was reported by a cultural geographer who had submitted a popular culture manuscript to the *Annals of the Association of American Geographers*. The editor informed the prospective author that to be taken seriously in the profession he should avoid research on "gays and country music."

The winds of change, however, began to blow steadily across the cultural geography field in the 1970s. In 1973, popular culture research was lent credibility when Wilbur Zelinsky (former Sauer student and venerable dean of American cultural geographers) wrote *The Cultural Geography of the United States*. His admonition to study music and dance, food and drink, sports and games, and clothing and adornment raised some eyebrows within a profession that had virtually ignored these culture traits. Moreover, he pointed out that cultural geographers had been wed too fastidiously to only the material culture of America. Zelinsky concluded that nonmaterial culture was just as much a part of our overall culture as the tangible artifacts.

The same year, David Lanegran and Risa Palm, former graduate student colleagues in the University of Minnesota geography department, assembled an anthology entitled *An Invitation to Geography*. It included several topics of a popular culture vein, such as rock music, sports, disease, print media, riots of the 1960s, and Vietnam. The editors emphasized that it was "unfortunate that American geographers writing for the beginning student or for the general public have often ignored the everyday concerns and curiosity about places on which a conceptual geographic structure could be built." They concluded that anthologies of that time were deficient of material written on subjects familiar to college students.

A third book in 1973, entitled *Geography and Contemporary Issues* and edited by Melvin Albaum, University of Colorado geography professor, examined numerous topics with an American popular culture bent, including poverty, black ghettos, violence and crime, campus unrest, riots of the 1960s, and "New Left" politics. Albaum's reasons for assembling such a collection were "to provoke a greater participation of geography as a research and teaching discipline in the study and analysis of contemporary issues" as well as bring together a collection of studies that "could be understood and which appealed to today's students." Although they did not specifically mention popular culture, it is evident that the editors of these two anthologies were implying a general lack of material on such studies. Clearly, these were novel topics that cultural geographers had not heretofore studied.

In 1974, a group of cultural geographers as well as other academics met in State College, Pennsylvania, and formed the Society for North American Cultural Survey (SNACS). One of its goals was to compile all maps on cultural matters from the existing literature into an informal atlas on North American culture. These so-called "scratch" atlases embraced a myriad of cultural topics including both folk *and* popular culture. They served as the genesis for *This Remarkable Continent: An Atlas of United States and Canadian Society and Culture* published in 1982. It covered an enormous range of topics, including food and drink, music and dance, sports and games, structures, and religion; culture traits long neglected by cultural geographers. For those interested in popular culture, this first-of-its-kind atlas of 387 maps was a stimulus for further research because it illuminated the possibilities for study on a number of popular culture items.

Noted cultural geographer John Fraser Hart's *The Look of the Land*, published in 1975, contained elements of popular culture. Although the book was primarily agricultural in nature, one section, "Impact of Leisure," highlighted camping, hunting and fishing, and use of Off-Road Recreative Vehicles (ORRVs) as potential uses of leisure time by farmers. He concluded that snowmobilers, skiers, suitcase farmers, and lawn worshipers need cultural analysis as cultural groups just as much as the Old Order Amish. Clearly, these were nontraditional topics that cultural geographers had disregarded.

Perhaps overlooked in the mid-1970s was the fact that geographers assumed an active role in the national Popular Culture Association meetings. Alvar Carlson, one of the cultural geographers who spearheaded efforts in this direction, was the first to organize a geography section in 1976. This has become an annual session chaired later by Charles Gritzner (South Dakota State University) and Walter Martin (University of North Carolina-Charlotte).

In 1978, two renowned cultural geographers, Joseph Spencer and Marvin Mikesell, spoke for more popular culture studies. Mikesell, in his presidential address to the Association of American Geographers, "Tradition and Innovation in Cultural Geography," observed that only a few of the universal elements of culture had been systematically studied by geographers. He admitted that "we know a lot about certain topics, but little about others" and "we know a great deal about material culture, but less about nonmaterial culture." He concluded that the field of cultural geography was plagued by many gaps and deficiencies. Spencer authored an article, "The Growth of Cultural Geography," published in *American Behavioral Scientist*, in which he encouraged cultural geographers to explore art, music, human adornment, clothing systems, and eating behavior. These were elements of culture, according to Spencer, that had not been effectively researched by geographers.

A year later, Donald Meinig, well-known historical-cultural geographer from Syracuse University, edited *The Interpretation of Ordinary Landscapes*, a provocative group of essays by some of the foremost cultural geographers. Perhaps the most appropriate and engaging of these essays was "Axioms for Reading the Landscape" by Peirce Lewis. He outlined seven points for interpreting ordinary, everyday landscapes. In the third axiom, Lewis criticized academics for excluding common landscapes, which he said was due to "negligence combined with snobbery," a reflection of the elitist attitude previously mentioned. He emphatically stated that a multiplicity of landscape features can "tell us a great deal about what kinds of people Americans are, were, and may become." Among the items that deserve attention, Lewis declared, were mobile homes, motels, gas stations, shopping centers, fundamentalist church architecture, water towers, city dumps, and carports. Moreover, he suggested that cultural geographers had yet to tap the nonacademic literature as a research source, a fact that revealed, noted Lewis, American scholars are too "snooty." Included in his list of alternative research sources were the writings of "new journalists" like Tom Wolfe (landscapes of drag racing and surfing), trade journals such as *Fast Foods*, and the "rare" book by the perceptive nongeographer, such as those written by Grady Clay and J. B. Jackson.

Also in 1979, John F. Rooney Jr., a cultural geographer specializing in sports and games, compiled a set of maps and text in paperback form, *A Social and Cultural Atlas of the United States*, a forerunner to the larger *This Remarkable Continent* compendium of maps printed in 1982. Rooney stated in the foreword that the atlas "requires utilization of much data hitherto ignored by scholars interested in the United States." Covered in this atlas were such popular culture topics as ethnic groups, voting behavior, religion, sports and recreation, music, food and drink, and crime. In the epilogue, Rooney concluded that the atlas is "an ongoing research effort by geographers who have probed and continue to seek a better understanding of our elusive and exciting character."

Finally, the 1970s ended with the first treatment of popular culture in the textbook literature when Terry Jordan and Lester Rowntree produced the second edition of *The Human Mosaic: A Thematic Introduction to Cultural Geography*. An entire chapter was devoted to popular culture in order to demonstrate that everyday culture could be approached from a geographical perspective and that geographic concepts could be applied to popular culture. Apparently, the authors must have struck a responsive chord because an expanded popular culture chapter remains in the sixth edition of the textbook published in 1994. It is also significant to note that a vast majority of human/cultural geography textbooks published in the 1980s and 1990s have incorporated popular culture topics including *The Cultural Landscape: An Introduction to Human Geography* (Rubenstein); *Human Geography: Cultures, Connections, and Landscapes* (Bergman); *Human Geography: Landscapes of Human Activities* (Fellmann, Getis, and Getis); and

Human and Cultural Geography: A Global Perspective (Shelley and Clarke). It was obvious by the end of the decade that several eminent cultural geographers were making overtures to address the matter of popular culture, albeit in a sometimes indirect manner.

The decade of the 1980s opened on a fortuitous note for the merger of popular culture with cultural geography when Alvar Carlson, Bowling Green State University cultural geographer, launched the *Journal of Cultural Geography* in 1980. In announcing the maiden issue, Carlson argued that academics had long overlooked many facets of culture, including popular culture. Yet, Carlson affirmed, cultural geographers, knowingly or unknowingly, had maintained an interest in various segments of popular culture, if not in their research, surely in their teaching. He reassured his colleagues, who may have felt uneasy about popular culture topics, that his new journal would be inclusive rather than exclusive. They would no longer have to be considered on "the fringes of what was the traditionally recognized core of their discipline."

After the positive reaction to Carlson's editorship of the 1978 *Journal of Popular Culture* volume, he seemed convinced that the time was right to propose an academic marriage between cultural geography and popular culture. Much credit must be given to Carlson for providing cultural geographers an opportunity to publish their findings on popular culture as well as for providing a forum for all cultural geographers to become aware of the popular culture research being produced by their peers.

As the 1980s progressed, there were more calls for the inclusion of popular culture into cultural geography. Donald Ballas and Margaret King proposed a "creative merger" in a *Journal of Cultural Geography* commentary. They suggested that because geography had maintained longstanding relationships with other fields such as anthropology and economics, it was time to augment these interdisciplinary endeavors with popular culture. Ballas and King outlined a number of geographic concepts pertinent to popular culture, including cultural regionalization, cultural diffusion, and cultural landscape. Moreover, they asserted that popular culturalists and cultural geographers share many common techniques of research, such as observation and field work. They concluded that many of its practitioners had urged cultural geography to "expand its horizons in both content and approach." Thus, popular culture was an avenue to explore a different set of phenomena in spatial terms.

The decade of the 1980s and the first half of the 1990s has proven to be productive times for popular culture's alliance with cultural geography. More than a dozen leaders in cultural geography have generated significant studies on popular culture, ranging from architecture to zoos. These studies have been widely acclaimed and cited in both the scholarly and textbook literature. Among the most prominent of these were Bob Bastian and Jim Curtis's work on popular architecture; Harm DeBlij's studies on wine; George Carney and Charles Gritzner's publications on popular music; John Rooney, John Bale, and Karl Raitz's research on sports; Leo Zonn's examinations of the media, especially film; John Jakle's analyses of the vernacular landscape, particularly drive-ins, gasoline stations, and motels; Dick Pillsbury's investigation of restaurant types; Dan Arreola's efforts on Mexican-American houses, murals, and fences; James Shortridge's findings on religion and literature; John Goss's exploration of the shopping mall; and Wilbur Zelinsky's inquiries on numerous popular culture items, including ethnic cuisine, signage, personal and town names, and vernacular regions. These as well as other studies bode well for the complete integration of popular culture into cultural geography. No longer considered a temporary aberration or that its practitioners are dilettantes, popular cultural geography, for the most part, is broadly accepted and received within the discipline.

Perhaps the quintessential validation of a unification of popular culture with cultural geography was Zelinsky's 1992 update of *The Cultural Geography of the United States*. He complimented cultural geographers for "flashing light into hitherto shadowy corners of the cultural cosmos." Some of the arenas in which he said "promising starts are visible" included the geography of sport, foodways, music, literature, and art. Furthermore, he paid tribute to a core of cultural geographers who had recognized the "value of decoding landscapes generated by popular culture." Finally, he encouraged cultural geographers to undertake studies on an infinite number of other popular culture items, including T-shirts, buttons, bumper stickers, graffiti, and billboards.

What were the overriding considerations for this gradual emergence of popular culture in geography? Five possible factors are offered. The first explanation is related to the quantitative revolution of the 1960s. As a reaction to this decade, there was a growing trend toward a more humanistic geography led by Yi-Fu Tuan, Anne Buttimer, and others. Their inclination was that not all human phenomena could be subjected to hard scientific scrutiny or that such phenomena could be structured into some mathematical formula. A second answer centers around the matter of zeitgeist (spirit of the times). Cultural geographers were influenced by the fact that sister disciplines, most notably sociology and history, had for more than two decades been engaged in the study of popular culture. Apparently, other academics saw value in researching these popular elements of American culture. Because cultural geographers had lagged behind, there was an abundance of popular culture topics to be studied from a geographic viewpoint. Moreover, several academics outside the discipline were providing encouragement to cultural geographers to add their perspective. Similarly, a number of cultural geographers interested in popular culture had matriculated graduate school in the 1960s and 1970s, when the social and ecological issues of those decades were principal concerns of that generation. And, importantly, popular culture was a vital component of those movements, from rock music to pop art. In short, subject matter was plentiful and there was ample material "out there" to study.

Increased interest in popular culture may also be attributed to the fact that it provided an opportunity to broaden the base of cultural geography. As previously mentioned, cultural geographers had demonstrated a clear bias toward the study of material culture in a rural context. Therefore, the study of popular culture with a more urban-oriented and nonmaterial culture bent was a mechanism to augment the historically restrictive dimensions of cultural geography.

Another explanation is associated with the conversion of an avocation into a vocation. What provided the inspiration for cultural geographers to turn to popular culture topics? John Rooney, an avid sports enthusiast since his high school years when he lettered in football and baseball and toyed with the idea of signing a semipro baseball contract, moved from his graduate work in environmental perception to his lifelong study of sports as a popular culture trait. George Carney was reared in the Ozark hills listening to and playing country music from hillbilly to bluegrass. This background was renewed when he began studying popular music from a geographical angle. Jim Curtis had maintained an abiding interest in literature since childhood, aspired to be a novelist during his undergraduate career, and had four short stories rejected by the *New Yorker* magazine. Curtis transformed his interest in popular literature into interpreting Steinbeck's Cannery Row and Mark Twain's Hannibal from a cultural geographer's viewpoint. John Jakle's fascination with gasoline stations, motels, and drive-ins had been nourished by his many years of travel along the highways and byways of America. Perhaps these geographers were more interested in popular culture per se than in the geography of popular culture. But in using their cultural geography training, they all saw the *what, where,* and *why* questions in popular culture and made a common commitment to answer those questions by using popular culture topics to enhance cultural geography. And by making a long-term investment in the study of these popular culture subjects, they eventually gained respect among their colleagues.

Finally, one might argue that the rise of popular culture among cultural geographers during the past twenty-five years was an attempt by a group of young geographers to stake a claim for themselves in the field. They wanted to be, or at least seem to be, different from their older-generation professors in cultural geography. Many were in search of a niche, or some sort of specialization, within the field of geography. Moreover, they were living in an era of specialization, when qualifying adjectives to precede "geography" and "geographer" became fashionable (i.e., "hyphenated" geographers).

The Geographic Approach to Popular Culture

If a discipline can be condensed into one word, we might agree that geology is rocks, botany is plants, history is time, and geography is *place*. Place refers to a location, but specifically to the values and meanings associated with that location. A place is a location that demonstrates a particular identity. For example, your address at 100 Anywhere Avenue is a location, but because it is your home, certain qualities attached to that location give it meaning to you, making it a place.

All places possess individual physical (e.g., landforms and climate) and cultural (e.g., religion and music) traits that make them different from other places. The distinctive characteristics loaded onto a place give it uniqueness. One of the important geographical ideas is that no two places on the earth's surface are the same. The precise qualities of a place are never exactly duplicated.

Geographers like to think in terms of place in space (earth-space). Each place maintains numerous attributes. It has a location in space. Distance and direction tell us about its relationships with other places in space. Places have an arrangement in space, a spatial distribution. There are differences between places in space, or spatial variation. Movement occurs from place to place in space, such as migration and diffusion. Interaction happens between places in space via connecting networks, such as transportation and communication. Finally, several places that are similar, in either physical or cultural characteristics, may be grouped together to form a region, areas that display internal sameness to make them different from surrounding space.

Geographers study places at various scales. This refers to the size of the unit studied. It may be at an international, national, regional, or local level. Scale in a technical sense tells us about the size of an area on a map as compared with the actual size of the mapped area on the earth's surface.

Geographers view elements of popular culture as making a contribution to the character of a place. These elements help make a place unique and different from other places. As a part of the cultural whole, popular culture gives human meaning to a place and helps assign unique images to a place. Cultural geographers have not abandoned their traditional methods of studying culture when employing popular culture traits. Laurence Carstensen's study of the growth of McDonald's restaurants portrays the *cultural diffusion* of this phenomenon from place to place. Stephen Tweedie's reinterpretation of the Bible Belt provides a classic case study of the religious characteristics that distinguish this *culture region* from other regions in the United States. Albert LeBlanc's essay demonstrates the interrelationships between two culture traits (clothing and music), or *cultural integration*. Finally, Barbara Weightman's research on religious pluralism in Los Angeles illustrates the visible imprint of diverse human beliefs and activities in space, or the *cultural landscape*.

In addition to matters concerning place, geographers ask four fundamental questions—*What* is it (phenomenon)? *Where* is it (pattern)? *Why* is it there (process)? *When* did it happen (period)? As a mental hook to help understand and remember the geographic approach, geographers pose the four "W" questions, answered by the four "Ps." The first "P" articulates that geographers analyze something (*phenomenon*), such as the number of MTV viewers. The second "P" is one that geographers are particularly interested in, as it stresses *pattern*, or the distribution and arrangement of the phenomenon over the earth's surface, presented in the form of a map. For example, the map might portray the number of MTV viewers in the United States, with a pattern indicating a high concentration of fans in New York and a low viewing audience in Montana. The third "P" focuses on the explanation or causes behind the pattern, or *process*. In interpreting the map of MTV viewers, the geographer is looking for reasons why the place-to-place variation exists between New York and Montana. A number of factors may come into play in solving the riddle of the map pattern. Perhaps a demographic profile of the population of the two states would reveal that New York has more young people than Montana. Data indicate that MTV targets an audience in the 14–34 age category. Age structure, however, may not be the only criterion to explain the state-to-state differences. The availability of cable television, ethnic and religious backgrounds of the population, and music preferences may also need to be considered. Lastly, geographers are concerned with the fourth "P" (*period*) because some knowledge of the history of the phenomenon helps explain its movement from where it originated to other places. Consequently, the origin and diffusion of a phenomenon over a period of time may provide clues to its present pattern on the map. In our MTV example, we know that this phenomenon was launched in 1981, but were all fifty states covered at the outset? New York, in all probability, was one of the major markets in 1981; however, it might be assumed that Montana was a cultural laggard when it came to adoption of MTV.

Geographers do not have all the facts at their fingertips when it comes to interpretation of patterns on a map. Therefore, they must rely on research from printed sources or produced by fieldwork, or a combination of both. In the case of MTV viewers, geographers would search for data sources that would give them the information needed for map interpretation.

This anthology by no means covers the field of American popular culture as studied by geographers. Comprehensiveness is an illusory goal for anything but a multivolume encyclopedia, and that would fall short in this age of exploding information. The absence in this anthology of numerous popular culture traits should not be taken as a denial of their importance. Selections were based on four practical considerations. First was the lack of space. Publishers do place limits on number of pages unless it is an encyclopedia. Second is the fact that cultural geographers have not yet explored a number of popular culture items, such as clothing and adornment, represented here by two essays authored by a specialist in costume history and one in textiles. Third is that several recent popular cultural geography articles were published in journals that charge exorbitant fees for permission rights to reprint them. Finally, these were the popular culture topics I have most often used in my introductory cultural geography course over the past twenty-five years.

The intent of this project was to put in print a set of readings on geography and popular culture as a means to interest geography majors as well as the nongeography major by using relevant topics in order to demonstrate the approaches and methodologies of cultural geographers. The ultimate goal is to convey to the student with little or no background in geography that the geographic approach and the basic geographic concepts can be illustrated by use of topics familiar to them.

In conclusion, the job of a cultural geographer is to interpret all levels of culture (high-low, elitist-populist, and folk-popular) and the manner they are manifested spatially. It should be the goal of all cultural geographers to promote an open-ended American cultural geography in which a multiplicity of voices are heard and published findings read, new topics whether folk or popular culture be investigated, and that rigor and depth of analysis are demanded.

Part I: Music

Cultural geographers have researched and written more on music than any other popular culture trait. See, for example, my anthology, *The Sounds of People and Places: A Geography of American Folk and Popular Music* (Rowman & Littlefield, 1994), which contains twenty articles on various music genres ranging from bluegrass to zydeco. The two articles selected for this reader, however, were not included in the music volume because they represent the most recent research on this popular culture topic by geographers. The first essay, by Warren Gill, a human geographer at Simon Fraser University-Vancouver, is a study on the Northwest Sound, a place-specific music that emerged in the Pacific Northwest in the 1950s, when rock and roll made its appearance on the American popular culture scene. Gill's research focuses on a particular region where this popular music phenomenon originated, evolved, and declined during the years 1958–66. The Northwest Sound was a result of local geographic conditions that produced a musical creativity that reflected teenage culture in the region. Although its impact beyond the region was limited at the time, the Northwest Sound helped mark the integration of a frontier into the mainstream of American culture and provided a foundation for the "grunge" rock sound associated with Seattle in the 1990s. In chapter 2, my analysis of Branson, Missouri, as the new "mecca" of country music provides a three-stage process through which this geographic center of country music evolved: use of local talent, introduction of nationally recognized veteran performers, and an infusion of a younger generation of stars. Branson has emerged as a focal point for country music because of its historical antecedents and its advantages over other country music centers. The latter includes low-cost, family-type entertainment clustered in one area, multiple theaters with greater seating capacities, and additional tourist-oriented amenities.

1

Region, Agency, and Popular Music: The Northwest Sound, 1958–1966

Warren G. Gill

The mass cultural phenomenon of rock music has been accorded limited attention in the geographical literature, yet for over thirty-five years, it has been the dominant popular musical art form within Western societies. While the music has been primarily commercial entertainment, it has also served as a symbol of rebellion, collective consciousness, and subcultural and regional identity. Although the goal of most rock and roll performers has been to achieve recognition within national and international markets, the various trends and styles of rock derive initially from conditions specific to particular regions, with local dance and bar bands often being the principal sources of innovation and change. These regional sounds are an amalgam of local forces set within the general framework of society at large and in the specific context of the commoditization of mass culture promoted by advanced capitalism.[1] This subject, with its interplay of cultural, social, and regional factors, would seem to be particularly attractive to geographers, yet the most expansive work to date has been produced by scholars from other disciplines—most notably Simon Frith,[2] Dick Hebdige,[3] and Russell Sanjek.[4] While a body of geographical research on music has been assembled,[5] the principal focus has not been rock and roll.

In an attempt to partially redress this neglect, this paper examines the geographical factors that produced a regional variation of rock that originated, flourished, and eventually expired in the Pacific Northwest region of

Reprinted by permission from the *Canadian Geographer* 37 (1993), 120–31.

North America in the period from 1958 to 1966. Known as the "Northwest Sound," this vernacular musical style was centered in the Seattle/Tacoma, Portland, and Vancouver areas, and while not one of the dominant forms of popular music nationally, it was in its day the driving force of youth culture in the region. The Northwest Sound was a form of "protopunk" music— loud, crude, simplistic, and accessible—a rock innovation that usually emerges locally, outside the influence of major corporate record labels. In the late 1950s the Pacific Northwest was still a relatively remote area, lacking both the indigenous popular music traditions of many other regions of North America and the musical production and distribution techniques of eastern hit makers. The rhythm-and-blues-based music of the dance halls of the region was, in its own way, as fresh an interpretation of the African American roots of rock and roll as that of the pioneers of the genre in the mid-1950s and the revival to come from the United Kingdom in the 1960s. In a period bereft of these elemental aspects of rock and roll, the Northwest Sound was not simply a return to a previously successful formula, but a different evolutionary direction in response to local conditions. Grounded as it was in regional economic and cultural development, the Northwest Sound offers a productive topic for geographic investigation; the challenge is to place the analysis within a theoretically meaningful context. Two approaches within the discipline offer guidance: (1) the geography of music and (2) "reconstituted" regional geography. It will be argued that regional geography—"reconstituted" around the questions of structure, agency, locale, and regionalization—is the most appropriate method for analysis. This is not to say that there are not useful lessons from the geography of music: a selective review provides context and helps point to the need for a more comprehensive theoretical base to explicate the case of the Northwest Sound.

Geography and the Analysis of Popular Music

Geographical research on music has largely developed around the pioneering work of George Carney of Oklahoma State University.[6] Drawing on the tenets of the Berkeley School,[7] such studies have been principally concerned with examining the diffusion of music across North America, particularly the rural blues, folk, and country and western styles emanating from the American South.[8] A secondary, and more humanistic, focus has been the interpretation of images of place or landscape as exemplified in the lyrics of specific songs. Topics have included the image of the city from rural[9] and urban[10] perspectives, perceptions of regions,[11] the effect of state policy on place images,[12] and the contextualization of rock lyrics around consistent themes[13] (A: see Appendix following the Notes).

Beyond country music and analyses of lyrics, there are few geographic publications on rock and roll to offer guidance. Larry Ford[14] identifies the culture hearths of the Mississippi Delta, Nashville, and places such as Chicago, Cleveland, and Detroit—cities that were repositories of significant African American migration from the South—as vital to the development of early rock. New York, where "Tin Pan Alley" was the locus of earlier forms of twentieth-century popular music, also played an important role as a force in opposition to which early rock and roll flourished. The clearest spatial patterns are observed in the first decade or so, as improvements in technology, increased availability of recording facilities, and the dispersal of artists eventually destroyed the unique advantages of a particular location[15], although in the late 1980s the emergence of place-specific incubators, such as Minneapolis; Athens, Georgia; and a revitalized Seattle scene, has again been observed.[16] The availability of venues featuring live artists and the presence of small independent record labels, such as Sun in Memphis and Chess in Chicago in the 1950s, are key factors in the formation of local music scenes. The perpetuation of local dance styles and place-names in records and the variability of local radio station and juke box playlists reflect the continuing power of regional taste "despite the seemingly monolithic nature of record companies—and the proliferation of rock and radio stations owned by the same company."[17] The essence of a regional sound can also reveal the local cultural context. In a recent example, the evolution of the "Miami Sound" of the 1970s and 1980s—where Latin musical traditions were fused with disco and rock to create a distinctive style—has been shown to be part of the larger process of acculturation of the younger generation of Cuban Americans.[18] Like the Northwest Sound, the Miami Sound is defined through patterns of instrumentation, vocal stylings, and musical interpretation, rather than lyrical content.

While some progress has been made in developing a geography of music, the focus on country and folk and the concentration on analyses of song lyrics has unnecessarily restricted the subject matter. Regions are clearly critical to innovation, and almost all styles—from rock-a-billy to rap—have their roots in a local scene. As the leading form of popular culture, rock provides the most accessible opportunity for individual citizens to express their identity and perhaps even achieve fame, demonstrating that "the utopian dream of everyman an artist can come true right here, in our suburban land of opportunity—the ultimate proof that rock and roll is the most democratic and all-American of art forms."[19]

To this end, an important point of entry has been the "garage band"—

most memorably commemorated in the song "Joe's Garage" by Frank Zappa—where teenagers come together musically in basements or garages to embark on a rock odyssey. This elemental genre is almost universal throughout North America, and in a few areas, such as the Pacific Northwest and to a lesser extent Texas and Southern California, a distinctive regional style evolved from this pool of amateurism.[20] The Pacific Northwest is not identified, however, by Larry Ford[21] or Richard Butler[22] in their tracings of the development of North American sounds in the 1960s. That the region is not grouped with such important centers as San Francisco, Los Angeles, and Philadelphia in these analyses is unsurprising, as so few of the bands left traditional evidence, such as national record chart success, of the diffusion of their influence. The Northwest Sound was primarily a local phenomenon, but one with an eventual, but more long run, impact on the development of rock. The question, then, is one of the conditions specific to the production of this distinctive regional style. Diffusion from cultural hearths is clearly important, but in this case, it is the interaction between cultural, social, economic, and geographic forces at the local and national levels that commands the greatest interest. Structure—in this case the isolation of the region and the control of cultural resources in the Northeast—was the framework within which this form of human agency flourished.

Given these concerns, "reconstituted" regional geography, with a basis in structuration theory, offers a foundation for the investigation. As the substantive contributions to this new regionalism have been reviewed recently elsewhere,[23] discussion will be limited to the application of this program to the Northwest Sound.

Region, Agency, and the Pacific Northwest

The resurgence of interest in regional analysis in geography in recent years following Derek Gregory's[24] call "that we need to know about the constitution of *regional* social formations, of *regional* articulations and *regional* transformations" (italics in original) has resulted in a number of studies reflecting a reconstituted regional geography.[25] This neoregional geographic research is set apart in that it is focused on specific questions and is informed by theory, rather than regional description,[26] however, elegantly constructed. As Nigel Thrift[27] has suggested, the region can be seen as the "meeting place of social structure and human agency, substantive enough to be the generator and conductor of structure, but still intimate enough to ensure that the 'creature-like aspects' of human beings are not lost."

Work in this area has been strongly influenced by Anthony Giddens's[28] concept of *structuration*, which has provoked considerable interest within the discipline.[29]

For the purposes of the present study, the most instructive elements of the concept are that the production and reproduction of social life are a result of a dynamic process of conflict between individuals or groups and the structural elements that constitute society. In reconstituted regional geography this process is revealed through analysis of *locale*—a specific setting for interaction such as a job site, a nightclub, or a defined spatial unit such as a neighborhood—and *regionalization*—the means by which differentiation occurs within or between locales. Of interest here are the power relations between center and periphery, particularly the control of *authoritative resources* that influence the social production of everyday life, leading to *time-space distanciation*—the extension and stretching of social systems across time and space.

These concepts offer a framework for the analysis of the Northwest Sound. In this case, the structural forces are (1) the geographic, social, and economic conditions of the Pacific Northwest in the 1950s and early 1960s, most particularly the peripheral relation of the region, and (2) the state of popular music continentally in the period as a result of the control of popular culture resources in the Northeast. The forms of agency are (1) the teenage social situation in the region, (2) the creativity of young musicians, and (3) the development of a local popular cultural infrastructure. The principal locale is the dance hall, in its multiplicity of locations across the region. The interplay of these elements led initially to the production of popular music tied to the social practice of the teenage dance, which became reproduced in a progressively distinctive form up to the point where it was subsumed by external forces and the regional popular culture integrated into the North American mainstream. Such connections must be drawn through the employment of a realist approach,[30] especially in terms of the thorny question of causation; the causal powers suggested are activated only in response to contingently related conditions. In this the hoary and methodologically charged claim of regional "uniqueness"[31] is justified to the extent that the Northwest Sound was an original interpretation, and yet one that can be understood only in terms of the larger forces that presented the opportunity for agency and eventually denied it again.

In the late 1950s these forces came to bear on a region divided politically but united geographically (B). Roughly coterminous with the old Oregon Territory, the region can be generally defined as the area west of the Rocky Mountains and north of California, including the states of Washington, Oregon, and Idaho and the mountain counties of western Montana and the province of British Columbia[32] (C). Dominated by the Coast and the Cascade ranges and by proximity to the Pacific Ocean, the major urban centers of Seattle, Portland, and Vancouver, are characterized by mild temperatures, abundant precipitation, and a generally overcast and drab climatic regime.[33] With a significant part of the Northwest comprising the great coastal rain forest, the economic and cultural base of the region has been centered on the harvesting and processing of natural, particularly forest, resources. The form of industrial relations and settlement patterns, as well as the character of everyday life, have been tied historically to the economic fluctuations of this export-driven industry.[34]

In the postwar period, while there was notable progress away from the traditional staples economy, the region remained focused primarily on boom and bust resource exploitation into the 1960s.[35] Boeing of Seattle can be considered an exception to this generalization, but the firm's technological linkages outside the region have reduced its impact on the economic growth.[36] While the region was sparsely populated in an overall sense, the vast majority of the population by the 1950s were urban dwellers from varied ethnic backgrounds, predominantly white, but with significant Asian minorities and a small but growing African American population in Seattle. The major urban centers were most similar to each other in terms of size, economic function, and social conditions,[37] and by 1960 the majority of the population of Vancouver and Seattle had been born in the region, a factor that contributed to a heightened sense of insularity.[38]

The persistence of geographic, social, and economic ties led Joel Garreau[39] to develop a unified conception of the area as part of "Ecotopia" in his popular regionalization of North America. The environmentally sensitive character ascribed by Garreau's term (and the more recent "ecocultural" description of "Cascadia")[40] stands in sharp contrast to the period before "quality of life" became a favored symbol in the popular press. While the principal cities were becoming more sophisticated in the postwar era, their more utilitarian seaport origins remained and they "retained a frontier roughness," as one Vancouver historian has described it.[41] The sense of continental isolation behind the mountain barrier, as well as the formative and remote nature of the area, were important defining characteristics before improvements to continental air transport and communications system in the 1960s brought wider influences. Within this setting the Northwest Sound evolved as a unique style of playing derived from the roots of rock and roll but translated for young white and Asian audiences in a society gradually being formed out of the juxtaposition of the baby boom and the accelerated development of the region. The local music mirrored the externality, physical and social ruggedness, and "newness" of the

Pacific Northwest and helped mark the transition of these rapidly urbanizing areas from frontier to metropolis.

The Northwest Sound: Subculture and Social Institutions

The key social institution in the creation of the distinctive style of the Northwest Sound was the teenage dance. With the postwar baby boom, the adolescent population burgeoned in the 1950s, when liquor laws were stringent and there were few entertainment facilities catering to teenagers. The first wave of rock and roll in the middle part of the decade had sensitized the young to a sound that symbolized the conflict of values between generations and represented the coming of contemporary society. The teenage dance was first a social event, but it was also an opportunity to hear the music of the postwar generation as it was meant to be played. This was important in that the technology of home playback equipment could not yet provide an adequate approximation of the live performance of a rock and roll band. As a consequence of these factors—as well as those related to Top 40 music discussed below—church, school, and private dances in the Pacific Northwest became leading social institutions, while dance halls, battles of the bands, and teenage fairs became an outlet and focus for the activities of adolescents.

The dances and dance halls were representative of the frontier nature of the region. Fistfights were so common that intimidating bouncers were employed to swiftly dispatch troublemakers with maximum authority. Although liquor was generally not available on the premises (the legal drinking age was 21 years in both Washington and British Columbia, and the clientele was almost exclusively teenage), alcohol often played a role in the development of the character of these places. Many patrons would either consume spirits purchased with fraudulent identification before coming to the dance or surreptitiously imbibe in the parking lot during the course of the evening. The music at the dances captured and created the excitement, power, and illicitness of the events and the physicality of worklife and even the climate of the Northwest. As 1990s star Guns 'n' Roses bass player Duff McKagan, a Seattle native, has noted, "You gotta understand Seattle, it's grunge. People are into rock & roll and into noise, and they're building airplanes all the time and there's a lot of noise, and there's rain and musty garages. Musty garages create a certain noise."[42]

At the pinnacle of local social activities were converted "big band" era ballrooms and other venues where promoters such as Seattle disc jockey Pat O'Day in Washington and Les Vogt—Vancouver's original rock and roll star—in British Columbia presented local groups. In the Seattle/Tacoma area, which was both the geographical and popular cultural center of the region, places such as Parker's Ballroom, Birdland, the Target, the Lake Hills Roller Rink, and the Spanish Castle became key centers for dances featuring groups like the Wailers, the Dynamics featuring Jimmy Hanna (with future jazz giant Larry Coryell on guitar 1959–63), the Viceroys, the Dave Lewis Combo, the Frantics, the Bumps, the Sonics, Merilee and the Turnabouts, the Galaxies, and the Counts; while the Chase, the Headless Horseman, the Lake Oswego and D-Street Armories were home to such Portland-based bands as the Kingsmen, Don and the Goodtimes, Gentlemen Jim & the Horsemen, and Paul Revere and the Raiders, the latter originally from Idaho.

The Vancouver area was less important to the development of the sound, but places such as Danceland, the Embassy Ballroom, the Hollywood Bowl (later known as the Grooveyard), and the Pacific National Exhibition Gardens often featured bands from south of the border and local Northwest Sound-inspired groups like the Nocturnals, the Vancouver Playboys, the Chessmen (with guitarist Terry Jacks, of "Seasons in the Sun"), the Classics (evolving over the years into Canadian music stalwarts the Collectors and Chilliwack), the Stags, the Imperials, the Shantelles (with Paul Dean, later of Loverboy, on guitar), the Shockers, the Accents, and the Spectres (led by Bruce Fairbairn, later producer of Bon Jovi, Aerosmith, and AC/DC).

The Northwest Sound: Context and Character

Musically, the Northwest Sound had its origins in the instrumental groups that proliferated throughout urban North America after the first great rock and roll explosion of 1955 to 1958. By the late 1950s rock and roll had become fully commercialized, and the various regional influences that had created this new style of popular music were integrated into a national market controlled through the authoritative power of a few corporate centers in the Northeast. The two dominant sounds of this era were the manufactured teen idol productions from Philadelphia (Fabian, Frankie Avalon) and the Ink Spot-inspired "doo wop" stylings of vocal groups, like the Diamonds and the Platters.[43] The Fleetwoods, from Olympia, Washington, gained international success in the latter idiom with two number one hits in 1959, "Come Softly to Me" and "Mr. Blue."

In this period, unlike the earliest days of rock and roll, many of the hit records were written in "Tin Pan Alley" factory style in New York by teams of writers such as Carole King, Gerry Goffin, and Neil Sedaka, who in a relatively brief time, produced 200 charted hits out of the Brill Building in New York.[44] These productions were the staple of Top 40 AM radio throughout North America, but their layered and artificial style of production made them difficult for local dance bands to reproduce in a live setting.

As a result, instrumental groups such as Johnny and the Hurricanes of Toledo, Ohio, developed as local dance hall alternatives. The simplicity of the instrumental style, building upon such national hits as Bill Doggett's "Honky Tonk" (1956), "Rebel Rouser" by Duane Eddy (1958), and "Rumble" by Link Wray and the Ray Men (1959), provided a point of entry for many groups into the roots of rock and roll in a period when the productions of the dominant market were particularly moribund. Initial recording successes of instrumental groups from the Northwest such as "Tall Cool One" (Billboard #36–#38 on re-release in 1964) and "Mau Mau" (BB #68) by the Wailers, "Straight Flush" (BB #91) and "Fogcutter" (BB #93) by the Frantics in 1959, "Walk—Don't Run" (BB #2) and "Perfidia" (BB #15) by the Ventures in 1960 and "Like, Long Hair" (BB #38) by Paul Revere and the Raiders in 1961 reflected the nationwide development of this instrumental sound (D). A local "scene" was beginning, with the Wailers offering inspiration to other Tacoma musicians, including Bob Bogle of the Ventures: "We really looked up to them. We thought they were absolute stars—thought they were all millionaires."[45]

The Ventures, with 37 charted albums to date, continued to have international success by interpreting current musical and popular cultural trends in their distinctive instrumental style, and reached the Top Ten twice more before the end of the 1960s. Their unique guitar sound, overlaid with reverb and vibrato, has been argued to be "the era's signature sound . . . inspiring legions of guitarists the world over."[46] By remaining in their chosen style, the Ventures did not follow the path of the further development of the Northwest Sound, as "their music wasn't raunchy like that of the Northwest groups . . . it was smooth, polished and technically precise."[47] It was this "raunchy" sound that provided the basis for further development.

Over the next two years, groups like the Wailers began to incorporate vocals into the instrumental style of "Tall Cool One." This evolved sound was essentially a white rhythm and blues very elementally constructed around either 12-bar blues progressions or a sustained repetition of the three basic blues chords—root, fourth, and fifth—featuring shouted lead vocals with limited harmony singing and powerful playing. Key instruments in most groups were Hammond electric organs and saxophones. When combined with simplistic but energetic drumming, dominant guitar lines, and extended instrumental solos, these elements created a very full, loud, hard-edged sound, with a driving dance beat. Vocal melody lines were minimal, and the lyrics simple and forcefully delivered, often punctuated by drawn-out, piercing screams before instrumental breaks. The inspiration for the Sound was rhythm-and-blues from the 1950s and early 1960s, but given the small African American community in the region, this was a music not generally heard on local playlists with the exception of black disc jockey Bob Summerrise's evening show on radio station KTAC in Tacoma, which many young musicians listened to and learned from.[48] Besides, what was to become the Northwest "classic"—Richard Berry's (1955) "Louie Louie"— interpretations of songs such as Barrett Strong's "Money" (1960)—the first self-released hit for Berry Gordy Jr., who would found Motown—Jessie Hill's "Ooh Poo Pah Doo" (1960), the Olympics' "Big Boy Pete" (1960), the Contours' "Do You Love Me" (written by Berry Gordy Jr., 1962), Jimmy Forrest's (1952) "Night Train," and Little Willie John's "Fever" (1956) became staples of the dance circuit and were featured on early local albums by both the Kingsmen and Paul Revere and the Raiders. Covers of Texas rock-a-billy artist Ray Sharpe's "Linda Lu" (1959), Rufus Thomas's "Walking the Dog" (1963), Marvin Gaye's "Hitch Hike" (1963), and Eddie Holland's "Leaving Here" (1964) were also regional favorites and assumed by many in the audience to be Northwest songs. (Paul Revere and the Raiders, later to become national teen idols, were in this period covering such tunes as Hank Ballard's [1954] salacious "Work with Me Annie.") The subtleties of the original versions of these songs vanished as they were transposed to the raucous dance hall style of the Pacific Northwest. The rhythm-and-blues influence extended to costumes and manner of performance: most groups had a distinctive uniform and presented simple dance routines, known as "steps," in the tradition of African American vocal groups, as supplemental entertainment. While grounded in rhythm-and-blues, the Sound also developed around many locally written hits, with songs such as the Wailers' "Tall Cool One" and "Dirty Robber," and instrumentals like "Turn on Song" by the Counts and "David's Mood" and "J.A.J." by Seattle organ player Dave Lewis (an influential soloist and one of the few African American musicians active in Seattle) being included in most repertoires. Song titles (and lyrics) were generally not geographically descriptive; however, a few, such as "Fogcutter" by the Frantics, "Seattle" by the Wailers, and "Tacoma" by the Galaxies, did reflect the locality. From this interplay of external and internally generated influences, a vibrant local music scene blossomed, similar in character to those of Liverpool and San Francisco in the 1960s and Seattle again at the birth of "grunge" rock in the 1980s (where "there was this one corner of the map that was busy being really inbred and ripping off each other's ideas.")[49]

In an era of studio-dominated rock, the Northwest Sound became a simple, creative, live-oriented alternative to Top 40 radio. From Oregon to British Columbia, regardless of what was on the national record charts, this was the music of the dance halls, armories, and teen fairs (as Oregon chronicler Don Rogers characterized it in his 1988 book). A local popular cultural phenomenon had developed, entirely separate from the major record labels and outside the influence of commercialized national taste. As Butler[50] noted, access to recording studios and distribution networks is crucial to the development of a local focus. Bob Reisdorff, a record distributor in Seattle, started his own label—Dolton—in 1958 after hearing a tape of the Fleetwoods' "Come Softly to Me," which he was convinced would be a major hit. Dolton Records went on to produce and release many Northwest bands, including the Frantics and the Ventures. After encountering difficulties with national distribution of their material (as musical decision makers in New York and Los Angeles "still thought we had cows in the streets"),[51] the Wailers, still only teenagers, formed Etiquette Records in 1960 to release both their own and other regional material (the Sonics, the Galaxies).

Other regional labels included Jerry Dennon's Jerden Records (the Kingsmen, Don & the Goodtimes) and Tom Ogilvy's Seafair-Bolo Records (the Viceroys, the Dynamics) in Seattle, Roger Hart's Sande Records (Paul Revere and the Raiders) in Portland, and Les Vogt's Jaguar Records in Vancouver (the Classics). These labels distributed cheaply made recordings from studios such as Al Reusch's Aragon Studios in Vancouver (originally established to record Highland Dancing music), Commercial Records (where the Wailers recorded "Tall Cool One" and other tracks in 1958 for $34.30), and Joe Bole's home basement studio in Seattle ("Walk—Don't Run" and other early Ventures tracks) to the regional market and occasionally beyond. Local singles and albums abounded, and the dance halls—as the embodiment of the regional youth subculture—were filled with enthusiastic proponents of the Northwest Sound. Popular bands were booked over a year in advance: in 1963 the Raiders worked more than two hundred dates and grossed almost $250,000.[52]

Mass communication was also important, but again in a regionally specific way. Seattle radio station KJR, which could be heard into southern British Columbia, had a critical influence in propagating the sound. KJR's leading disc jockey, Pat O'Day, was an early convert to Northwest rock, and his very popular program featured Northwest recordings and served as a promotional vehicle for both the bands and the dances where they played. O'Day also ran a major booking agency, later to become Concerts West, which controlled much of the dance circuit in Washington.[53] KISN in Portland, where music director Ken Chase owned teen nightclubs and top DJ

Roger Hart promoted local dances (and eventually became manager of the Raiders) and CFUN in Vancouver, where disc jockey/drummer Fred Latremouille had a regional instrumental hit called "Latremotion" with the Classics 1964, played similar roles at a time when radio playlists were much more open. In Vancouver in the 1950s, disc jockey Red Robinson had prepared the ground for acceptance of the Northwest Sound by "making Vancouver a rock-a-billy town, instead of wimp city, and for that we should be grateful."[54]

If the Northwest Sound was the music of a new generation in a new environment, the anthem was a dialogue with a bartender about returning to meet a fondly remembered lover in Jamaica entitled "Louie Louie." Originally written on a piece of toilet paper in 1955 for his Latin-style band by Richard Berry, "Louie Louie" became the hallmark of the Northwest Sound. Berry's version was discovered in a delete bin in 1960 by vocalist Rockin' Robin Roberts, who made the song his trademark, ad-libbing the famous "yeah, yeah, yeah, yeah" tag line that became emblematic of the song in the seminal version he recorded with the Wailers in 1961. "Louie Louie" became an important local hit on the Etiquette label but was not successful nationally, as Liberty Records were convinced that it would not receive airplay because it was not "programmable."[55]

In the Northwest, however, the song was an inspiration, and almost every group in the region began playing the three-chord opus. The best-known recorded version is by the Kingsmen. Produced for $37 in Portland, it reached number two on Billboard, with over two and a half million copies sold nationwide in 1963, edging out a competing version by Paul Revere and the Raiders recorded the following day in the same studio.

Jack Ely's garbled, ersatz R&B-style vocal, shouted on tiptoes through the braces on his teeth at a ceiling-hung microphone, created a legendary controversy over the alleged sexual content of the lyrics and prompted proposals to ban the song and even to launch an FBI investigation.[56] The unique and primitive character of the Northwest Sound was summed up by some black friends of Richard Berry's who, upon hearing the Kingsmen's version, told him that "these white guys recorded your song and it's awful . . . they really messed it up." Berry thought it was kind of interesting that "Louie Louie" had become a white kids' record, and when he finally heard it, he described it as "raggedy and real funky," very unlike the smooth treatment he had given it himself in 1956 as the incongruous B side to his own cover of "You Are My Sunshine."[57]

Somewhat contradictorily the Kingsmen were released nationally on Wand Records, until then a label exclusively for African American artists. To help foster the illusion that they were a black group, no pictures of the group appeared on their first album cover.[58] In its simplicity and style, "Louie Louie" was the epitome of the dance hall song of the Pacific Northwest, and thousands of teenagers marked their passage through adolescence with the immortal refrain:

> *Louie Louie, oh no,*
> *Said me gotta go*
> *Yeah yeah yeah yeah.*
> *(Limax Music Inc.)*

The song has become so emblematic of the region that it has been twice nominated as the official Washington State song. Discussions of the song's suitability have produced some unusual debates and high theater in the state legislature. With the failure of the Washington State efforts, a bill proposing official adoption of the song was put forward in Oregon, with discussion also taking place in Idaho, as both states could claim direct association through the Kingsmen and the Raiders.[59] Further recognition of both the universality of the song and its centrality to the region came when Seattle cartoonist Gary Larson depicted a humpback whale singing the chorus to a research ship's suspended microphone in a 1984 "Far Side" cartoon. Since 1985 the *Seattle Times* has offered annual Louie Awards to "acknowledge dubious achievements and bizarre occurrences which shape life in the Northwest."[60] The controversy over the lyrical content of the song was revived to satiric effect by Denver cartoonist Berke Breathed in his Bloom County strip during the 1988 U. S. presidential campaign when he offered fictionalized interpretations by candidates George Bush and Michael Dukakis. Approximately 800 versions have been recorded worldwide, with sales of some 300 million units. Unfortunately, Richard Berry sold the rights to the song—along with four others—in 1957 for $750.[61]

If the Wailers were the beginning of the Northwest Sound, the Sonics were the ultimate evolution. As *Creem* magazine writer Robot A. Hull commented, "If punk rock was music created on the jagged edge, then The Sonics were its exemplars."[62] Motivated by the success of their fellow Tacomans, the Sonics formed in 1963, and took their name from the sonic booms endemic to living with Boeing. Starting out essentially copying the Wailers' sound, they began playing local dances and writing original material. They were signed to the Wailers' label, Etiquette, and in their first recording session almost destroyed the studio and "ended up sounding like a trainwreck" in a quest to achieve on tape the brutally raw sound of their live performances.[63]

Their first single, "The Witch" backed with "Psycho," was an aural assault, with subject matter and lyrical content not heard on radio. Pat O'Day was at first unwilling to play the song on KJR, but eventually gave in after insistent demands from local teenagers. "The Witch" reached number two on the KJR chart in early 1965, staying at that position for three weeks, surpassing "Granny's Pad" by the Viceroys (1962) as the best-selling Northwest single. While the record received airplay in other markets, including Orlando, San Francisco, and Pittsburgh, it did not break onto the national charts, perhaps because the sound was too raw and the songs "too demented for most radio programmers in the rest of the country."[64] Their sound and subject matter has made the Sonics admired by everyone from Bruce Springsteen to the Sex Pistols,[65] but they remained confined to the local dance and recording market with two, now widely prized, albums for Etiquette, and one less successful one for Jerden (distributed by ABC) before the original band members left in 1967. As drummer Bob Bennett said in retrospect, "We were a wild, dirty, kickass band," perhaps best described in the liner notes to the release of their two Etiquette albums on compact disc: "three chords, two tracks and one hell of a band."[66]

The Northwest Sound: Decline and Demise

With the exception of a few major hits like "Louie Louie," the Northwest Sound remained essentially a regional style, partly through the combination of bad luck, bad timing, and the poor decision making that characterized the Wailers' national efforts. The group was taken by surprise in 1959 when Cleveland disc jockey Alan Freed refused to air their instrumental "Mau Mau," as he felt the title would be offensive to blacks. This "had never occurred to these white kids from insulated Tacoma," and the song was not a success in cities with large African American populations. The group rejected the offer of GAC, the biggest booking agency in the United States, to stay in New York in 1959: "The high school kids didn't like being away from home. They missed their cars. They missed their girlfriends. They went back to Tacoma. The next year they called the talent agency, asking if the offer was still open. It wasn't. A hundred other rock groups had been more than willing to uproot themselves."[67] As we have seen, by 1961 when they were better prepared for success, "Louie Louie" was not promoted nationally by Liberty Records. While international stardom was lost to the Wailers, it is clear that without their presence on the local scene, the Northwest Sound would not have developed with the same strength and vigor.

Throughout the early 1960s, rock and roll as a popular art form was clearly in need of revival, but the prime force for rejuvenation came from

Great Britain rather than the Pacific Northwest. The scale of creative activity, in terms of population alone, was much larger in Great Britain and the level of musical interaction consequently higher. The "British Invasion" of 1964 thrust a reborn rock and roll upon North America. Although the Northwest Sound was a creative alternative and shared some similar roots with the new music of the United Kingdom, the British sound was cleaner, more polished, and more melodically and vocally sophisticated. While the Beatles, the Who, and the Kinks have acknowledged the influence of Northwest groups in their own musical development,[68] the sounds coming out of Britain had a pop sensibility and appeal to the younger baby boom generation that the crudity of the Northwest Sound could not match. The British bands also drew from the simplicity of early rock and roll, but infused their music with a songwriting craftsmanship lacking in the Northwest. What began as regional sounds in the United Kingdom quickly became, through the force of marketing and the media (as well as natural appeal), the dominant style of North American popular culture.

This musical onslaught from overseas completely altered the musical charts across North America, yet the Northwest Sound remained an important local force with occasional national success through 1966. The Kingsmen had three Top 40 albums in this period and made the national singles charts eight more times, having a Top 20 hit with "Money" in 1964 and reaching number four in 1965 with "Jolly Green Giant," their novelty reworking of "Big Boy Pete." Northwest-style songs "Just Like Me" (BB #11) and "Steppin Out" (BB #4) by Paul Revere and the Raiders became national hits in 1965 and 1966, before the group was sanitized as the "house band" on *Where the Action Is*—an insipid Dick Clark-produced American national daily after-school television show. Even the hard luck Wailers, who continued to successfully release singles and albums to the local market, almost broke through once again in 1966 with "It's You Alone." In Canada, the Nocturnals had two nationally charted songs in 1965 and 1966, while in the Northwest such local hits as "Leaving Here" by Jimmy Hanna & the Dynamics and "Bacon Fat" by the Viceroys received heavy airplay. Perhaps the ultimate testament to the regional power of the Northwest Sound was the release in 1965 of an Etiquette Records Christmas album (reissued on compact disc in 1991), featuring original seasonal songs by the Wailers, the Sonics, and the Galaxies.

The Northwest bands were still in demand for local dances, although some began to include adapted versions of suitable British songs in their repertoire. The other major musical innovation of the early 1960s—the surfing sound from Southern California—became a staple of the local airways (and helped sensitize the youth of the region to a new subculture—as depicted in Sandy Wilson's films (*My American Cousin* and *American Boy-friends*), and while influencing oddities like the Wailers' "We're Going Sur-fin" of 1963, it was not the principal force for change.

In the Vancouver area, the Northwest Sound groups gradually drifted in two directions, which, although divergent, were consistent with the origin of the local style. Some turned toward the music of the Rolling Stones, while others moved into straight rhythm-and-blues with the increasing impact of soul music on the pop charts in 1965. This latter trend provided one of the more unusual footnotes in Vancouver musical history. For a few years in the mid-1960s, Vancouver remained a musical anomaly in that many of its leading bands comprised local white sidemen fronted by a black singer, playing both "Louie Louie" and such polished Motown hits as the Temptations' "Get Ready." Both of these forms of local dance activity remained viable into 1968, when the new psychedelic sound emerging from the Bay Area remade the definition of current rock and established a final break with the Northwest Sound era. As Roger Skinner of the Nocturnals noted, "We were a dance band and changed as the times changed, up until the hippy era anyway—we just couldn't get into that."[69]

The entirely new international popular culture of the psychedelic era effectively replaced the event of the teenage dance with the concert; local dance halls that did not adapt to the new format went into rapid decline. With the increased availability of liquor licenses and a lowering of the age of consumption in British Columbia in the late 1960s, nightclubs became more important on the social scene as the early baby boom teen cohort moved into adulthood. A Vancouver nightclub audience was noticeably confused in 1970 when the Spectres, by now a Blood, Sweat and Tears-style band, chose to recall their Northwest Sound roots by concluding the last engagement of their career by playing "The Witch."

In the United States, the Wailers initially responded to the British influence by "softening their sound, doing harmony vocals [and] discarding most of their trademark instrumentals" and later tried, but failed, to adapt to the psychedelic era, eventually breaking up in 1968.[70] (Guitarist Jimi Hendrix, the great psychedelic innovator and Seattle native, made his career outside the region, although he did offer a eulogy to the Northwest era in his song "Spanish Castle Magic"—which commemorated the legendary Seattle dance hall.) Leading groups such as the Kingsmen, Don & the Goodtimes, the Viceroys, and the Dynamics had all disbanded or converted to psychedelia by 1968, while the Raiders continued to be successful into the 1970s with the more polished sound they developed on moving to Los Angeles. As the old groups and music faded away, the transition of the region from an isolated center of musical creativity to one that was part of the mainstream of North American youth culture was complete. Perhaps most ironically, the Sonics entered the late 1960s (eventually with a complete change of personnel) as the antithesis of their origins and became purveyors of commercialized pap on the national nightclub circuit.

Region and Agency in Retrospect

Given this inauspicious finale, the history of the Northwest Sound can be broadly encapsulated in John Agnew's remark that "the increasingly global organization of production, the increased homogenization of human practices through the influence of mass media and national education systems, and the 'surveillance' of national governments over their populations have helped to make the practices reproduced in different places more and more alike."[71] On the other hand, however, the production of this regional style can also be seen to affirm the notion that mass culture does not always lead to uniformity, as separatist feelings "derive their vigor from affirming their own iconographies against the forces which threaten them."[72]

In Vancouver, an element of the Northwest Sound legacy remains, as the various popular music sounds and scenes to this day have "arisen out of a spirit of independence and proceeded with a willful individuality" that is not well understood by those outside the region[73] (E).

Seattle emerged again in the late 1980s as the center of an innovative local music scene, with bands such as the Screaming Trees, Queensryche, Nirvana, Pearl Jam, and Alice in Chains playing a "cussed, aggressive, incisively individualistic style . . . with its own attitude."[74] These new groups recognize the heritage of the Northwest Sound and expand on it in "their own tinnitus-inducing ways" with "an overall scruffy feel that is in stark contrast to much of mainstream rock."[75] Whether Nirvana's anthem "Smells like Teen Spirit," with four, rather than the traditional three, chords will be the "Louie Louie" of the 1990s remains to be seen.

In conclusion, the rise and regional dominance by the Northwest Sound can be seen as a product of distinctive local conditions within the broader continental context of the state of popular music in the late 1950s and early 1960s. As a grassroots musical movement, the Northwest Sound grew out of Top 40 radio, but developed its character largely outside the sphere of the national market. The processes that led to the decline of the Sound also served to create conditions to enable its reproduction in altered forms appropriate to new structural and local conditions, clear evidence that agency does affect structure. More recent musical genres, including those as diverse as the "heavy metal" of the American Midwest, the punk music of New York and London, and the new "grunge" sound of Seattle, have clearly been influenced by the Northwest Sound.

At the local level, many popular dance bands still pay homage to the Northwest Sound, often in front of audiences who were not even born until the 1970s, by playing "Louie Louie" (F). Now, as then, the dance floor fills with enthusiasts chanting the chorus in ritual fashion, demonstrating that at least some continuity with the region's musical past remains. If it can be argued that local garage or bar bands are the staple of the unpretentious (and thus perhaps purest) aspects of rock, the Northwest Sound stands as an original interpretation. While it may be an overstatement that it is one of the three distinctive North American contributions, together with "Psychedelic" and "Surf" music, to the development of rock and roll in the 1960s (as suggested by Vancouver journalist Michael Willmore),[76] the Northwest Sound remains a legacy of the region. As Scott McCaughey, of current stars the Young Fresh Fellows, has noted, "Those bands have never been forgotten around here, there was always a core of people who looked at that music as the Northwest tradition."[77] The limited appeal of the Northwest Sound beyond the local area is an indictment of the commercial deficiencies of the style, but it is also a highlight of the way in which expressions of popular culture, such as rock music, can capture the character of a region.

Notes

1. Theodor W. Adorno, *Prisms* (London: Neville Spearman, 1967) and Daniel Bell, *The Cultural Contradictions of Capitalism* (New York: Basic Books, 1978).

2. Simon Frith, *Sound Effects: Youth, Leisure and the Politics of Rock 'n' Roll* (New York: Pantheon, 1981).

3. Dick Hebdige, *Subculture: The Meaning of Style* (London: Methuen, 1979).

4. Russell Sanjek, *American Popular Music and Its Business: The First Four Hundred Years*, Vol. 3 *From 1900 to 1984*, (New York: Oxford University Press, 1988).

5. George O. Carney, ed., *The Sounds of People and Places: A Geography of American Folk and Popular Music* (Lanham, Md.: Rowman & Littlefield, 1994).

6. Ibid.

7. Phil L. Wagner and Marvin W. Mikesell, eds., *Readings in Cultural Geography* (Chicago, Ill.: University of Chicago Press, 1962).

8. George O. Carney, "Geography of Music: A Bibliography," *Journal of Cultural Geography* 1 (Fall–Winter 1980), 185–86.

9. Louis A. Woods and Charles F. Gritzner, "The Contemporary Pastoral: A Case for Country Music," presentation at Western Social Science Association Conference, San Diego, 1981.

10. Larry R. Ford and Floyd M. Henderson, "The Image of Place in American Popular Music: 1890–1970," *Places* 1 (March 1974), 31–37.

11. James R. Curtis, "Woody Guthrie and the Dust Bowl," *Places* 3 (July 1976), 12–18.

12. John C. Lehr, " 'Texas (When I Die)': National Identity and Images of Place in Canadian Country Music Broadcasts," *Canadian Geographer* 27 (Winter 1983), 361–70.

13. Bob Jarvis, "The Truth Is Only Known to Guttersnipes," in *Geography, the Media and Popular Culture*, eds. Jacquelin Burgess and John R. Gold (London: Croom Helm, 1985), 96–122.

14. Larry R. Ford, "Geographic Factors in the Origin, Evolution, and Diffusion of Rock and Roll Music," *Journal of Geography* 70 (November 1971), 455–64.

15. Richard W. Butler, "The Geography of Rock: 1954–1970," *Ontario Geography* 24 (1984), 1–33.

16. Jay Cocks, "Seattle's the Real Deal," *Time* (March 23, 1992), 55.

17. Richard V. Francaviglia, "Diffusion and Popular Culture: Comments on the Spatial Aspects of Rock Music," in *An Invitation to Geography*, eds. David A. Lanegran and Risa Palm (New York: McGraw-Hill, 1978), 126.

18. James R. Curtis and Richard F. Rose, " 'The Miami Sound': A Contemporary Latin Form of Place-Specific Music," *Journal of Cultural Geography* 4 (Fall–Winter 1983), 110–18.

19. Lester Bangs, "Protopunk: The Garage Bands," in *The Rolling Stone Illustrated History of Rock & Roll*, revised edition, ed. Jim Miller (Toronto: Random House, 1980), 261–64.

20. Robot A. Hull, "That's Cool, That's Trash: A History of the First Punk Era," *Creem* 2, 30–31 and 60–62.

21. Ford, *Journal of Geography*, 455–64.

22. Butler, *Ontario Geography*, 1–33.

23. Andrew Jonas, "A New Regional Geography of Localities?" *Area* 20 (June 1988), 101–10; Mary Beth Pudup, "Arguments Within Regional Geography," *Progress in Human Geography* 12 (September 1988), 369–90; Barney Warf, "The Resurrection of Local Uniqueness," in *A Ground for Common Search*, eds. Reginald G. Golledge, Helen Couclelis, and Peter Gould (Goleta, Calif.: Santa Barbara Geographical Press, 1988), 51–62; Derek Gregory, "Chinatown, Part Three? Soja and the Missing Spaces of Social Theory," *Strategies* 3 (1990), 40–104.

24. Derek Gregory, *Ideology, Science and Human Geography* (New York: St. Martin's Press, 1978), 171.

25. Derek Gregory, *Regional Transformation and Industrial Revolution: A Geography of the Yorkshire Woollen Industry* (London: Macmillan, 1982); Alan Pred, *Place, Practice and Structure: Social and Spatial Transformation in Southern Sweden, 1750–1850* (Cambridge: Polity Press, 1985); Ed W. Soja, *Postmodern Geographies: The Reassertion of Space in Critical Theory* (London and New York: Verso, 1989).

26. John Fraser Hart, "The Highest Form of the Geographer's Art," *Annals of the Association of American Geographers* 72 (March 1982), 1–29.

27. Nigel Thrift, "On the Determination of Social Action in Space and Time," *Environment and Planning D: Society and Space* 1 (1983), 23–57.

28. Anthony Giddens, *The Constitution of Society: Outline of the Theory of Structuration* (Berkeley: University of California Press, 1984); Anthony Giddens, *A Contemporary Critique of Historical Materialism: The National-State and Violence*, Vol. 2 (Berkeley: University of California Press, 1987).

29. Anthony Giddens, "Time, Space and Regionalization," in *Social Relations and Spatial Structures*, eds. Derek Gregory and J. Urry (London: Macmillan, 1985), 265–95; A. I. Moos and Michael Dear, "Structuration Theory in Urban Analysis: Theoretical Exegesis," *Environment and Planning* A 18 (February 1986), 231–52; Derek Gregory, "Structuration Theory," in *The Dictionary of Human Geography*, eds. R. J. Johnston, Derek Gregory, and David M. Smith, second edition (Oxford: Basil Blackwell, 1986), 464–69; Derek Gregory, "Areal Differentiation and Post-Modern Human Geography," in *Horizons in Human Geography*, eds. Derek Gregory and Rex Walford (London: Macmillan, 1989), 67–96.

30. E. M. Gibson, "Realism," in *Themes in Geographic Thought*, eds. M. E. Harvey and B. P. Holley (London: Croom Helm, 1981), 148–62; Andrew Sayer, "Realism and Geography," in *The Future of Geography*, ed. R. J. Johnston (London: Methuen, 1985), 159–73.

31. R. J. Johnston, "The World is Our Oyster," *Transactions of the Institute of British Geographers* 9 (1984), 443–59.

32. Stewart Holbrook, Nard Jones, and Roderick Haig-Brown, *The Pacific Northwest* (Garden City, N.Y.: Doubleday, 1963).

33. Tom L. McKnight, *Regional Geography of the United States and Canada* (Englewood Cliffs, N.J.: Prentice-Hall, 1992).

34. Barney Warf, "Regional Transformation, Everyday Life, and Pacific Northwest Lumber Production," *Annals of the Association of American Geographers* 78 (June 1988), 326–46; Eric Grass and Roger Hayter, "Employment Change During Recession: The Experience of Forest Product Manufacturing Plants in British Columbia, 1981–1985," *Canadian Geographer* 33 (Fall 1989), 240–52.

35. Kenneth G. Denike and Roger Leigh, "Economic Geography 1960–70" in *Studies in Canadian Geography: British Columbia*, ed. J. L. Robinson (Toronto: University of Toronto Press, 1972), 69–86; Douglas C. North, "Location Theory and Regional Economic Growth," in *Regional Policy: Readings in Theory and Applications*, eds. J. Friedmann and W. Alonso (Boston: Massachusetts Institute of Technology, 1975), 332–47.

36. Rodney A. Erickson, "The Regional Impact of Growth Firms: The Case of Boeing, 1963–1968," in *Systems of Cities: Readings on Structure, Growth, and Policy*, eds. Larry S. Bourne and James W. Simmons (New York: Oxford University Press, 1978), 402–11.

37. A. Phillip Andrus et al., *Seattle* (Cambridge: Ballinger, 1976).

38. Norbert MacDonald, "Population Growth and Change in Seattle and Vancouver 1880–1960," in *Historical Essays on British Columbia*, eds. J. Friesen and H. K. Ralston (Toronto: Gage, Carleton Library No. 96, 1980), 201–27.

39. Joel Garreau, *The Nine Nations of North America* (Boston: Houghton Mifflin, 1981).

40. Eileen V. Quigley, "Cascadia," *The New Pacific* 2 (Winter/Spring 1990), 2–3.

41. Patricia E. Roy, *Vancouver: An Illustrated History* (Toronto: James Lorimer and National Museum of Man, National Museums of Canada, 1980).

42. Michael Azerrad, "Grunge City: On the Seattle Scene," *Rolling Stone* 628 (April 16, 1992), 44.

43. Jim Miller, *The Rolling Stone Illustrated History of Rock & Roll*, revised edition (Toronto: Random House, 1980).

44. Sanjek, *American Popular Music and Its Business*, 1988.

45. Steve Kolanjian, "Who Would Have Thought That Don Wilson's Job at His Father's Used Car Lot in Tacoma, Washington, Would Lead to the Formation of the Ventures?" Liner notes. *Walk—Don't Run: The Best of the Ventures* (Dolton Records, 1990).

46. Jean Charles Costa, "The Ventures," in *The Rolling Stone Record Guide*, eds. Dave Marsh and John Swenson (New York: Random House, 1979), 400.

47. Greg Shaw, "The Instrumental Groups," in *The Rolling Stone Illustrated History of Rock & Roll*, revised edition, ed. Jim Miller (Toronto: Random House, 1980), 105–6.

48. Erik Lacitus, "Northwest Rock: A History, Part 1," *Seattle Times–Seattle Post-Intelligencer* (July 29, 1984), G1, G2, G8.

49. Azerrad, "Grunge City: On the Seattle Scene," 44.

50. Butler, "The Geography of Rock: 1954–1970," 1–33.

51. Lacitus, "Northwest Rock: A History, Part 1," G8.

52. Don Rogers, *Dance Halls, Armories and Teen Fairs* (Hollywood: Music Archives Press, 1988).

53. Erik Lacitus, "Northwest Rock: A History, Part 3—Super DJ Pat O'Day Was the Force Behind the Northwest Sound," *Seattle Times-Seattle Post-Intelligencer* (August 12, 1984), G29.

54. Michael Willmore, *The History of Vancouver Rock and Roll: In the Beginning*, Vol. 1 (Vancouver: Vancouver Record Collectors Association, 1987), 6.

55. Erik Lacitus, "Northwest Rock: A History, Part 2—The Wailers," *Seattle Times–Seattle Post Intelligencer* (August 5, 1984), G2.

56. Bob Shannon and John Javna, *Behind the Hits* (New York: Warner Books, 1986); Dave Marsh, *The Heart of Rock and Soul: The 1001 Greatest Singles Ever Made* (New York: New American Library, 1989).

57. Bob Greene, "The Man Who Wrote 'Louie Louie' (Richard Berry)," *Esquire* 110 (September 1988), 63–67.

58. Rogers, *Dance Halls, Armories and Teen Fairs*, 1988.

59. " 'Louie Louie': Classic Goes With 'Nut Bills,' " *Seattle Times* (March 26, 1989), B8; Alf Collins, "Column," *Seattle Times* (May 20, 1985), D3.

60. Jack Broom, "The Louie Awards, 1987: From Ridiculousness of an Olympia Cover-Up, to Sublimity of a Theater Without Enough Cover," *Seattle Times* (December 27, 1987), B1.

61. Greene, "The Man Who Wrote 'Louie Louie' (Richard Berry)," 63–67.

62. Hull, "That's Cool, That's Trash: A History of the First Punk Era," 60.

63. Erik Lacitus, "Northwest Rock: A History, Part 6—The Sound Never Dies, But It's Up To Us To Keep It From Fading," *Seattle Times–Seattle Post Intelligencer* (September 2, 1984), F1.

64. Rogers, *Dance Halls, Armories and Teen Fairs*, 43.

65. Azerrad, "Grunge City: On the Seattle Scene," 44.

66. Peter Blecha, *The Ultimate Sonics*, Liner notes, Seattle: Etiquette Productions, 1991.

67. Lacitus, "Northwest Rock: A History, Part 2," G2.

68. Lacitus, "Northwest Rock: A History, Part 1," G1, G2, G8.

69. Michael Willmore, *The History of Vancouver Rock and Roll: Vancouver A-Go-Go*, Vol. 2 (Vancouver: Vancouver Record Collectors Association, 1985), 8.

70. Lacitus, "Northwest Rock: A History, Part 2—The Wailers," G2.

71. John A. Agnew, "Sameness and Differences: Hartshorne's 'The Na-

ture of Geography' and Geography as Areal Variation," in *Reflections on Richard Hartshorne's The Nature of Geography*, eds. J. Nicholas Entrikin and Stanley D. Brunn (Washington, D.C.: Association of American Geographers, 1989), 127.

72. Brian S. Osborne, "The Iconography of Nationhood in Canadian Art," in *The Iconography of Landscape: Essays on the Symbolic Representation, Design and Use of Past Environments*, eds. Denis Cosgrove and Stephen Daniels (Cambridge: Cambridge University Press, 1988), 175.

73. Tom Harrison, "All Over the Underground," in *Shakin' All Over: The Rock and Roll Years in Canada*, eds. Peter Goddard and Philip Kamin (Toronto: McGraw-Hill Ryerson, 1989).

74. Cocks, "Seattle's the Real Deal," 1992.

75. David Browne, "Seattle Rock: Out of the Woods and Into the Wild," *New York Times* (November 18, 1990), Section 2, 31.

76. Michael Willmore, "They All Played Louie, Louie," *Vancouver Sun* (October 24, 1980), L6–7.

77. Azerrad, "Grunge City: On the Seattle Scene," 48.

Appendix

A. John C. Lehr [*Canadian Geographer* 27 (Winter 1983), 361–70] analyzed images of place in country songs on the playlists of two Manitoba radio stations after the imposition of Canadian content requirements. Although the material broadcast conformed to the new Canadian Radio and Television Commission regulations in that it was performed or produced by Canadians, the place images represented were revealed to be predominantly American. Bob Jarvis (*Geography, the Media and Popular Culture*, 96–112), apparently unaware of North American research, but well versed in British sociological analysis, usefully attempted to overcome some of the failings of lyrical analysis through the contextualization of rock songs around six consistent themes that can be generalized as the road, cars and "girls," promised lands, escapism, urbanism, and social disillusionment.

B. Since Expo 86, and particularly with the Canada-U.S. Free Trade Agreement, there has been tremendous growth in cross-border traffic and a revival of interest in a unified conception of the region with organizations such as the Pacific Corridor Enterprise Council (PACE) and the Pacific Northwest Economic Region (PNWER) actively promoting the "Cascadia" concept and the "economic and culture consolidation of the VanSeaPort 'super region.'" See Brian Buchanan, "Brave New West," *BC Business* 20

(1992), 27–37, and Dona Sturmanis and Jim Oakes, "Forging Links," *BC Business* 19 (1991), 27–35.

C. As it is the contention in this paper that place was critical to the development of the Northwest Sound this "definition of the region" follows Nigel Thrift's [*Environment and Planning D: Society and Space* 1 (1983), 39] prescription that "any reconstituted regional geography" should proceed from a compositional analysis of physical geographic features through "an account of the organization of production in the region"—with a concentration on labor processes and social and class structure.

D. National chart positions have been determined for the United States from Joel Whitburn's trilogy: *Bubbling Under the Hot 100: 1959–1981* (Menomonee Falls, Wis.: Record Research, 1982); *Top Pop Singles: 1955–1986* (Menomonee Falls, Wis.: Record Research, 1986); and *The Billboard Book of Top 40 Albums* (New York: Billboard Books, Watson-Guptill, 1991). For Canada, national chart positions were taken from Brendan J. Lyttle, *A Chartology of Canadian Popular Music from January 1965 to December 1976 Inclusive* (Toronto: RPM Music, 1978). For local rankings, consult Michael Nightingale, *Raincoast Rock: A Musical History of the Artists That Made the Northwest Sound 1955 to 1990* (Victoria, B.C.: Oak Bay Copy Center, 1990), and Don Rogers, *Dance Halls, Armories and Teen Fairs* (Hollywood: Music Archives Press, 1988).

E. The early days of Vancouver rock have been commemorated on vinyl in Volumes 1 and 2 of *The History of Vancouver Rock and Roll* (Vancouver Record Collectors Association) available through Neptoon Records, 5766 Fraser Street, Vancouver, B.C., Canada, V5W 2Z5, and in reunion concerts in 1986 and 1990—portions of the latter event having been aired by the Canadian Broadcasting Corporation as "Vancouver Rock Classics" in December 1990. Representative works by the Kingsmen, Paul Revere and the Raiders, the Ventures, and the Sonics are all now on compact disc, with most other U.S.-based groups available on vinyl compilations by Jerden Records (*The Original Great Northwest Hits—3 Volumes*). Information on delisted albums and re-releases by Etiquette Records and other local labels is available from Park Avenue Records, P.O. Box 19296, Seattle, WA 98109.

F. Richard Berry has suggested that one reason for the continued worldwide popularity of "Louie Louie" is a result of the infamous toga party scene in the 1978 film *Animal House*, where John Belushi and other fraternity members sang the song to riotous effect. The mythology of the song is such that it has even become the subject of study in high school courses on popular culture. In the mid-1980s, a "Louie Louie" parade, attracting over 60,000 participants annually in Philadelphia, was described by its founder as "a parade for no reason . . . and no reason would be 'Louie Louie.'" For further details on this phenomenon, see *People Weekly* 27 (May 25, 1987), 34–35. Reason or not, the song and the bands that made it famous have remained part of the psyche of the Northwest: somewhat bizarrely, a surprise performance by the Kingsmen was the highlight of a major black tie social event in Vancouver in November 1990.

2

Branson: The New Mecca of Country Music

George O. Carney

If you like country music in the city,
you'll love country music in the country—
Ozark Mountain Country.[1]

Among the many phenomena that cultural geographers have examined are geographic centers of music, as found in works by Peter Nash, Larry Ford, and Richard Butler.[2] More specifically, they have also investigated the influence of new centers of country music, such as Austin, Texas, on the more established nodes, such as Nashville, Tennessee, and Bakersfield, California.[3] One such center that has emerged and challenged Nashville in the last decade is the Ozark town of Branson, Missouri. This study offers a three-stage process to illustrate how Branson has evolved as a country music center, analyzes the advantages Branson holds over Nashville and other centers for both country music entertainers and fans, and assesses Branson's future as the new mecca of country music.

Historical Background

The 1941 *Missouri: A Guide to the "Show Me" State* described Branson, population 1,011, as "predominantly a resort town." Its business district

Reprinted by permission from the *Journal of Cultural Geography* 14 (1994), 17–32.

consisted of cafes, taverns, drug stores, and novelty shops, all of which catered to the tourists and residents who participated in the water-based recreation (swimming, fishing, and boating) associated with nearby Lake Taneycomo. Recommended points to visit included cultural landscape features such as Matt's Cabin and Uncle Ike's Post Office, frequent settings for the principal characters in Harold Bell Wright's 1907 novel, *Shepherd of the Hills,* and physical landscape attractions such as Marvel Cave, reported as one of the largest limestone caves in Missouri.[4]

Over the years, local residents witnessed a lack of nighttime entertainment for the growing number of tourists.[5] This resulted in Branson's first country music show in 1959. It was no coincidence that country music became the dominant form of entertainment.[6] The surrounding Ozarks possessed a rich heritage in country music hearkening back to the Anglo-Saxon ballads brought to the region by Appalachian settlers in the first half of the nineteenth century.[7] The traditional or "old-timey" substyle of country music had been firmly entrenched in the cultural mosaic of the Ozarks for 150 years.[8] In the late 1940s, nearby Springfield was the site for one of the most widely acclaimed country music shows—the Ozark Jubilee. Rivaling the Grand Ole Opry in Nashville, the Ozark Jubilee was broadcast over local radio station KWTO. By 1956, it gained ABC national television network status with Red Foley as host. Featured guests included Porter Wagoner from the Ozark town of West Plains, Missouri; Leroy Van Dyke from Sedalia, Missouri; Brenda Lee; Sonny James; and Hank Williams Sr. Bill Malone, a noted country music historian, called the Ozark Jubilee "the king of the televised barn dances."[9] In addition to the Ozark Jubilee, KWTO ("Keep Watching the Ozarks") had developed a longstanding reputation as one of the major country music radio stations west of the Mississippi.[10] Thus, the cultural foundation for Branson's emergence as a country music center had been laid over a long period of time (Fig. 2–1).

Evolution of Country Music

The association of country music with Branson occurred in three stages: (1) use of local talent from 1959 to 1982 (similar to the Grand Ole Opry in Nashville during its infant years of the mid-1920s, when local artists from the surrounding countryside performed in Ryman Auditorium); (2) introduction of nationally known veteran country music performers from 1983 to 1990 (older, more seasoned artists who had fallen from the hit charts for several years, e.g., Roy Clark and Mel Tillis); and (3) an infusion of the

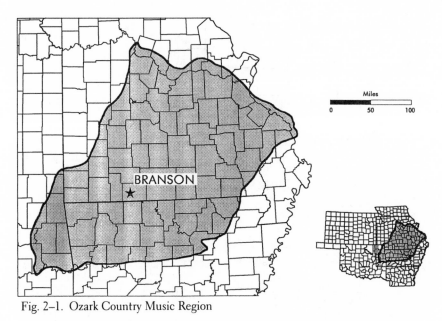

Fig. 2–1. Ozark Country Music Region

younger-generation entertainers (neotraditionalists) from 1990 to 1994 who were riding high on the hit charts (e.g., Randy Travis and Reba McEntire).[11]

The first stage emerged when the Mabe Brothers, a local country music band, started performing on Springfield radio and eventually joined the Silver Dollar City theme park in Branson as a featured attraction. Because of their popularity at the theme park's daytime shows, the Mabes decided in 1959 to open a country music show on Saturday nights in the fifty-seat basement of the Branson Community Center. Known professionally as the Baldknobbers, the group's success resulted in their movement to a nearby pavilion that seated three hundred people. Encouraged by the enthusiastic crowds, the Baldknobbers in 1965 purchased the town's skating-rink building. They quickly outgrew that facility and in 1968 constructed a new indoor theater on Missouri Highway 76.

During the next fifteen years, six more local groups from the Ozarks opened country music productions along "The Strip" (Highway 76). The Presley Family became known locally in the early 1950s in the Brighton area north of Springfield, where they performed at various social functions such as pie suppers and church dinners (Fig. 2–2). As a result, the group was invited to appear on a Springfield radio station. After an engagement in Branson in 1958, they began an eight-year stint at Fantastic Caverns, a local commercial cave complex. In 1966, Presley's Mountain Music Jubilee was

Fig. 2–2. Sources of Local Country Music Talent for Branson

inaugurated in a new indoor facility on Highway 76. After formation of the Foggy River Boys in Joplin, Missouri in 1969, the group moved to Kimberling City, a resort community west of Branson in 1971. After closing their theater, they moved to Branson in 1974. The Plummer Family came to Branson in 1973 from the southeastern Missouri town of Farmington, which they had used as a base for performances throughout Missouri and Illinois. Bob Mabe left the Baldknobbers to open the Bob-O-Links Country Hoedown Theater on Highway 76 in 1977. Another Ozark family act from the Bonne Terre area south of St. Louis, the Wilkinson Brothers moved to Branson in 1981 after making the country music circuit in Missouri, Arkansas, and Illinois. Finally, the Ozark Country Jubilee, a spin-off of the Ozark Jubilee of the 1950s, moved from Springfield to Branson in 1981 to join the other groups on "76 Country Music Boulevard," the new promotional name for Highway 76.[12]

These locally produced shows were performed in theaters with seating that ranged from five hundred to two thousand people and, according to Gary Presley of the Presleys, were filled to capacity each night during a forty-night summer season by 1980.[13] Dubbed "mom and pop" operations by local journalists, the Branson shows were initiated by families dedicated to the preservation of Ozark country music and "getting it out to the ears of tourists visiting the area."[14] Branson had become a regional showplace for homegrown talent.

The second stage in Branson's emergence as a country music center was launched in 1983 when Roy Clark, longtime "Hee Haw" television show star who lived in Tulsa, Oklahoma, opened an indoor theater on Highway 76 (Fig. 2–3). His name recognition was responsible for attracting guest appearances by several Nashville stars (e.g., Boots Randolph and T. G. Sheppard). Four years later, Boxcar Willie, an old-line Grand Ole Opry star, was the first to build a theater and move to Branson permanently (Fig. 2–4). During the past decade, more than seventy established Nashville entertainers have appeared in Branson (Table 2–1).

This dramatic influx of veteran country music talent into Branson is attributed to four factors. First was the opportunity to perform on a regular basis and in a permanent location, thereby eliminating the one-night stands commonly experienced by entertainers. Clark, the pioneer in the national star contingent, stated: "Most veteran country music stars have toured, made themselves a name and now want to get off the road and go where there is an audience."[15] Johnny Cash, a country music elder, added, "We're tired of putting in a million miles a year on the road."[16] A June 1990 *Billboard* headline read "Veterans Find 2nd Home in Branson." The article concluded that longtime performers were delighted to let the fans do the

Fig. 2–3. Roy Clark Celebrity Theater in Branson

Fig. 2–4. Box Car Willie Theater in Branson

driving.[17] But perhaps Tillis, another senior member of the country music fraternity, best expressed it when he humorously summarized their feelings: "You can go to church every Sunday and put your underwear in the same drawer every night."[18]

A second reason seasoned performers were attracted to Branson was because they could appear before a live, attentive audience in a drug-free venue where shows concluded before midnight. Veteran artists preferred this atmosphere when compared to playing in front of a rowdy, heavy-drinking clientele in a smoke-filled honky tonk or bar until the wee hours of the morning. Roger Miller observed before his recent death: "Branson's a good place to go for what we call a sit-down job."[19] The family-type atmosphere of the shows has undoubtedly been a crucial point in attracting the veteran artists.[20]

A third point that has contributed to Branson's popularity among the older entertainers is the physical and cultural landscape of the Ozarks region. The easy-living, laid-back lifestyle of Ozarkians appeals to performers like Jim Stafford, who says it is a place where veteran stars can "plant roots." He concluded, "I'm staying here and may even join the Rotary Club."[21] One established Nashville star commented, "I have the opportunity to take my family, eat some down-home Ozark cooking, go trout fishing, and play a round of golf."[22]

Finally, many of the old-line performers see Branson as an investment opportunity. Rick Frye, community development director for Branson, em-

Table 2–1. Veteran Country Music Artists and Groups Who Have
Performed in Branson

(1) Alabama	(38) Montgomery, Melba
(2) Anderson, Bill	(39) Nelson, Willie
(3) Anderson, Lynn	(40) Oak Ridge Boys
(4) Asleep at the Wheel	(41) Overstreet, Tommy
(5) Atkins, Chet	(42) Owens, Buck
(6) Bare, Bobby	(43) Parton, Dolly
(7) Brown, Jim Ed	(44) Perkins, Carl
(8) Campbell, Glen	(45) Price, Ray
(9) Cash, Johnny	(46) Pride, Charley
(10) Cash, June Carter	(47) Pruett, Jeannie
(11) Cash, Tommy	(48) Rabbitt, Eddie
(12) Coe, David Allen	(49) Randolph, Boots
(13) Conlee, John	(50) Reed, Jerry
(14) Cornelius, Helen	(51) Rich, Charlie
(15) Davis, Danny	(52) Riley, Jeannie C.
(16) Fairchild, Barbara	(53) Rodriquez, Johnny
(17) Fender, Freddy	(54) Rogers, Kenny
(18) Fricke, Janie	(55) Royal, Billie Joe
(19) Gatlin Brothers	(56) Russell, Johnny
(20) Gosden, Vern	(57) Seely, Jeannie
(21) Greenwood, Lee	(58) Sheppard, T.G.
(22) Haggard, Merle	(59) Smith, Connie
(23) Hall, Tom T.	(60) Sons of the Pioneers
(24) Hamilton, George IV	(61) Spears, Billie Joe
(25) Harris, Emmylou	(62) Statler Brothers
(26) Husky, Ferlin	(63) Thomas, B.J.
(27) Jennings, Waylon	(64) Tucker, Tanya
(28) Jones, George	(65) Twitty, Conway
(29) Kendalls	(66) Wagoner, Porter
(30) Kershaw, Doug	(67) Wariner, Steve
(31) Lane, Cristy	(68) Watson, Gene
(32) Lee, Brenda	(69) Wells, Kitty
(33) McDaniel, Mel	(70) West, Dottie
(34) Mandrell, Barbara	(71) Wiseman, Mac
(35) Mandrell, Louise	(72) Wynette, Tammy
(36) Miller, Roger	(73) Young, Faron
(37) Milsap, Ronnie	

phasizes that $25 million was invested in new construction and $5 million on remodeling during the 1980s. Kenny Rogers, an established star, formed a partnership with Silver Dollar City owners in 1990 and plans to invest $100 million over the next ten years, according to Frye.[23] Several other country music veterans have either built or purchased theaters as well as invested in new hotels and restaurants. Among these are Tillis, Loretta Lynn, Mickey Gilley, Moe Bandy, and Charley Pride. Tillis summarized, "I went to Nashville and I guess I spread the word a little too good. I said 'Boys, there's gold in them thar hills.' "[24] In addition to theaters, hotels, and restaurants, seasoned performers are sinking money into media outlets. "Branson USA," a syndicated country music show, is currently being broadcast on country music radio stations stretching from Shreveport, Louisiana, to Omaha, Nebraska, including several with 50,000-watt signals. The Branson Entertainment Network, a new superstation satellite network, similar to Chicago's WGN and Atlanta's WTBS, will carry programming patterned after the Nashville Network (TNN) and Country Music Television (CMTV).[25]

The third stage of Branson's evolution as a country music center during the 1990s involves the newer generation of country artists. As late adopters of Branson's importance, the newcomers see the significance of live shows as a means to increase contact with fans. Recording in Nashville to secure marquee value, they make the trek to Branson to draw audiences. Moreover, the opening of the larger capacity theaters (e.g., the Grand Palace which seats 4,000) has guaranteed the newer stars a profitable booking when they perform in Branson (Fig. 2–5). These younger entertainers view Nashville as the recording and publishing center whereas Branson is the performance outlet. Twenty of the biggest names in contemporary country music have appeared in Branson since 1990, including Country Music Association award winners Vince Gill, Randy Travis, and Reba McEntire (Table 2–2).

A Tale of Two Cities

Situated 360 miles to the west of Nashville, Branson has become the "Toyota" of the country music industry (i.e., it's a great copy, less expensive, and more efficient). In comparing this upstart center of country music with Nashville, the "mother lode" of country music, one sees the advantages that Branson has captured over its competitor. Perhaps the major reason for Branson's success is its fan-orientation, whereas Nashville is production driven. The consumers of country music (fans) view Branson as a form of hands-on entertainment where they can mix and mingle with their

Fig. 2–5. Grand Palace Theater in Branson

**Table 2–2. New Country Music Artists and Groups Who Have
Performed in Branson**

(1) Black, Clint	(11) Restless Heart
(2) Brown, T. Graham	(12) Sawyer Brown
(3) Dunn, Holly	(13) Skaggs, Ricky
(4) Forester Sisters	(14) Stone, Doug
(5) Gill, Vince	(15) Sweethearts of the Rodeo
(6) Highway 101	(16) Tillis, Pam
(7) Jackson, Alan	(17) Tippin, Aaron
(8) Loveless, Patty	(18) Travis, Randy
(9) McEntire, Reba	(19) Van Shelton, Ricky
(10) Morgan, Lorrie	(20) Wild Rose

favorite stars via autograph sessions and photo opportunities. Moreover,
many of the entertainers have made a long-term commitment to Branson,
thus ensuring fans that their favorite artists will be there when they visit.
The fans see Nashville as a commercialized country music center where
they take bus tours of the stars' homes, but rarely see any of them. As Tillis
succinctly put it, "You go to Nashville, you see the stars' homes. You come
to Branson, you see the stars."[26]

Nashville retains its role as a high-profile media-exposure outlet, where the stars crank out their latest recordings while maintaining a behind-the-scenes attitude in terms of contact with their followers. In contrast, audiences are encouraged to stay after the Branson performances and press the flesh with the veteran stars who routinely thank their guests for enabling them to be off the road. Branson boasts of more than thirty theaters featuring live country music shows while the Grand Ole Opry remains the only show in Nashville (Fig. 2–6). As the late Conway Twitty, a staunch supporter of Nashville until he appeared in Branson, observed: "Nashville blew it. The Grand Ole Opry fought like a tiger to stay the only show in town and keep everybody else out. Well, Branson stepped in and took over."[27] That is the principal reason why Branson has claimed a clear-cut advantage over Nashville in the group tour market and was the number one destination point of the American Bus Association in 1993.[28] Demographic profile data on tourists and their points of origin are gathered by the Silver Dollar City entertainment complex. Unfortunately from a geographer's perspective, efforts to obtain such data were denied to the author because they are proprietary. Statistics on the number of tourists to the Branson area have been recorded since 1986. They show an increase from 3.1 million tourists in 1986 to 5.6 million in 1993, a growth rate of more than 80 percent in a matter of seven years.[29]

A second explanation for Branson's popularity lies in the spatial arrangement of the theaters. Shows are clustered along one highway much like the casinos in Las Vegas. One does not have to motor or walk far to find various country music performances. If one show is sold out, another one down "The Strip" may have available tickets. In contrast, live entertainment outside the Grand Ole Opry is scattered throughout Nashville, a metropolis of 500,000, where the fan is forced to drive in traffic congestion across town in order to locate live country music. And in all likelihood, the fan will not find major stars on the Nashville club scene. Combined with the clustering of live music is the matter of cross-selling, a business technique effectively used by the Branson theater operators to foster a spirit of cooperation in advertising each other's shows.

A third advantage that Branson has over Nashville is its ability to offer the fans low-cost opportunities to see live country music. This viewpoint was best summarized by a booking agent in Nashville: "For three days in Branson fans can partake in all-you-can-eat restaurants for less than $10 per person, stay in a comfortable hotel room for $40 a night, and take in three to six shows that range in price from $10 to $25 per ticket; all for less than $200. In Nashville, the same money might get you a hotel room and a couple of meals."[30] Although data are sketchy when comparing the types of

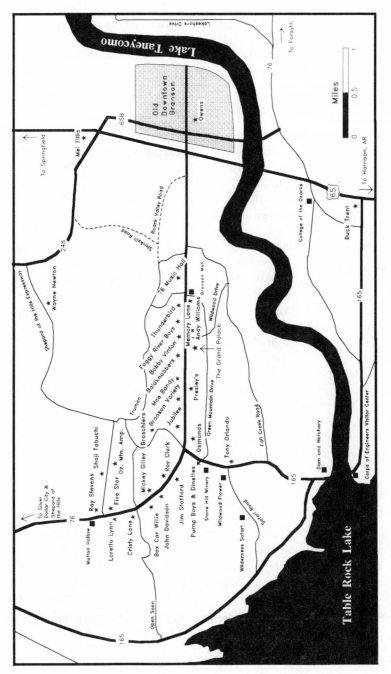

Fig. 2–6. Location of Branson Theaters

fans drawn to the two places, it appears that Branson has captured a different clientele, both demographically and geographically. Branson likes to boast that it shows are "family-friendly" performed in a "down-home" atmosphere. Ozark Marketing Council tourist statistics seem to substantiate this fact. Indicators show that families are the primary visitors during the summer season, while retirees comprise the bulk of Branson's vacationers in the winter.[31] From a geographic perspective, Branson's location within a 600-mile radius of major metropolitan areas where country music remains popular has given it impetus for growth as a country music mecca. These metropoles include Chicago, Kansas City, St. Louis, Des Moines, Little Rock, Omaha, Ft. Worth, Dallas, and Oklahoma City (Fig. 2–7).

Finally, Branson's appeal to the country music fan can be attributed to its cultural and natural amenities. Charles Gritzner's observations that the typical country music fan is of a blue-collar, rural or small-town background has contributed to Branson's popularity.[32] The laid-back, small-town, "just plain folks" atmosphere attracts the country music purist who feels more comfortable in Branson's cultural milieu than in the teeming metropolitan corridors of Nashville. Before performances begin, tour groups, couples with anniversaries, and individuals celebrating birthdays are recognized and allowed to applaud themselves and their hometowns. So accessible are the entertainers that they routinely mingle with customers at local businesses. Local tour guides tell fans that if they want to see the stars, go to Wal-Mart. Furthermore, the surrounding Ozark hills, lakes, and woods lure the outdoors-minded country music fans. The area offers opportunities to fish in world-class trout streams; engage in swimming, water skiing, and boating; view scenic foliage in the fall; and tour one of the majestic limestone caves. Branson has capitalized on this easy-going, pastoral setting with its "You'll love country music in the country" slogan.

Conclusions

More than fifty years after it was depicted as a little resort community nestled in the quiet and quaint Ozark hills, Branson is today referred to as the "Las Vegas of Country Music," "Country Music Show Capital of the World," "Broadway of Country Music," and "Music Country, USA" (a play on Nashville's title of "Music City, USA"). Most observers agree that Branson and Nashville offer two completely different venues based on the same music genre. An obvious complementary effect is at work—those who are attracted to country music in one place wind up spending some of their entertainment dollars to benefit another place (e.g., a fan may pay to see

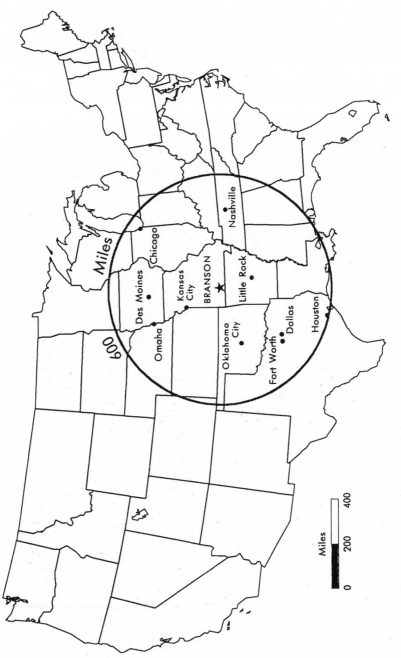

Fig. 2–7. Cities within a 600-Mile Radius of Branson

and hear Johnny Cash in Branson and purchase one of his tapes or compact discs produced in Nashville). The Country Music Association, based in Nashville, has embraced Branson because it views growth in both places as contributing to the overall strength and popularity of country music. Bill Ivey, executive director of the Country Music Foundation, also based in Nashville, sees a symbiotic relationship between the two locations.

> I see Branson as a phenomenon that enhances the overall scene. It reaches a somewhat different audience than Nashville does, not only in age (older) but geography. . . . In the big picture I see Branson as something that enhances Nashville's role as Music City, the place where music is created. . . . I want all these artists to have places to perform in front of live audiences, not just Garth Brooks and Alan Jackson.[33]

Some commentators on country music believe that Branson has peaked in popularity and is plagued with multiple internal and logistic problems (e.g., failure to meet building codes, lack of zoning and planning ordinances, and most importantly, accessibility—only one major highway [U.S. 65] leads to Missouri Highway 76 in Branson and the closest airline connections are in Springfield). Others claim that Branson lacks the seventy-year tradition of Nashville and with its garish strip and neon marquees lacks the soul of the Grand Ole Opry and the dignity of Nashville. Despite the disadvantages, it appears likely that Branson will take its place alongside Bakersfield, California, and Austin, Texas, as focal points for country music. Competition from these new centers of country music keeps Nashville "honest." Branson's unabashedly "y'all come" attitude coupled with a solidly populist appeal to the "common person" has made Nashville more aware of its critics, who portray "Music City, USA" as overly commercial, elitist, and a franchiser of country music. Regardless of the outcome, Branson, Nashville, and the other centers are all tied to a common industry and promote the same objective—to allow artists, veterans or newcomers, an opportunity to make a decent living and to maintain country music as America's fastest-growing popular music.[34]

Notes

1. Ozark Marketing Council Promotional Advertisement, 1990.
2. Peter Hugh Nash identified centers of classical music in "Music and Environment: An Investigation of Some of the Spatial Aspects of Production, Diffusion, and Consumption of Music," *Canadian Association of University Schools of Music Journal* 5 (Spring 1975), 42–71. Larry Ford and

R. W. Butler investigated centers of rock and roll music in the United States and Great Britain in "Geographic Factors in the Origin, Evolution, and Diffusion of Rock and Roll Music," *Journal of Geography* 70 (November 1971), 455–64, and in "The Geography of Rock: 1954–1970," *Ontario Geography* 24 (Spring 1984), 1–33.

3. George O. Carney, "Country Music and the South: A Cultural Geography Perspective," *Journal of Cultural Geography* 1 (Fall/Winter 1980), 16–33.

4. *The WPA Guide to 1930s Missouri* (Lawrence: University Press of Kansas, 1986), 486. This is the same volume that was published in 1941 in the American Guide Series.

5. For an analysis of the impact of tourism on Branson, see LaRue Boyd, "Economic Growth as a Result of Tourism in the Branson/Lakes Area of Missouri 1980–1993" (unpublished Master's thesis, Oklahoma State University, Department of Geography, 1993). Geographers use "lack of intervening opportunities" to explain this supply and demand situation. See John F. Rooney Jr., *A Geography of American Sport: From Cabin Creek to Anaheim* (Reading, Mass.: Addison-Wesley, 1974), 138–42.

6. Country music, according to most scholars, defies precise definition. It is a hybrid form of American music that originated in the rural South during the colonial period. Eclectic in nature, it drew upon a myriad of ballads, dance tunes, and instrumental pieces brought to North America by Anglo-Celtic immigrants, gradually absorbing a variety of vocal and instrumental influences from different ethnic groups, including Blacks, Cajuns, and Mexicans. It was simply called southern rural folk music until the 1920s, when journalists began to refer to it as "hillbilly" music. This description was retained until the late 1940s, when several recording artists suggested the name of the music be changed to "country" in an effort to improve its image.

7. George O. Carney, "The Ozarks: A Reinterpretation Based on Folk Song Materials," *North American Culture* 6 (Fall/Winter 1990), 40–55.

8. The traditional or "old-timey" substyle of country music most clearly resembles the early southern rural folk music of the eighteenth and nineteenth centuries. Its vocal characteristics retain a strong ballad influence and the lasting effect of church singing-school harmony. Instrumentally, this substyle continues to rely on the fiddle and banjo combination, or with the addition of a second fiddle and guitar, a rural string ensemble is formed. For a fuller analysis of this country music substyle, see Carney, *Journal of Cultural Geography*, 24–26.

9. Bill C. Malone, *Country Music, U.S.A.* (Austin: University of Texas Press, 1968), 270.

10. For an examination of country music radio stations, see George O.

Carney, "From Down Home to Uptown: The Diffusion of Country-Music Radio Stations in the United States," *Journal of Geography* 76 (March 1977), 104–10.

11. Andrew Vaughan, *Who's Who in New Country Music* (New York: St. Martin's Press, 1989).

12. "Over 25 Years of Music History," *Southwest Missourian* (Kimberling City, Mo.), February 20, 1986, 1, 19, 24.

13. Ibid.

14. *Business Journal* (Springfield, Mo.), May 27, 1990, 1, 13.

15. *Business Journal* (Nashville), April 22–26, 1991, 31.

16. *USA Today*, June 17, 1991, 2D.

17. The *Billboard* article was discussed in the *Arkansas Gazette* (Little Rock), June 10, 1990, E–1.

18. Tillis's quote appeared in the *Capital-Journal* (Topeka, Kans.), July 24, 1992, D–1.

19. *News-Leader* (Springfield, Mo.), April 8, 1990, 13–A.

20. For a religious denomination's viewpoint of Branson's family-type programming, see the Missouri Baptist Association's publication *Word and Way*, September 17, 1992, 6.

21. *USA Today*, June 17, 1991, 2D.

22. *News-Leader* (Springfield), April 8, 1990, 13–A.

23. Personal interview with Rick Frye, community development director for Branson, April 8, 1990.

24. *USA Today*, April 30, 1992, 1–D.

25. *Broadcasting* (Washington, D.C.), July 27, 1992, 26–27, and *Business Journal* (Nashville, Tenn.), September 30–October 4, 1991, 13.

26. "Move Over, Nashville," *Post-Dispatch* (St. Louis), September 11, 1988, 12.

27. "Hillbilly Haven," *People Magazine* 36 (October 21, 1991), 60.

28. *Atlanta Journal-Constitution* (Atlanta), "First There was Nashville . . . Then Came Branson," July 4, 1993, N–4.

29. Ozark Marketing Council Reports for 1986 and 1993, Springfield, Mo.

30. *The Tennesseean* (Nashville), October 20, 1991, J 1–2.

31. Boyd, 12.

32. Charles F. Gritzner, "Country Music: A Reflection of Popular Culture," *Journal of Popular Culture* 11 (Spring 1978), 857–64.

33. "Branson, Mo.: Will Music Country's Boom Mean Music City's Bust?" *The Tennesseean* (Nashville), October 20, 1991, J–2, and a telephone interview with Bill Ivey, executive director of the Country Music Foundation, October 10, 1993.

34. *USA Today*, May 26, 1994, 1–D.

3

Selected Reading I

Chapters 1 and 2

Carney, George O. (ed.). *The Sounds of People and Places: A Geography of American Folk and Popular Music*. Lanham, Md.: Rowman & Littlefield, 1994 (3rd ed.).

Chase, Gilbert. *America's Music: From the Pilgrims to the Present*. Urbana: University of Illinois Press, 1987 (rev. 3rd ed.).

Cooper, B. Lee. *Popular Music Perspectives: Ideas, Themes, and Patterns in Contemporary Lyrics*. Bowling Green, Ohio: Popular Press, 1991.

Curtis, Jim. *Rock Eras: Interpretations of Music and Society, 1954–1984*. Bowling Green, Ohio: Popular Press, 1987.

Ferris, William, Jr. *Blues from the Delta*. New York: Da Capo, 1984.

Gillett, Charlie. *The Sound of the City*. New York: Pantheon, 1984.

Klingsbury, Paul, and Axelrod, Alan (eds.). *Pickers, Slickers, Cheatin' Hearts, and Superstars: Country Music and the Musicians*. New York: Country Music Foundation and Abbeville Press, 1988.

Malone, Bill C. *Southern Music-American Music*. Lexington: University Press of Kentucky, 1979.

————. *Country Music, U.S.A.* Austin: University of Texas Press, 1985.

Miller, Jim (ed.). *The Rolling Stone Illustrated History of Rock & Roll*. New York: Rolling Stone, 1980.

Oliver, Paul. *The Story of the Blues*. New York: Chilton, 1969.

Pareles, John, and Romanowski, Patricia (eds.). *The Rolling Stone Encyclopedia of Rock & Roll*. New York: Summit, 1983.

Roberts, John Storm. *The Latin Tinge: The Impact of Latin American Music in the United States*. New York: Oxford University Press, 1979.

Shaw, Arnold. *Black Popular Music in America*. New York: Schirmer, 1986.

Szatmary, David P. *Rockin' in Time: A Social History of Rock and Roll*. Englewood Cliffs, N.J.: Prentice-Hall, 1991 (2nd ed.).

Part II: Clothing and Adornment

When it comes to research on clothing and adornment, the geography body is bare, despite calls by eminent cultural geographers such as Wilbur Zelinsky and Joseph Spencer more than twenty years ago for such studies. Hence, the two essays in this section are by professionals outside the field of geography.

In the context of popular culture, clothing includes dress worn by ordinary people in everyday life. Clothing shapes and defines our identities, reveals how we spend our working hours and leisure time, and reflects our gender, occupations, and group affiliations. Some knowledge of the terminology related to clothing is needed in order to understand its relationship with popular culture. "Style" is a concept that refers to clothing with particular characteristics that distinguish it from other garments of the same type. A style may vary in popularity over time, but its distinctive features do not change. Bell-bottom jeans, for example, may fluctuate in acceptance at given times, but the shape of the flared legs differentiate them from pegged or tapered jeans. The style or styles that are accepted or popular at a particular time in a particular place are called "fashions." The way in which fashion changes is explained as the "fashion cycle." When a style remains fashionable for an extended period of time, it is called a "classic" such as a long-sleeved crewneck sweater. One of the enduring clothing styles in America are jeans.

Jeans are an American icon. For the past 150 years, they have signified different lifestyles, from the self-reliant cowboy to the rebellious hippie. Today, Levi's, the original brand of jeans, offers more than two hundred variations. Clearly, there is a choice for everyone, ranging from denim coveralls for small children to baggies for hip-hoppers. According to industry estimates, approximately 430 million pairs of jeans were sold in 1993, a whopping $7.2 billion worth.

Al LeBlanc, a professor of music at Michigan State, contributes an insightful treatment of how musicians create a persona, or image, through clothing and adornment. It is a sound piece of research on a topic sorely neglected by cultural geographers and others. His imaginative approach gives popular culturalists a missing link in the study of clothing and music. The essay is nicely pieced together in chronological order so as to elucidate the dynamics of music artists and their wear. LeBlanc examines the relationships between clothing and music styles, influences that musicians have had on each other's dress, and the impact of music artist's clothing on the public.

Beverly Gordon, textiles and design professor at the University of Wisconsin-Madison, provides a fascinating essay on the origin, development, and current status of jeans. Her astute observations of this clothing phenomenon focuses on historical periods, especially changes in jeans color, decor, and fits as well as the function of jeans in popular culture. It is a refreshing and perceptive piece on clothing's role in popular culture—the evolution of jeans from work clothes to fashion to an American symbol of popular culture around the world.

4

All Part of the Act:
A Hundred Years of Costume in
Anglo-American Popular Music

Albert LeBlanc

Cos-tume n. 3. A set of clothes appropriate for a particular occasion or season. (American Heritage Dictionary)

The leading performers of popular music have always been the celebrities of popular culture. Never has their celebrity status been greater than it is today, with their music presented on an almost continuous basis by the many broadcasters who specialize in popular music, and with their images before the public in settings as varied as televised rock videos and the covers of magazines and tabloids that line the supermarket checkout counter.

A crucial part of any popular musician's success is his or her persona—an image of personal style for public consumption. Costume is the most important visual ingredient of the persona, and popular musicians rely on it to develop the image they want to project.

Prominent popular musicians are the leaders, not the followers, in setting the dress styles of the popular culture of their times. It is quite possible that they were not the first individuals to adopt a particular form of dress, but very often they are the people who introduce new styles to the general public because they are the first public figures that a large segment of the

Reprinted by permission from *Dress and Popular Culture*, eds. Patricia A. Cunningham and Susan Voso Lab (Bowling Green, Ohio: Popular Press, 1991), 61–73.

public sees wearing a new style. This chapter describes a century of fashion leadership by prominent performers of popular music.

To the general public, costume may be the most noteworthy and memorable aspect of today's performers of popular music. Musicians tend to invest more money and time in developing their costumes than the average individual invests in a comparable proportion of a wardrobe. In appearance, musicians' costumes are more expensive looking, more trendy, more flashy, and they often have a better fit, though fit is sometimes exaggerated for effect. Musicians' costumes are more humorous, more sexual, more androgynous, more formal, and sometimes even more conservative than the clothes of the general public. In effect, the costume of popular music performers stands out from what the public wears, is noticed by the public, and influences the public. An onlooker does not need a musical education to notice and remember how a musician looks.

What is the background over the past hundred years of the costume of popular music performers? What trends have emerged? What are some of the most noteworthy examples of performer costume during the past century, and how do popular musicians make use of the costumes they wear in advancing their careers and their music? This review examines these questions, emphasizing musicians' onstage attire rather than what they wear in "everyday life." It is doubtful, in fact, that popular music performers even have an "everyday life" within the contemporary environment of electronic media. The popular musicians of today expect to be noticed and photographed any time they are accessible to the public, and they dress accordingly.

To go back a century in popular music covers a lot of ground—from the time of John Philip Sousa and Scott Joplin to the time of Madonna and Sting. In general, the costumes of popular music performers in 1890 were considerably more conservative than what is the norm today. Minstrel show and vaudeville musicians probably had the most eccentric costumes, if they were performing on stage rather than being hidden in an orchestra pit. But the majority of popular music performers tended to wear a quasi-military band uniform or some version of their Sunday best—a "nice" set of dress clothes.

This period was the heyday of the professional concert band, in both military and civilian versions, and each variety espoused the military form of dress. The United States Marine Band, which Sousa conducted in the 1880s, had a highly elaborate uniform. When Sousa formed his own professional civilian band in 1892, he selected a uniform that was military in style, but was distinctly more conservative than that worn by the Marine musicians. Nowhere is the change more evident, nor more attractive, than in two famous portraits of Sousa, first as conductor of the Marine Band and in his white uniform as leader of his first civilian band.[1] In *Bands of America*, H. W. Schwartz chronicles the rise and fall of the professional concert bands and offers many examples of their quasi-military uniforms.[2]

The professional concert bands had their imitators everywhere, and an essential part of the imitation was the uniform. Because many of these imitators were impecunious members of town bands, fraternal organization bands, or just groups of friends who played wind instruments, there was less money available and less pressure to wear a fancy uniform. Even Scott Joplin, the future King of Ragtime, appeared in quasi-military uniform as a member of the Queen City Negro Band in 1896.[3] Circus and carnival bands were also much in evidence, and they also tended to wear the quasi-military uniform. Many of the minstrel-show pit bands wore a uniform in the same style.

While the quasi-military uniform was much favored near the end of the nineteenth century, it is very likely that the average practitioner of popular music wore some version of his Sunday best to perform. The average popular musician of the day was not a member of a professional concert band, was not involved in vaudeville or minstrelsy, and did not have to keep up with today's tradition of costume notoriety. Al Rose and Edmond Souchon present numerous photographs of the small black bands in and around New Orleans at the turn of the century, and it is a comparatively rare group that appears in uniform.[4] Yet suits, neckties, and hats abound for these musicians, almost exclusively male. It is evident that many of these performers are low-income people wearing their Sunday best. The look of Sunday best can be seen in ragtime and early country music as well as in the earliest groups to perform New Orleans jazz.

What was worn by musicians who made a living playing in bordellos? One might expect these people to approximate the oversexed look of some of today's rock musicians, but that does not seem to be the case. Most surviving pictures of ragtime musicians show them posing in Sunday best for a formal portrait, or sitting at the keyboard in formal attire with little else in the background. A famous portrait of Tony Jackson shows the celebrated pianist wearing a tuxedo as he sits at his piano.[5] Photographers would not normally be welcome in a bordello, but there is a fascinating picture of the women of one of New Orleans' most elegant houses posing for the camera while Jelly Roll Morton serenades them at the keyboard.[6] Morton appears to be wearing a conservative business suit.

In the hundred years since Sousa became established as a public figure, the costume of popular musicians has become more flamboyant, more sensationalized, and very often more sensual. With many contemporary musicians, the costume worn on stage and electronically transmitted to living rooms across the nation is considerably more sexually provocative than what their musical forebears would have worn to actually perform in a bordello.

Why has costume changed in this way? There have been changes in the underlying culture, with the culture becoming a great deal more liberal. At least equally important is the emergence of new styles of music that did not exist in the last century. Rock music would be the prime example of this. It can be shown that the style of music that is played influences what a performer wears more strongly than anything else.

A study of performer costume may safely begin with the clothing that is worn, including color, pattern, material, adornment, fit, accessories, and manner of wearing all of the above. Especially in the case of rock musicians, any study of clothing must also survey that which is not worn.

In the area of color, Deborah Harry's wearing of black[7] greatly influenced the punk rock subculture of the late seventies, and Tanya Tucker's bright red jumpsuit worn for an album cover in 1978[8] signaled a shift to a more adventurous persona. Color is extensively used by even the most conservative performers of country music to enhance their stage presence. Sometimes color has been used as a personal trademark, for example by country singer Johnny Cash, nicknamed The Man in Black.[9] Cash embraced the color black long before it became fashionable in the late seventies and early eighties. Popular musicians have not been reticent in their use of color, often wearing striking hues that members of the general public would not dare put on.

Pattern has also served popular musicians well. Bill Haley's plaid and printed sport coats gave an upbeat appearance to his band,[10] while paisley prints served to tie musicians into the styles of the psychedelic era. Animal coat prints, such as imitation leopard skin,[11] tiger skin, and even zebra[12] have been popular with both male and female rock performers. Rock singer Harry has used the animal skin look extensively in developing her persona.

Visually striking material has often been used to make performer garments. An often-cited example of this would be Elvis Presley's gold lamé suit of the 1950s,[13] but the field also includes black leather worn with élan by Elvis and Jim Morrison in the sixties, the rhinestones especially favored by country musicians, and sequins, spandex, rubber, plastic, gauze, velveteen, and other unusual materials too numerous to mention.[14]

Perhaps the most memorable use of black leather was made by Presley when he wore a complete suit of it in his televised comeback special of 1968.[15] Morrison of the Doors used a rather standard (for rock musicians) black leather suit early in his career,[16] but shifted to a gray leather, which gave a strong reptilian effect,[17] perhaps intended as a tie-in with the "Ceremony of the Lizard" used in his stage act.

A standard approach to costume notoriety has been to start with a striking fabric in a striking color and a striking cut, and add ornamentation, usually with some combination of rhinestones and sequins. Aging country musicians of the most conservative lifestyle have dropped all vestiges of conservatism in their own efforts to develop memorable costumes. Hank Snow and Porter Wagoner[18] typify this approach, though Presley in his later years equaled them for rhinestone-studded splendor.[19] A typically flamboyant Hank Snow costume is on exhibit at Nashville's Country Music Hall of Fame and Museum. While he was not considered a practitioner of country music, the late pianist Liberace had a healthy appetite for rhinestone-encrusted costumes.[20] Among the younger generation, Michael Jackson is making sure the rhinestone tradition survives.

Blue denim served as the uniform of the rock culture, and rock idol Bruce Springsteen appeals to its historical roots by wearing a pair of ancient red tag Levi's in a cut that was popular in the fifties.[21] It is probably no accident that red tag Levi's in the same cut and featuring the venerable button-up fly sold very well in the mid-eighties as Springsteen's popularity soared.

Fit is one aspect of costume in which popular music performers have often departed from public norms while also influencing the evolution of style. As might be expected, fit has run the entire gamut, from very loose to very tight. Band leaders Cab Calloway and Louis Jordan helped to popularize the loose-fitting men's zoot suit of the forties, and this garb enjoyed a British comeback during the rock era.[22] Liberace appeared in capes of magnificent expansiveness, and some of the most outrageously attired punk and heavy metal rock bands have used capes to create a contrast with costumes that are either skin tight or very largely missing.[23]

Tight-fitting clothes became a virtual uniform of the rock culture during the seventies, though they were strongly in evidence both before and after that decade. An early classic example was the very fitted leather jeans worn by Jim Morrison early in his career,[24] but their tightness was soon eclipsed by creations of the seventies, as exemplified by Rod Stewart's imitation leopard skin tights[25] and Tanya Tucker's jumpsuit worn for the cover of her "TNT" album of 1978.[26] Other musicians carried the trend to what must have been its limits.[27]

Accessories have always been an easy way to personalize one's dress style, and popular musicians have not overlooked this opportunity. For years they have used hats, gloves, scarves, and various other artifacts to express an individualistic way of dressing.

Hats are one of the most widely used fashion accessories in popular music, and who could quickly forget the cowboy hat Bob Wills wore to front his Western swing band;[28] Thelonious Monk's beret, which became an emblem of bebop jazz in its infancy;[29] or Frank Sinatra's mainstream hat,[30] which became such a recognizable part of his image in the fifties? The most famous hat in American popular music may be Cousin Minnie Pearl's flowery straw hat with its prominent attached price tag, worn for years on broadcasts of the Grand Ole Opry.[31]

Gloves have not been overlooked in the quest of popular musicians for a distinctive appearance. Sousa launched his return to civilian life after World War I by ordering one hundred dozen pairs of white calfskin gloves, to be used in conducting his professional concert band.[32] Paul Bierley maintains that Sousa's conducting gloves were made of kid rather than calfskin, and offers a photo.[33] Michael Jackson is a famous contemporary wearer of gloves. He is known for cutting off the fingertips, adding a great many sequins, and he often wears only one glove for additional accent.

Artifacts that distinguish specific performers would include such things as Bob Wills's cigar, which was as famous as his hat.[34] Sousa was quoted as admiring the company of a good cigar more than most other creature comforts, and he made them a part of his style by having his favorite brand prepared with a drawing of himself on the wrapper.[35] It is reported that the origin of Rudy Vallee's megaphone was the singer's weak voice, but the resulting visual trademark stood him in good stead when he appeared in print media.[36]

The manner of wearing accessories has been almost as important as the accessories themselves in creating a memorable image for a performer. Frank Sinatra's hats were usually a standard menswear product, but he wore them at a jaunty angle, often far back on his head,[37] but sometimes far down over his brow.[38] Deborah Harry of Blondie wore a standard pair of tight-fit Levi jeans. What was different was the fact that they were badly torn.[39] In 1987, teenagers paid a premium price for worn and torn jeans bought new in a shopping mall. The different thing about Cousin Minnie Pearl's hat was its prominently displayed price tag.

It is probably fair to say that the clothing that is not worn has led to as much costume notoriety among popular musicians as that which is worn. Varying degrees of undress also make a costume statement. Elvis Presley contributed to a male dress style trend of many years running by simply leaving an extra button undone below the collar of his shirt. His single open buttonhole soon became two,[40] and near the end of his life the open gap approached his expanding waistline.[41] The look depended on the absence of an undershirt, and it flourished thus during the sixties and seventies, worn mainly by rock and disco performers and their audiences. Much to the relief of undershirt manufacturers, the men's open-shirt look of the middle and late eighties came to reveal a brightly colored tank top rather than bare skin.

As rock music matured, levels of male undress escalated. Singer Jim Morrison was merchandised as a sex symbol, a persona he carefully cultivated in 1967, asking a Hollywood hair stylist to shape his mane like that observed on a statue of Alexander the Great,[42] and posing shirtless for photo sessions with 16 and *Vogue* magazines and for Elektra Records photographer Joel Brodsky. Judging from the frequency with which they have been reprinted, Brodsky's photos of the shirtless Morrison were a visual bonanza for Elektra, and one of them became known as the "Young Lion" shot.[43] Mick Jagger, Iggy Pop, and Ted Nugent all made shirtless performance a part of their style. Pop's shirtless condition gave his audience a better view of his blood when he chose to cut himself as part of his stage act.

While male musicians were shedding their shirts, some of their female counterparts were getting rid of their bras, and making sure that their audiences noticed the results. Punk rocker Patti Smith wore the braless look on the cover of her *Easter* album (Arista 4177, 1978) and assumed a pose in which she appeared to be looking down at her own slip. The irrepressible Deborah Harry went braless often,[44] and women performers in music styles other than rock also espoused this look in the seventies, for example folk singers Kate and Anna McGarrigle,[45] country rock singer Rita Coolidge,[46] and soul singer Chaka Khan.[47]

While male rock musicians have sometimes removed clothing in a performance, female rockers have occasionally worn see-through garments in concert. Rose Simpson of the Incredible String Band wore a see-through dress of sheer white gauze to perform at the Woodstock Festival,[48] and Linda Ronstadt wore a similar but less revealing dress for one of her album covers.[49] Diana Ross,[50] Claudia Barry,[51] and Deborah Harry[52] were other female performers who embraced the see-through look of the late sixties and seventies.

A female bare-chested look was suggested by the symbolism of one of Madonna's costumes for her "Who's That Girl" tour of 1987. Over the breast section of an opaque black garment in the style of a corset, the pop star wore glossy imitation nipples of bright copper color.[53] At one point in the act, black tassels were suspended from the tops of the ornaments.[54] Madonna looked conservative compared to punk rocker Wendy O. Williams, who wore similar but more exaggerated ornaments.[55] The difference was that Williams wore them over bare skin, a decision that may have contributed to her arrest for indecent exposure.[56]

The ultimate female breast-baring of the sixties came from a performer who was not even engaged in popular music. Classical cellist Charlotte Moorman established a reputation for various forms of nudity in her performances, with her first topless concert in New York City leading to her arrest in mid-recital and earning her the night in jail. Her unique approach to the traditions of art music was more successful in Europe, where she completed without arrest a performance in which movie cartoons were projected on her nude body while she sat astride a metal "bomb" and bowed it with a saw.[57]

Williams and Moorman were hardly alone among musicians in being arrested for indecent exposure. A highly celebrated case was Jim Morrison's arrest, but he chalked up the added notoriety of being charged with "lewd and lascivious behavior" for a 1969 performance in Miami.[58]

Rock performer nudity, originally espoused with an eye toward occasional sexual excitement, came to be an overworked convention that could leave the jaded beholder with an impression of general tastelessness. Many of the open-shirted males in Robert Ellis's *Pictorial Album of Rock* are in a state of physical development that would look better covered up. The Tubes' extreme of nudity and attempted sexuality shows how far some rock groups were willing to go.[59]

The category of performer grooming involves hair style, including facial hair, fingernails, and use of makeup. Hair style can become an easily recognizable trademark, and some classics in this area were the tenderly boyish bangs of the early period Beatles,[60] Bill Haley's famous spit curl,[61] and Little Richard's rampant pompadour.[62] Earlier eras saw the slicked-down look of Paul Whiteman and Bix Beiderbecke. Total baldness has always made a strong visual effect, and early jazz man King Oliver and latter-day soul man Isaac Hayes[63] wore the look with élan. Oliver's baldness gave him a special poignant dignity.[64]

Some performers have changed the color of their hair for visual effect. Deborah Harry is a natural brunette, but began a ritual of routine bleaching of her hair to front the rock group Blondie.[65] At one point she used peroxide to render it silvery white for the production of a picture disc.[66]

Eyebrows can be present or absent, and accentuated or not. Light but geometric eyebrows are essential to the look of Annie Lennox of the Eurythmics.[67] Eyebrow geometry is also essential to Boy George.[68] Lennox uses eye shadow makeup as an important part of her overall look, and male performers Michael Jackson and David Bowie use eye shadow as much as do women.

Moustaches offer male musicians an opportunity for a distinctive facial look, and this look has ranged from the pencil-thin moustache of dapper society band leader Shep Fields,[69] through the slightly heavier versions worn by Paul Whiteman,[70] the young Duke Ellington,[71] and Bix Beiderbecke,[72] to the full-grown drooping moustache worn by Frank Zappa.[73]

Sideburns became an Elvis Presley trademark fairly early in his public life, and he sported a stylish pair for the filming of his 1968 television special. Unfortunately they kept expanding and seemed almost parodistic near the end of his life.[74]

Male performers have used beards to attain a wide variety of looks. It is especially fascinating to note a progression of bearded looks on the same performer, and Jim Morrison may be the best example because of his very short public life. As a young sex symbol, Morrison was clean shaven.[75] As he turned to blues in his musical style he dropped his slinky costumes in favor of a white T-shirt and blue denim. Meanwhile, he grew a full beard.[76] His beard continued to develop into a long, curly, guru look.[77] In short, the beard fit the persona. For his trial in federal court for obstructing the duties of an airline flight crew, the usually scruffy Morrison appeared clean shaven wearing a blazer and necktie.

Long a target of patronizing commercials, the dusky precursor of male beard formerly known as five o'clock shadow has enjoyed unprecedented acclaim in the eighties. While some have hypothesized that it cost Richard Nixon at least one election, it has become an indicator of male coolness after its favorable introduction to the public on the successful television series *Miami Vice*. Jim Morrison was actually one of its pioneers,[78] but it took popular contemporaries such as Sting to get the look better established among musicians. George Michael and Jon Bon Jovi are two of the newer performers to wear the look.[79]

If Sting typifies the currently popular shadow-beard look, country musician Kenny Rogers is a good example of the more traditional beard—fuller and longer, but very neatly trimmed.[80] Rock musicians Ian Anderson of Jethro Tull, Jerry Garcia of the Grateful Dead, and Billy Gibbons and Dusty Hill of ZZ Top have modeled some the longest and fullest beards in popular music.[81]

The color of a beard can also convey a message. Sousa's dark full beard worn when he assumed command of the Marine Band gave an impression of youth as well as authority. On the other hand, the gray beard of Kenny Rogers speaks of maturity and experience, and this impression also surfaces sometimes in the lyrics of his songs. There is something of a graybeard tradition in country music, with recurrent admonitions that one had better show respect for a graybeard.

Makeup is an aspect of grooming which is associated almost exclusively with females by the general public. This is not the case with performers, who all need some of it to avoid a deathly pallor under the intensity of stage or television lighting. Rock musicians, however, have hardly stopped at the moderate amounts of makeup needed to ward off pallor. During the glitter rock era of the seventies, David Bowie wore stabbing streaks of makeup across his face in the shape of a lightning bolt.[82] By the end of the decade, Kiss had established a painted-face look which made Bowie seem conservative.[83] At that point in their career, the members of Kiss so valued the look that they refused to be interviewed or photographed without full makeup.

For many people eyeglasses are merely a necessity for seeing, but popular music performers have even turned their mundane spectacles into personal trademarks. Pince-nez glasses were a Sousa trademark,[84] while Benny Goodman and Glenn Miller wore wire-rim models which were almost frameless.[85] Buddy Holly could be recognized by his black plastic eyeglass frames, and it would appear that he and Roy Orbison must have gone to the same optician.[86] Blind musician Ray Charles has dark glasses in frames similar to Holly's. For him they have become a timeless and very personal trademark.[87]

In the sixties, John Lennon espoused wire-rim frames which contrasted with the plastic frames of the fifties, and Grace Slick performed at the Woodstock Festival in rose-tinted wire-rim octagons.[88] The glasses Janis Joplin wore at Woodstock were tinted orange and quite oversize in contrast to Slick's.[89] Among contemporary performers, eyewear styles have ranged from the Ben Franklin frames worn by country musician Grandpa Jones,[90] through the very highly styled plastic frames favored by Elton John.[91]

Musicians have generally remained close to the trends of their times in selection of eyewear, but sometimes they are responsible for creating new trends. It would require methodical historical investigation to determine whether they created a style or helped to popularize a style which had been originated by others.

Jewelry is a standard means of personal adornment, and popular musicians of both sexes have made ample use of it. Liberace may be the classic example, but Presley and Morrison used it to good effect in designing their own looks. One of the most striking uses of jewelry has been made by soul performer Isaac Hayes, who has often appeared shirtless wearing very heavy gold chains arranged in a way reminiscent of suspenders.[92] Jelly Roll Morton had a front tooth which displayed a diamond embedded in gold.[93] Sadly, he had to pawn his famous ornament for living expenses near the end of his life.

The tattoo is another form of personal adornment used by musicians. Actress-musician Cher may have the most famous tattoo in popular music. It is located on her buttock, and she has worn costumes which display it.[94]

In summary, what uses have popular music performers made of costume? They have used it to define a persona. They have used it to differentiate roles within a group, and these roles have been as varied as band leader, sideman, clown, or sex object. They have used costume to create and maintain a specific personal trademark. They have used costume to stay up-to-date, always remaining stylish and current. Some have decided not to stay up-to-date, instead giving the public another view of styles already proven to be popular. Many have used costume to show unanimity with the conventions of a musical style. Others have used costume to defy convention and create outrage, saying that they are only doing what the public really wants to do but does not dare.

For its own part, what has been the public's reaction to the costume of popular music performers? Sometimes the public denounces it, sometimes the public imitates it, but always the public notices it. And that is what performers want more than anything else.

Notes

1. Paul E. Bierley, *John Philip Sousa: American Phenomenon* (Englewood Cliffs, N.J.: Prentice-Hall, 1973), 6, 13.

2. H. W. Schwartz, *Bands of America* (Garden City, N.Y.: Doubleday, 1957).

3. Peter Gammond, *Scott Joplin and the Ragtime Era* (New York: St. Martin's Press, 1975), 95.

4. Al Rose and Edmond Souchon, *New Orleans Jazz*, revised edition (Baton Rouge: Louisiana State University Press, 1978).

5. Al Rose, *Storyville, New Orleans* (University, Ala.: University of Alabama Press, 1974), 108.

6. Chris Albertson, *Jelly Roll Morton* (Alexandria, Va.: Time-Life Records, Giants of Jazz Series, 1979), 6–7.

7. Debbie Harry, Chris Stein, and Victor Bockris, *Making Tracks: The Rise of Blondie* (New York: Dell, 1982), 35.

8. Ted Polhemus and Lynn Procter, *Pop Styles* (London: Vermilion, 1984), 65.

9. Patrick Carr, ed., *The Illustrated History of Country Music* (Garden City, N.Y.: Doubleday, 1979), 258.

10. Timothy White, *Rock Stars* (New York: Stewart, Tabori, and Chang, 1984), 89.

11. Polhemus and Proctor, 48.

12. Harry, Stein, and Bockris, 34.

13. Martin Torgoff, ed., *The Complete Elvis* (New York: Delilah, 1982), 195.

14. See Polhemus and Proctor, *Pop Styles*.

15. Albert Goldman, *Elvis* (New York: McGraw-Hill, 1981), 290.

16. Danny Sugerman, *The Doors: The Illustrated History* (New York: Morrow, 1983), 37.

17. Ibid., 146.

18. Jerry Strobel, ed., *Grand Ole Opry: WSM Picture-History Book* (Nashville: WSM, 1976), 106, 115.

19. Torgoff, 218–19.

20. Polhemus and Proctor, 95.

21. Roger Dean and David Howells, *The Ultimate Album Cover Album* (Englewood Cliffs, N.J.: Prentice-Hall, 1987), 195.

22. Polhemus and Proctor, 113.

23. Ibid., 20–21.

24. Sugerman, 37 and 83.

25. White, 184–85.

26. Polhemus and Proctor, 65.

27. Ibid., 126–27.

28. Charles R. Townsend, *San Antonio Rose: The Life and Music of Bob Wills* (Urbana: University of Illinois Press, 1976), 271.

29. William P. Gottleib, *The Golden Age of Jazz* (New York: Simon and Schuster, 1979), 115.

30. John Howlett, *Frank Sinatra* (New York: Simon and Schuster, 1979), 80.

31. Jack Hurst, *Nashville's Grand Ole* Opry (New York: Abrams, 1975), 163.

32. Schwartz, 284–85.

33. Bierley, 134.

34. Bob Wills, *King of Western Swing* (MCA-543, 1973).

35. Bierley, 102.

36. George T. Simon, *The Best of the Music Makers* (Garden City, N.Y.: Doubleday, 1979), 583.

37. Howlett, 65, 87, 107.

38. Ibid., 95.

39. Harry, Stein, and Bockris, 132.

40. Torgoff, 94, 135.

41. Goldman, 290.

42. Jerry Hopkins and Danny Sugerman, *No One Here Gets Out Alive* (New York: Warner, 1980), 144.

43. Ibid., 165.

44. Harry, Stein, and Bockris, 99.

45. Kristin Baggelaar and Donald Milton, *Folk Music: More Than a Song* (New York: Crowell, 1976), 283.

46. Fred Dellar and Roy Thompson, *The Illustrated Encyclopedia of Country Music* (New York: Harmony, 1977), 58.

47. Jon Futrell et al. *The Illustrated Encyclopedia of Black Music* (New York: Harmony, 1982), 163.

48. Jean Young and Michael Lang, *Woodstock Festival Remembered* (New York: Ballantine, 1979), 58.

49. Ethan A. Russell, *Dear Mr. Fantasy* (Boston: Houghton Mifflin, 1985), 236.

50. White, 191.

51. Polhemus and Proctor, 106.

52. Lester Bangs, *Blondie* (New York: Simon and Schuster, 1980), 73.

53. Rich Elias, "Madonna Live," *Rock Scene Presents Concert Shots* (March 1988), 13.

54. Ibid., 31.

55. Polhemus and Proctor, 107.

56. Ibid., 83.

57. "A Unique Cello Recital," *The Instrumentalist* (November 1968), 10.

58. Hopkins and Sugerman, 236 and 238.

59. Robert Ellis, *The Pictorial Album of Rock* (New York: Crescent, 1981), 204–5.

60. Nick Logan and Bob Woffinden, *The Illustrated Encyclopedia of Rock* (New York: Harmony, 1977), 27.

61. Ibid., 101.

62. Tony Palmer, *All You Need Is Love* (Harmondsworth, England: Penguin, 1977), 220–21.

63. Futrell et al., 152; Polhemus and Proctor, 104.

64. Rose, 119.

65. Bangs, 53, 55.

66. Polhemus and Proctor, 86.

67. Annie Lennox and Dave Stewart, *Eurhythmics in Their Own Words* (Sydney: Omnibus, 1984), 28–29.

68. Polhemus and Proctor, 78.

69. George T. Simon, *Simon Says: The Sights and Sounds of the Swing Era 1935–1955* (New Rochelle, N.Y.: Arlington House, 1971), 65.

70. Leo Walker, *The Big Band Almanac* (Pasadena: Ward Richie, 1978), 423.

71. Stanley Dance, *Duke Ellington* (Alexandria, Va.: Time-Life Records, Giants of Jazz Series, 1978), frontispiece.

72. Curtis Prendergast, *Bix Beiderbecke* (Alexandria, Va.: Time-Life Records, Giants of Jazz Series, 1979), 31.

73. Ellis, 222–23.

74. Goldman, 290.

75. Frank Lisciandro, *Jim Morrison: An Hour for Magic* (New York: Delilah, 1982), inside cover.

76. Ibid., 70.
77. Ibid., 89, 157–58.
78. Ibid., 6.
79. *Creem Rock Shots* (March 1988), 18, 51, 67.
80. Dellar and Thompson, 200.
81. Ellis, 102, 111; Polhemus and Proctor, 137.
82. Polhemus and Proctor, 75.
83. Polhemus and Proctor, 77; Ellis, 120.
84. Bierley, 83
85. Simon, *Simon Says*, 48, 433.
86. Polhemus and Proctor, 50.
87. White, 49.
88. Young and Lang, 63.
89. Ibid., 62.
90. Hurst, 145.
91. Ellis, 113.
92. Futrell et al., 119, 152.
93. Albertson, 26.
94. "Cher's Bottom Line," *People Weekly* (January 14, 1980), 63.

5

American Denim: Blue Jeans and Their Multiple Layers of Meaning

Beverly Gordon

Blue jeans, the now-ubiquitous denim garments that almost constitute a uniform on high school and college campuses, have been an integral part of the American scene for more than one hundred years. In that time they have embodied many different messages, and functioned in different ways—as symbols of rebellion; outlets for personal creativity; emblems of up-to-date, fashionable awareness; and evidence of generational longing and insecurity. Changes in jeans styling, embellishment, and marketing are closely tied to changes in the society as a whole, and these changes serve as a subtle but accurate barometer of trends in contemporary popular culture. The jeans phenomenon merits serious attention on the part of the popular culture scholar.

The Blue Jean: The Wild West and the Farmer

Jeans first appeared in their now-familiar form in California in the second half of the nineteenth century. Levi Strauss, a Bavarian immigrant, came

Reprinted by permission from *Dress and Popular Culture*, eds. Patricia A. Cunningham and Susan Voso Lab (Bowling Green, Ohio: Popular Press, 1991), 31–45.

to San Francisco in 1850 with a supply of strong canvas cloth that he hoped to sell to people making tents and wagon covers, but when he saw the kind of hard wear the gold prospectors gave their clothes, he had it made into sturdy pants. "Levi's" were really born when Strauss switched to a heavy denim fabric a few years later. Copper rivets were added at the stress points in 1873.[1] Jeans first evolved, then, as practical rather than fashionable clothing and were associated with hard-working physical laborers, especially those from the rough and rugged West. By the early twentieth century, when Levi's competed with other brands such as Wrangler and Lee, jeans and related denimwear such as protective overalls were the modal garments for farmers. By 1902 the Sears and Roebuck catalogue offered five different denimwear styles.[2] Again, individuals who wore these garments were not "fashionable," they were not making a statement of any kind; they were simply choosing serviceable, affordable clothing.

The Blue Jean as Anti-Fashion: The First Association

Jeans were first adopted as a kind of anti-fashion—a conscious, pointed statement that goes against the fashion norm and says, "I am different, I am not like you"—by a group of artists in the Santa Fe area in the 1920s.[3] Generally well-educated individuals of both sexes took to wearing jeans as a badge of their own group identity and special status. They were identifying themselves with the ruggedness, the directness, and the earthiness of the laborer, and were placing themselves as a part of the Western scene. They also adopted a unisex look long before it was the norm.

This group of artists continued to sport jeans in the 1930s, but something of the same impulse was also promulgated in the mainstream fashion world. Levi Strauss executives began encouraging Easterners who were taking the newly popular "dude ranch" vacations to outfit themselves with jeans or overalls, and the garments even became available for the first time in up-scale New York stores. Levi Strauss ran an ad in the April 1935 Vogue: "true Western chic was invented by cowboys."[4] Although the trend did not really take off at this time outside the dude ranch context, this was perhaps the first instance where fashionable consumers were encouraged to take on the aura of a particular lifestyle by wearing jeans.

The Blue Jean as War Hero: Widening the Base of Support

World War II was a turning point for blue jeans in America. Materials were scarce as resources were diverted to the war effort, but with the increasing number of workers in the factories and munitions plants, great quantities of durable work clothes were needed. Jeans were declared "essential commodities," and to serve the needs of thousands of Rosie the Riveters, the Blue Bell company came out with a special Wrangler dungaree style dubbed "the Jeanie."[5] Once again these were not really fashionable garments—they were work clothes. They were still used only in a particular context. Because factory war work was seen in a positive light, however, the garments were perceived as part of the patriotic, all-pitching-in spirit, and were thought of fondly. To women workers who had been used to wearing dresses and more constricting garments, they must have also seemed liberating and refreshingly comfortable. Wartime fashion was changing, also, and taking much of its detailing from the rather unfashionable wartime scene. Head wraps or turbans, originally used in the factories to keep long hair out of the machinery, became part of acceptable evening wear. Shoulder pads, originally seen in military uniforms, became an indispensable part of women's civilian garments. Jeans were associated with a particular war-era lifestyle, and were poised somewhere in the middle on the fashion/anti-fashion continuum.

The Blue Jean Anti-Fashion: Tomboys, Bad Boys, and Bohemians

After the war, jeans were no longer just unfashionable; they came to have widespread distinct anti-fashion associations. The hard-edged, square-shouldered female styles gave way in the high-style world to the ultra-feminine and very dressy "New Look," and the more rugged, unisex denim garments began to be associated with youth, freedom, and rebellion. Bennington College students, who were generally known as "artistic" and rather unconventional, adopted jeans as a "virtual uniform" on their Vermont campus.[6] They too used their clothing to symbolize freedom—freedom from the norms of conventional society.

Sometimes this freedom was simply the prerogative of youth, and was seen as innocent and harmless. Eddie Fisher crooned *Dungaree Doll* in the late 1940s,[7] and evoked the image of a happy-go-lucky bobby soxer, a tomboy who would eventually, in the words of another postwar era song, "trade her bobby sox for stockings." Another type of freedom emerged in the early 1950s, however, which was seen as much more sinister. There was a group of disenfranchised individuals who could not find a place in the conformist climate of Cold War America and who reacted to it with alienation and disdain. These were the young people symbolized in Marlon Brando's *The Wild One* and James Dean's *Rebel Without a Cause*, the angry or confused or simply no-good "juvenile delinquents" who at their most extreme flashed switchblades and tire irons and terrorized neighborhoods. These young people, also, wore jeans: jeans and leather jackets were the anti-fashion wardrobe that symbolically flaunted the mores of the frightened society at large. Jeans were so strongly associated with these outcasts, in fact, that a 1959 movie about an unwed teenage mother was tellingly titled *Blue Denim*.[8] The good-versus-bad connations were symbolized by a "dress right" campaign launched by the American Institute of Men's and Boy's Wear and aimed particularly at blue jeans.[9]

Associations with the Wild West actually strengthened or reinforced the anti-fashion statement that jeans made in the 1950s. This was the era of the Gray Flannel Suit and the Organization Man (A). It was a time permeated by what author Peter Beagle characterizes as "a strangled, constipated idea of a proper life."[10] It was also the era of the Hollywood and TV Western. Good and bad cowboys were sometimes differentiated by the color of their hats, but they all wore jeans. The Western simultaneously replayed the good guys/bad guys scenario of the Cold War and represented an escape from it, a foray into a still wild or "untamed" past where people did not have to fit into such carefully prescribed niches. Baby-boomers who grew up with Western heroes grew up with images of jeans, and wore them for their creative play. They wore them when they wanted to step into a fantasy world that was outside the world of piano lessons, visiting relatives, and other dutiful activities.

Anti-Fashion at Its Peak: The "Jeaning of America" and the Personalized Jean

It was in the 1960s that the "jeaning of America" occurred, and jeans took on a new role. The first signs of the shift really began in the late 1950s, when another type of rebel, the bohemian or "beatnik," began to adopt them with black sweaters for everyday wear. Unlike the Brando/Dean "bad boy" rebel, this was a dissenter, an urban intellectual who came to an anti-fashion statement of this sort from a thought-out position about the materialistic, conformist society of the day. To wear plain jeans and dark colors was to reject the more-is-better, new-is-better mentality of the Organization Man world. According to Levi Strauss executive Alfred Sanguinetti, 1962 marked the "breakout" point in jeans sales, with sales figures doubling in just three years. They further quintupled between 1965 and 1970[11] (B). By 1967 the anti-fashion statement was screaming across the land, for jeans were one of the most visible symbols of the rapidly increasing numbers of disenfranchised youth. The late 1960s were, of course, the turbulent period in which there was a marked escalation of the undeclared war in Vietnam, a war that polarized the society and led to a widespread rejection of mainstream social norms on the part of the younger generation. The youth-dominated counterculture, which was made up of the same baby-boomers who had worn jeans as play clothes and had grown up with James Dean and other such cultural icons, turned to jeans very naturally. Jeans were practical, long-lasting, and unchanging; they were the very antitheses of the mainstream "straight" world where fashion was by its very nature ever changing and quickly obsolescent. They were cheap, comfortable, and associated with physicality; they represented freedom from dutifulness, and because they were simultaneously associated with work and play, came to stand for a society where there really was no distinction between the two. As Valerie Carnes put it in a 1977 article entitled "Icons of Popular Fashion,"

> Denim jeans became [in the 1960s] the ultimate no-fashion put-down style—a classless, cheap, unisex look that stood for, variously, frontier values, democracy, plain living, ecology and health, rebellion *a la* Brando or Dean, a new interest in the erotic import of the pelvis, or, as Charles Reich suggested in *The Greening of America*, a deliberate rejection of the "artificial plastic-coated look" of the affluent consumer society.[12]

Jeans may have been the common anti-fashion denominator among the young, but not all jeans were alike. Jeans wearers avoided the plastic veneer and the sameness and artificiality it represented by the very act of wearing their jeans. Jeans conformed more and more to particular body shapes as they were worn and washed (cotton denim shrinks and stretches each time it is washed and reworn). Over time jeans came to carry particular "scars"—stains, rips, frayed areas, patches—that could be associated with remembered events and experiences. A pair of jeans became intensely personal. A small hole might be left alone as a "badge" of experience, or great deliberation might go into the choice of an appropriate fabric with which to cover it. Soon, counterculture youth were *glorifying* their jeans—decorating and embellishing them, making them colorful and celebratory, and making them into visible, vocal personal statements. Silk, velvet, leather, feathers, bells, beads, rivets, sequins, paint—anything that could be applied to denim fabric was applied to someone's jeans, jeans jackets, and related accessories. Men who had never learned to sew and who under most circumstances would think of embroidery as unmanly learned the necessary stitches to work on their own clothes. The unisex garment that symbolized the alternative youth culture was an appropriate vehicle for the breakdown of gender roles, and besides, one's jeans were too personal to trust to anyone else. By 1974 imaginatively adorned jeans were such a pervasive and interesting phenomenon that the Levi Strauss company sponsored a national "denim art" contest and was deluged with entries. Entrants repeatedly stated that they found it difficult to part with the garments long enough for them to be displayed in the exhibition; they felt they were giving up a part of themselves. "I feel most myself when I have my jeans on" was a typical comment from an entrant. Others said: "My jeans are an extension of me" and "my shorts [are] my autobiography on denim."[13]

The Blue Jean as Fashion: Absorbing the Counterculture with a Designer Label

In some ways it had by this time become almost necessary to dramatically personalize one's jeans in order to still make an anti-fashion statement. Many of the outward signs and even some of the underlying ideas of the counterculture had been adopted (some might say usurped) by the mainstream culture at large. Blue jeans in and of themselves were so well accepted in the establishment that even such political figures as New York City Mayor John Lindsay and presidential candidate Jimmy Carter were happy to be photographed wearing them. Anti-fashion had not only been absorbed by fashion, but had become part of its very essence. John Brooks, writing in The New Yorker in 1979, attributed the fashionable usurpation of the jeans phenomenon to the early 1970s "search for the fountain of youth,"[14] but it may have been as much a sign of an underlying widespread hunger for life-affirming values in what was a confused and dark time.

Jeans and other denim garments were also seen in the early 1970s as quintessentially American. Jeans had been developed in the United States, of course, and had long carried associations of the American West, but once they had filtered into the international fashion scene, they came to stand for the country as a whole. In 1973 the American Fashion Critics presented a special award to Levi Strauss for "a fundamental American fashion that . . . now influences the world." Nieman Marcus also gave Levi Strauss its Distinguished Service in Fashion Award that same year[15] (C). The popular press began to print rhetorical questions like "after all, what's more American than denim?"[16] and in 1974 American Motors Corporation contracted with Levi Strauss to provide blue denim fabric for upholstery for its Gremlin and Hornet cars.[17] The Gremlin, which was promoted as America's answer to the Volkswagon Beetle, was meant to be both upbeat and patriotic, and denim furnishings were thought to communicate both qualities.

Jeans sales continued to climb. By 1977 over 500 million pairs were sold in this country alone—more than twice the number of the total population.[18]

Fashion and anti-fashion came exceedingly close during this period, but there were continually two thrusts to the jeans craze. The counterculture continued to thrive and maintained and fostered a do-your-own, personalize-your-clothing vision. Numerous instruction books published between 1973 and 1977 carried a power-to-the-people message and told people how to fashion and refashion their own denim clothing. Publications with such titles as *Clothing Liberation, Make It in Denim, The Jeans Scene, The Jeans Book,* and *Native Funk and Flash*[19] continued to advocate inexpensive and comfortable clothing that made use of worn garments and other available materials. Cast-offs and odds and ends could not only be salvaged, but creatively used.

At the same time, there was a high-fashion version of this democratic, anti-fashion trend. Couturiers who saw these creative outfits on the streets and in such legitimizing exhibitions as Wesleyan University's "Smart Ass Art" (1973) and Levi Strauss's "Denim Art" at the Museum of Contemporary Crafts (1974) moved in and produced their own high-style versions of counterculture styles. Givenchy designed an entire denim wardrobe for film star Audrey Hepburn, for example, and Giorgio outfitted Dyan Cannon and Ava Gardner.[20] A $2,325 denim-lined mink jacket and mink-cuffed jeans were shown on the fashion runways in Paris in 1974, and professionally designed embroidered, sequinned, and nail-studded ensembles were going for about $500 in New York boutiques.[21] Recycled and well-worn fabrics— hallmarks of the counterculture look—were part of this style. Giorgio's jeans outfits that sold for $250 were made from already-used denim, for example, and designer shops in department stores like Lord and Taylor sold recycled jeans for three times the price of new ones.[22]

By the late 1970s, when the baby-boomers had been largely absorbed into the work force and the responsibilities of parenting, and the counterculture vision had become diffused, the high-style fashion forces won out over the anti-fashion style. Couture denim filtered down into the ready-to-wear market. Designer labels became an obsession; "designer jeans" were "*the* pants in America," according to a Saks Fifth Avenue retailer. Calvin Klein, who drew attention to jeans sporting his label with an erotic advertising campaign, sold 125,000 pairs a week in 1979.[23] Designer jeans were in such demand that there was a thriving counterfeit trade, and by 1981 *Good Housekeeping* magazine ran a feature advising consumers how to make sure they were buying the "real thing"[24] (D).

Designer jeans were often based on anti-fashion prototypes (both Calvin

Klein and Oscar de la Renta are known to have sent photographers out into the streets of New York to document what people were wearing),[25] but they tended to be subtle: they did not, in the early Reagan era, generally sport embroidered patches and tattered fringe. Often nearly indistinguishable (except by the small designer label sewn on the back pocket), they offered ostentatious but restrained snob appeal. Jeans were no longer the "great American equalizer"(E). Homemade and recycled garments did not have a place in the less democratic age—or rather, they had a place, but it was back with the poor and have-nots. Designer jeans were made to fit and flatter the body, but they were made to be long-lasting and uniform rather than to age and change with the individual. In 1984 several fabric manufacturers came out with new polyester/denim blends that were intended to stretch with the body and keep their shape. The Sydeco company introduced "Forever Blue," a new fade-resistant jeans fabric that was designed to "look new longer."[26]

The Blue Jean as Fashion: Prepackaged Experience

The Aged Jean

It seems fitting to begin the most recent chapter of the jeans saga in 1985, with the story of the "Authentic Stone." This was a product developed by Marshall Banks, who got the idea when he discovered a small piece of pumice stone in the pocket of his newly purchased jeans. Banks learned that the stone was accidentally left behind from the "stone washing"—the preconditioning process—that the jeans had been subjected to. Small pieces of pumice, which is an abrasive material, had been added to a premarket washing order to soften the garment (F). As the earlier description of innovative 1984 jeans fabrics makes clear, stone-washing and other preconditioning treatments were not yet de rigueur. Banks stated, presumably with his tongue in his cheek, that he hoped to appeal to the "do-it-yourselfer" with his Authentic [pumice] Stone packaged in its own "bed of denim." He felt his product blended "the whole 60s look with a status connotation"; it was a symbolic prepackaging of experience, a fashionable way of referring to the anti-fashion of the past. One hundred thousand Authentic Stones had been sold to leading department stores by 1986.[27]

The 1960s anti-fashion style had indeed been a look of well-used, lived-in jeans. The Vietnam years were enormously intense—every day brought the promise of incredible revelation of impending apocalypse—and experience was highly charged (G). The jeans one wore were part of the experience; they were faithful companions, they had been there. Even if they weren't heavily decorated, they were "encrusted" with memories,[28] and held the accumulated charge (H). Small wonder that aged, faded, tattered jeans were treasured: they were not only comfortable, but were far richer and more meaningful than those that were new and unmarked.

The best jeans were those that had aged naturally, over the course of time and experience, but there were numerous homegrown or do-it-yourself methods to speed up the aging process in order to look presentable. Folk wisdom suggested the best way to soften and shape one's jeans was to repeatedly get them wet and wear them until they dried. This could be done by soaking in the bathtub, but the sun and saltwater of the ocean beach environment was much preferred (I). New jeans were also home-treated by rubbing sandpaper and pumice stones across the fabric, by burying them, or by adding washing soda or bleach to a tubful of water.[29] The bleach treatment was controversial, largely because it weakened the fabric in the wrong places and made it look bleached rather than worn.[30]

The faded look was commercially imitated in a prebleached fabric for the first time in 1969, presumably inspired by the sun-bleached denims seen on the Riviera, and the look was popular in France.[31] Some very high-priced customized jeans were prefaded; items taken to "Robbie's Stud and Rhinestone Shop," an establishment that serviced fashion-conscious celebrities in Los Angeles, for example, were sent to a denim fading lab before the studding process began.[32] A few American laundry companies developed fading treatments in 1973 and jeans manufacturers like H. D. Lee contracted with them for several thousand faded garments,[33] but bleached fabrics were still not the norm. More and more "prewashed" denims were on the market by the late 1970s, but the phenomenon crept in slowly. A 1981 *Mademoiselle* fashion column spoke of the "new, faded look," but disparaged it for its extra costliness. Readers were advised to use inexpensive commercial color removers or fading products on their jeans if they liked the look of prewashed fabric.[34]

The prewashed look was characteristic of jeans manufactured by Guess, a company started in 1981, interestingly enough, by four brothers who had emigrated to the United States from France. Guess jeans achieved their well-worn look through a stonewashing process that took up to twelve hours, and by 1986 the company was already having trouble finding launderers with whom they could subcontract, as the treatments were breaking even the strongest washing machines.[35] Guess products, though expensive, began "flying off department store shelves" almost as soon as they were stocked,[36] and Guess captured a significant piece of the youth market by the mid-1980s. Other companies quickly found ways to emulate the prewashed look. *Rolling Stone* magazine proclaimed in May 1986 that the "best jeans available" were triple bleached and double stonewashed,[37] but the sentiment was still by no means universally accepted. One commentator writing in *Esquire* protested that hastening the aging process was a form of "faddish dishonesty." "To wear jeans is to create a life mold of oneself in denim," he exclaimed; preworn jeans are not a reflection of the "person within."[38] Numerous "upscale" American designers were using denim in their new lines, but were concentrating on less casual items such as dresses and coats, and aging treatments were not part of their design process.[39]

The Guess prototype and its "worn to death" look (J) continued to permeate the retail denim market, however, and it effectively dominated the 1987–88 fashion season. With fierce competition for the many dollars spent on jeans and other denim items (more than thirteen pairs of jeans were sold every second in 1986),[40] it was not surprising that novelty would be at a premium, but there was another, more fundamental reason that such products caught on. The 1980s crop of worn and faded-looking denimwear provided its primarily young customers with a costume that had *lived*. It carried a feeling or ambience, an illusion of experience. It, even more seriously than the Authentic Stone, represented a prepackaged kind of experience that was risk-free (K).

The actual intense and heady experiences of the counterculture Vietnam generation are not available to today's youth. "Free love" and easy sexuality have been tainted by the terrifying fear of AIDS, and optimistic faith in expanded consciousness through mind-altering drugs has been destroyed by the specter of crack and other lethal substances. The world no longer seems full of unending promise. It is no longer possible to take to the road with the certainty that there will be "brothers" who will provide places to stay along the way; this is the age of the homeless, and people avert their eyes. The realities of child abuse, incest, alcoholism, and family violence are ever more evident. There is no groundswell of passionate feeling to tap into, no clear vision of a better future. Unlike the children of the 1960s, then, the children of the 1980s are cautious and rightfully afraid. I maintain that they have taken to the washed-out tattered garments because they *imply* experience, adventure, and drama, and offer a vicarious (though not really conscious) experience of it. These clothes provide the security of the most up-to-date fashion, but the fashion itself alludes to the anti-fashion of an earlier time, and plays upon a longing for the (counter) culture that produced it.

Distressed Denim

The terms used to describe the new denimwear are quite telling. Denim is now subjected not only to stones, but to acid; it is "abused," "distressed," "sabotaged" and "blasted"; it has been "washed out." It is also cold and frigid: it is "frosted," "frozen out," and "iced"; and "glacier" or "polar-washed." At first these terms seemed reminiscent of the words used in the Vietnam era for the drug experience (stoned, wasted, wiped out), but in reality they have a much harder, more anguished edge. One was stoned or wiped out from an abundance of experience, now one has simply weathered the storm ("Storm Riders," and "White Lightning" are two contemporary jeans styles). Today's "Get Used" fashions echo the underlying desperation of the age.

Descriptive labels that come with this aged denimwear try to be comforting. "This garment is made to look used and soft," one states. "It is broken in just for you." Customers are reassured that the jeans are "inspired by the faded, comfortable character" of well-worn clothing, or by the "comfortable good looks and free-wheeling spirit of aviators and prairie hands." This is "authentic apparel," state the labels; these garments are "like three years old." The underlying message is that the world out there is a tough one, but the clothing has been through it and has already taken it. It is protective, for it acts as a foil and absorbs the shock so its owner doesn't have to. It is soothing: "worn denim is man's best friend" (L).

The 1988 season denimwear also borrowed from the free-spirited, make-your-own, recycle-it trend of the mid-1970s. Couturiers were beginning to show this look in about 1989, but now increasing numbers of ready-to-wear garments are designed to look as if they were made from several pairs of cut-up and reused jeans. There are waistband details tucked into bodices or turned upside-down on the bottom of jackets; there are odd pockets and belt loops sewn in at jaunty diagonal angles. Contrasting color patches, particularly in mattress ticking prints, are also evident.

Sadly, all these trendy looks are mere facades. Prewashed jeans are not really made "just for" anyone; they hold no one's individual contours. Jackets may have extra waistbands and added pockets or patches, but they do not have the free-spirited spontaneity and freshness of the make-your-own era. Much of the tattered quality of contemporary denimwear also looks contrived and unnatural. Wear and tear that develops during consecutive hours of laundering does not necessarily occur in areas that would be naturally stressed or worn, and sewn-in fringed selvages look too regular to be real. When a whole line of jackets even bears a "rip" in the same place and the rip is always outlined with rows of stitches, the point is exceedingly forced. These clothes may first allude to another era, and may offer the illusion of experience and comfort, but illusions are all they offer. They are in reality prepackaged, just like the Authentic Stone. They set up a facade for their wearers, a facade that makes them seem larger than they may be able to be. The look has struck a responsive chord, for it speaks to a yearning on the part of the young jeans customer, a yearning for a time when the world was not just tough, but exciting, and full of promise and imminent discovery.

Selling the Image

Photographs used in magazine advertisements for this denim clothing support the thesis developed above. Jeans manufacturers take it for granted at this point that their product is desirable, but they struggle to create memorable images that prospective customers will identify with. Consequently, the photographs do not feature the garments as much as create a mood or tell a story. The stories are dreamy and "mythic"[41] (M) and full of implications. Sometimes they imply a free and uninhibited sexuality—Calvin Klein ads featuring photographs by Bruce Weber consist of ambiguous images such as one woman surrounded by four men, two of whom are shirtless, or an odd tangle of bodies on the grass. Guess advertisements often include unbuttoned and unbuckled garments, and glimpses of lacy underwear beneath. A recent Jordache ad was headlined, "I Can't Get No Satisfaction," and simulated a young man's internal monologue: "I don't know what's with you girls. . . . Your body says yes but your lips say no . . . but you, Sandy, you're not like the rest. You wouldn't play with my head. . . ." The story had a happy ending, for in the next frame Sandy and the young man are entwined together, and he is peering soulfully into her denim jacket. Even where there is no explicit sexuality, there is a sensual undertone. Characters in Guess ads are always positioned suggestively, leaning, stretching, or slouching with studied ease.

Many of the vignettes include references to the adventurous past of the blue jean. There are couples leaning on motorcycles (Calvin Klein) and men in black leather gloves (Guess); rugged rodeo riders or free-wheeling Western characters with bolo ties or bandana neckerchiefs (Guess, Levi's); and even a young girl with a head kerchief that looks as if she just stepped off the wagon train (Guess). There are aviators and wavy-haired workers from the World War II era (Work Force—the Gap), and sullen bohemian-types dressed in black (Calvin Klein).

The characters in these advertisements are uniformly young and attractive, but they rarely seem full of vitality, joy, or optimism. Often, they face completely away from the camera or have their faces totally or partially obscured by unkempt long hair (itself a reference to the 1960s) or by shadow. Where faces are visible, expressions tend to be enigmatic: dreamy or thoughtful, perhaps, or petulant, sad, or weary. This enigmatic quality is quite anonymous, and suitably enough it allows potential customers to project themselves into the scene and become one of the characters. The scenes hint, in a rather desultory way, of experience and adventure, and imply that the worn garments the characters wear will bring that experience within the reach of even the most unadventurous or inexperienced teenager.

Blue jeans and related denim garments have, in sum, come to stand not just for the Wild West or the rugged laborer or the hardworking farmer— they have become an integral part of the whole American (and perhaps the worldwide) scene. They have been bleached, ripped, washed with acid, washed with stones, patched, cut up, decorated, distressed, and "worn to death," but they are resilient, and seem to always be able to return in yet another guise and take on yet another layer of meaning. They have at different times seemed matter-of-fact and part of the scenery, and at other times have called out for notice and attention. They have served as symbols of the culture at large and of subsets of that culture, and of rebellious, outspoken counterculture groups; they have been fashionable, unfashionable, and hallmarks of anti-fashion. They have embodied many of the longings, beliefs, and realities of the generations that have worn them. We must watch and try to understand them as they continue to evolve.

Notes

1. Elaine Ratner, "Levi's," *Dress* 1 (1975), 1–2; Robert Shea, "Yesterday's Leggings Are Today's Fashion Craze," *Today's Health* (March 1975), 31; John Brooks, "Annals of Business: A Friendly Product," *New Yorker* (November 12, 1979), 64–65.

2. Becky Rupp, "In Praise of Bluejeans: The Denimization of America," *Blair Ketchum's Country Journal* (December 1985), 83.

3. Brooks, 58.

4. Ibid.; John Berendt, "Blue Jeans," *Esquire* (September 1986), 24.

5. Brooks, 71; Carin C. Quinn, "The Jeaning of America—and the World," *American Heritage* (April 1978), 19; Shea, 31.

6. Brooks, 58.

7. Sharon Rosenberg and Joan Wiener Bordow, *The Denim Book* (Englewood Cliffs, N.J.: Prentice-Hall, 1978), xi.

8. Shea, 30.

9. Brooks, 72.

10. Peter Beagle, *American Denim: A New Folk Art* (New York: Abrams, 1975), 14.

11. Brooks, 73–74.

12. Valerie Carnes, "Icons of Popular Fashion" in *Icons of America*, eds. Ray N. Browne and Marshall Fishwick (Bowling Green, Ohio: Popular Press, 1978), 237.

13. Beagle, 14, 73.

14. Brooks, 60.

15. Carnes, 236.

16. "Do it up Denim!" *Mademoiselle* (February 1978), 142.

17. Barbara Fehr, *Yankee Denim Dandies* (Blue Earth, Minn.: Piper Press, 1974), 73.

18. Brooks, 58.

19. Eve Harlow, *The Jeans Scene* (New York: Drake, 1973); Alexandra Jocopetti, *Native Funk and Flash* (San Francisco: Scrimshaw Press, 1974); Jann Johnson, *The Jeans Book* (New York: Ballantine Press, 1972); Sharon Rosenberg and Joan Wiener Bordow, *The Denim Book* (Englewood Cliffs, N.J.: Prentice-Hall, 1978); Hazel Todhunter, *Make It in Denim* (New York: Taplinger, 1977); Laura Torbet, *Clothing Liberation: Or Out of the Closet and Into the Streets* (New York: Ballantine Press, 1973).

20. Fehr, 55, 66; Shea, 29.

21. Fehr, 27, 45.

22. Ibid., 46.

23. Jacqueline McCord, "Blue Jean Country," *New York Times Magazine* (April 29, 1979), 115.

24. *Good Housekeeping* (April 1981), 202.

25. Carnes, 235–36.

26. "Institute Report: Denim Update," *Good Housekeeping* (September 1984), 124.

27. "A Six Dollar Stone Wash," *Newsweek* (September 22, 1986), 77.

28. Fehr, 11.

29. Beagle, 39–40; Fehr, 62–64.

30. Todhunter, 26–27.

31. Carnes, 235; McCord, 115.

32. Fehr, 55.

33. Fehr, 64; Herbert Koshetz, "Laundry Offers New Way to Age Jeans," *New York Times* (August 7, 1973), 47.

34. "Denims: Here's How to Buy the Best and Fade Them Fast," *Mademoiselle* (August 1981), 258.

35. Steve Ginsburg, "Despite a Feud, Marcianos Make Guesswork Pay," *Women's Wear Daily* (November 25, 1986), 4–5.

36. Gary Slutsker, "The Smoking Bun," *Forbes* 25 (March 1985), 210.

37. Laurie Schecter, "Red-Hot Blues," *Rolling Stone* (May 8, 1986), 67–71.

38. Berendt, 25.

39. Wendy Goodman, "Upscale Blues," *New York* 10 (February 1986), 48–51; "Designing the Blues," *New York* 17 (November 1986), 78–79; Ruth La Ferla, "Singing the Blues, *New York Times Magazine* (July 13, 1986), Section 6, 60; "Denim Rides Again," *Life* (September 1986), 76–78.

40. "Denim Rides Again," 76.

41. Jennet Conant, "Sexy Does It," *Newsweek* (September 15, 1986), 64.

Appendix

A. See Douglas A. Russell, *Costume History and Style* (Englewood Cliffs, N.J.: Prentice-Hall, 1983), 48, for a discussion of the gray flannel suit imagery. The movie by that name came out in 1957. See also William Hollingsworth Whyte, *The Organization Man* (New York: Simon & Schuster, 1956).

B. John Brooks reports that the Levi Strauss company commissioned a survey in 1965 that indicated most people still associated the jeans with farmers, but the turning point in the popular association must have occurred very shortly thereafter.

C. Alison Lurie in her *The Language of Clothes* (New York: Random House, 1981) attributed the popularity of Levi's in Europe to the belief among European teens that "the power and virtue of America" was contained in the jeans, and would rub off on anyone who wore them.

D. Counterfeiting of jeans had actually begun some time before this date, with the bulk of the bogus products going overseas. Thirty-five thousand pairs of forged Levi's and Wrangler jeans were confiscated in West Germany in 1977. See "West Germany: A Booming Market in Counterfeit Jeans," *Business Week* (August 8, 1977): 38–39.

E. This epithet (and a similar one, the "great common denominator") had been bandied about considerably in the late 1960s and early 1970s. See Barbara Fehr, *Yankee Denim Dandies* (Blue Earth, Minn.: Piper Press, 1974), 35, and Robert Shea, "Yesterday's Leggings Are Today's Fashion Craze," *Today's Health* (March 1975): 29.

F. Barbara Fehr in her *Yankee Denim Dandies* claims that the original derivation of the phrase "stone wash" comes from a preindustrial era when garments were softened by a long exposure to running water. The garments were buried in streams, she says, and held down by rocks or stones. I have been unable to confirm this explanation, and rather suspect it is more likely related to the fact that fabric was long cleaned by rubbing over stones in the stream beds.

G. I speak from memory.

H. The thesis that clothing and other objects can hold a psychic charge has been developed at length by Mihaly Czikszentmihalyi and Eugene Rochberg-Halton in *The Meaning of Things: Domestic Symbols and the Self* (Cambridge: Cambridge University Press, 1981). Although this feeling about jeans was probably at its strongest in the Vietnam era when the jeans were still symbolic of counterculture beliefs, it has clearly not died out. In 1985 sculptor Bob Edlund offered to preserve the spirit of one's jeans forever by "freezing" them in characteristic poses with several coats of fiberglass resin. Edlund said he came up with this idea because jeans "are the hardest things in the world to part with." He even planned to coat children's overalls in this manner, much in the spirit of bronzed baby shoes. See "For a Mere $1,250, Sculptor Bob Edlund Will See To It That Your Jeans Never Wear Out," *People* (November 11, 1985), 79.

I. John Brooks in "Annals of Business: A Friendly Product," *New Yorker* (November 12, 1979), 80, claims he was given this advice when he bought his first pair of jeans in 1979; jeans "connoisseurs" had the benefit of years of experience when they told him what to do. Peter Beagle also discusses this process at length in *American Denim: A New Folk Art* (New York: Abrams, 1975), 39–40.

J. This was the actual phrase used by *Rolling Stone* fashion editor Laurie Schecter in *Rolling Stone* (May 8, 1986), 68.

K. It is somewhat outside the parameters of the jeans story, but another type of fashion that caught on in the mid-1980s was the safari-look, made up primarily of cotton khaki garments. The look was spurred on by such popular movies as the *Raiders of the Lost Ark* and *Out of Africa*, but it was first marketed by an innovative company named Banana Republic. When it was a new company, Banana Republic bought up lots of used army and safari clothing and restyled them for its customers. These safari-type clothes also provided a safe fantasy—a vicarious sense of adventure.

L. These adjectives and statements were all taken from labels on denimwear found in a variety of department stores in Madison, Wisconsin, in February 1988.

M. There are even some jeans advertisements that are framed and titled, like slice-of-life or art photographs. *Seventeen* magazine carried an ad for Jeanjer denimwear in September 1986, for example, that featured a snapshot-like image of a sensual girl in jeans and a denim jacket, outlined in black and clearly set off against the page. It was captioned "'Desert Blues,' 1986."

6

Selected Reading II

Chapters 4 and 5

Cunningham, Patricia A., and Lab, Susan Voso (eds.). *Dress and Popular Culture*. Bowling Green, Ohio: Popular Press, 1991.

Davis, Fred. *Fashion, Culture, and Identity*. Chicago: University of Chicago Press, 1992.

DeLong, Marilyn Revell. *The Way We Look: A Framework for Visual Analysis of Dress*. Ames: Iowa State University Press, 1987.

Ewing, Elizabeth. *History of Twentieth-Century Fashion*. Totowa, N.J.: Barnes and Noble, 1986.

Fiske, John. "The Jeaning of America" in *Understanding Popular Culture*, ed. John Fiske. Boston: Unwin Hyman, 1989.

Hoffmann, Frank, and Bailey, William G. *Fashion and Merchandising Fads*. Binghamton, N.Y.: Haworth Press, 1994.

Joseph, Nathan. *Uniforms and Nonuniforms: Communication Through Clothing*. New York: Greenwood Press, 1986.

Jones, Mablen. *Getting It On: The Clothing of Rock 'n' Roll*. New York: Abbeville Press, 1987.

Kaiser, Susan. *The Social Psychology of Clothing and Personal Behavior*. New York: Macmillan, 1985.

Kidwell, Claudia B., and Steele, Valerie (eds.). *Men and Women, Dressing the Part*. Washington, D.C.: Smithsonian Institution Press, 1989.

Lurie, Alison. *The Language of Clothes*. New York: Random House, 1981.

Polhemus, Ted, and Proctor, Lynn. *Fashion and Anti-Fashion: An Anthropology of Clothing and Adornment*. London: Thames and Hudson, 1978.

Roach, Mary Ellen, and Eicher, Joanne B. *The Visible Self: Perspectives on Dress*. Englewood Cliffs, N.J.: Prentice-Hall, 1973.

Rubenstein, Ruth P. *Dress Codes: Meanings and Messages in American Culture*. Boulder, Colo.: Westview Press, 1995.

Storm, Penny. *Functions of Dress: Tool of Culture and the Individual*. Englewood Cliffs, N.J.: Prentice-Hall, 1987.

Wilson, Elizabeth. *Adorned in Dreams*. Berkeley: University of California Press, 1987.

Part III: Food

Wilbur Zelinsky, the dean of American cultural geographers, reported some twenty years ago that the geographic cupboard was empty when one looks for literature on food. Despite the inattention by cultural geographers, few popular culture topics occupy a larger place in the American psyche than food. Similar to architecture, food pervades our everyday existence. It offers one of the oldest and most evocative systems of cultural identification; defining ethnic, regional, racial, and spiritual differences throughout America.

Because of a geographically mobile society, the franchising of food in America was inevitable. It began as early as the 1920s, with the registration of the "A & W" brand name; however, the boom years were the 1960s, when "Big Boy" and "Kentucky Fried Chicken" were among the early franchisers of that decade. By 1980 almost 400 firms had franchised some 65,000 fast-food outlets. Fast food has tended toward certain kinds of menus with the dominant fares centered on hamburgers, hot dogs, roast beef sandwiches, chicken, seafood, pizza, and pancakes. Both articles that follow deal with the franchising of food, one of the most common traits in American popular culture.

John Jakle, a University of Illinois geographer, details the historical background of the roadside restaurant in America, beginning with the curb-service roadside stands of the 1920s to the modern fast-food outlets. Fast food's popularity is linked to several factors, including quick preparation, relatively low cost, and appeal to a highly mobile populace that seeks security in standardized products and services. Large corporations have dominated highway-oriented restaurants since 1960 through what Jakle describes as "place-product-packaging": the coordination of building design, decor, menu, service, and pricing under a distinctive logo. Roadside eateries have become a popular institution in American society, concludes Jakle, because they are safe and predictable places for travelers away from home.

Laurence Carstensen, a geographer at Virginia Tech, contributes an insightful statistical study on the largest of the fast-food franchises—McDonald's. Using data from the 1970s and 1980s, he provides a valuable investigation into the origin and diffusion of this fast-food phenomenon across the United States during its infant stages. His cartographic analysis and interpretive remarks give us a fuller understanding of the "McDonaldization" of America into the 1990s. Today, McDonald's golden arches are one of the most recognizable symbols of American popular culture throughout the world, from Tokyo to Moscow.

7

Roadside Restaurants and Place-Product-Packaging

John A. Jakle

Widespread use of automobiles for travel in the twentieth century created logistical problems. Whether touring for pleasure or traveling on business, motorists required gasoline, lodging, and food. Petroleum companies organized dealer networks before World War I. Gasoline brand names, reflected in gasoline station buildings and logos, reassured motorists of standardized products and services, thus rendering the roadside less alien.[1] Tourist homes, campgrounds, and cabin courts provided lodging, although not until the 1950s did standardization through referral and franchise chains come to characterize the accommodations industry.[2] Food was the last of the traveler's needs to be standardized, for the franchised restaurant did not appear in large numbers until the 1950s.

This study concerns the twentieth-century roadside restaurant. It discusses how automobile convenience encouraged the standardization of food and service in eating places as "place-product-packaging."[3] The creation of place expectations by relating building types, products, service, decor, and prices under highly visible corporate logos has been a significant development underlying recent landscape change along America's highways. How and why was the roadside restaurant so affected? How did it impact roadside landscapes? How does it serve the traveler as a distinctive kind of place?

Reprinted by permission from the *Journal of Cultural Geography* 3 (1982), 76–93.

Cafes, Tearooms, and Diners

In cities, early motorists used restaurants located downtown or at street-car stops along business thoroughfares. In small towns, the traveler was part of the "Main Street" cafe clientele. Cafes were less formal than hotel dining rooms and their fast service was more suited to anxious motorists hoping to "make time" in the face of uncertain roads and frequent breakdowns. Many restaurants and cafes occupied storefronts as did other small retail establishments. In most cafes interior space was organized perpendicular to the street, with a soda fountain along one wall and tables or booths along the other (Fig. 7–1).

Most early travelers carried their own food for picnics by the roadside, but by World War I "tearooms" had come to line most of the nation's major highways. These were rural establishments frequently located in old farmhouses, barns, grist mills, or other "historical" structures. Often run by farm women, tearooms provided a shady spot to stop and refresh with "home-cooked" light meals. Tearooms were popular near large cities as destinations for short trips, but the largest establishments served long-distance travelers in isolated locations (Fig. 7–2). Success lay in prompt service, simplicity of menu, reasonable prices, quality of food, and attractive and cool surroundings.[4] Tearooms were frequently tied into cabin courts and other automobile-oriented enterprises (Fig. 7–3).

Fig. 7–1. Cafe in Newark, New Jersey (1920)

Fig. 7–2. Tearoom in Buchanan Summit, Pennsylvania (c. 1920)

Fig. 7–3. Tearoom and Cabin Court at Coeur d'Alene Lake, Idaho (c. 1925)

After World War I standardized "fast food" appeared in small "diners." Early diners were pedestrian- or streetcar-oriented, but by the 1930s many had been built to serve highway traffic (Fig. 7–4). Chains such as the White Castle and White Tower systems featured look-alike buildings covered in white brick or porcelain enamel to symbolize cleanliness.[5] Whereas many early diners were converted railroad cars, by the 1930s most buildings only

MONTEAGLE DINER – MONTEAGLE, TENN. U.S. 41-64   I-T-190 CLINE PHOTO

Fig. 7–4. Diner in Monteagle, Tennessee (c. 1940)

simulated railroad architecture. For tax purposes, these prefabricated buildings were considered personal rather than real property, and relative to other kinds of restaurant buildings, they could be depreciated at faster rates, bringing short-run tax savings.[6]

Roadside Stands

Although rooted in the cafe, the tearoom, and the diner, the highway-oriented restaurant owed more to the roadside stand. Shedlike refreshment stands had been common to fairs and carnivals and to public parks and beaches. Many foods now basic to the American diet were first popularized at fairs as exotic dishes served at stands. The ice cream cone, for example, originated at the 1904 St. Louis World's Fair (where the hot dog and hamburger were also popularized).[7] The refreshment stand was a logical mechanism for selling to motorists because, until the 1920s, motoring was still a warm-weather proposition. Stands required relatively little capitalization and could be boarded up in the off-season. Highway selling was ideal for entrepreneurs willing to experiment with limited capital, and the roadside stand was hailed as one of America's last remaining "frontiers" for independent businessmen.

The first stand to offer "curb service" was opened by the Pig Stands Company of Dallas in 1921. Food was served to customers parked in their automobiles at curbside because the stand did not have an off-street parking lot. In 1923, the company's second establishment did include a parking lot, as did an A & W Root Beer stand opened in Sacramento, California, the same year.[8] As diagrammed, the concept of the roadside stand was simple (Fig. 7–5). A small building with open or screened windows faced a driveway that provided easy access on and off the adjacent highway. Motorists placed their orders at windows or, as in the case of drive-ins, were served in the automobiles by "carhops." Some roadside stands were very elaborate, such as, for example, the Freda Farms establishment near Hartford, Connecticut (Fig. 7–6).

Architectural experimentation was a hallmark of the late 1920s and early 1930s. Stands were built as giant oranges and lemons, milk cans, ice cream cartons, and even inverted ice cream cones. "Dutch windmills" may have been the most popular of the exotic building types. Relatively few stands, judging by the commentary of the day, were considered attractive. Their flimsy construction and utilitarian aspect compounded by unimproved driveways, lack of landscaping, and garish signs brought widespread condemnation. Stands were viewed as a form of highway blight, with the term "hot dog kennel" coined as a derisive descriptor.[9] Several design contests sought to improve roadside stands, but to small avail since "design" went counter to the very idea of fast food at low prices with outdoor informality.[10]

Highway Coffee Shops

The growing market for dairy products, especially ice cream, brought the first revolution in roadside restaurants. In the 1930s dairy bars or soda fountains in conjunction with dairy sales stores appeared along peripheral highways outside small towns and cities. Howard Johnson innovated by combining soda fountains with dining rooms to create the highway-oriented "coffee shop," a motif which persists to this day as a predominant restaurant form.[11] Many companies adopted the new idea (Fig. 7–7). The motorist parked and entered through a vestibule: the dining room to one side of the entrance and the soda fountain to the other. The Interstate Company's seven Glass House restaurants of the Middle West and South were among the early roadside eateries so arranged.

Howard Johnson's restaurants came to epitomize the new style in the popular mind. Johnson pioneered franchising as a means of capitalizing rapid chain expansion. By 1940, 130 Howard Johnson Restaurants had been opened with half locally owned but operated under Johnson's franchise supervision.[12] Bankers were reluctant to mortgage highway restaurants, con-

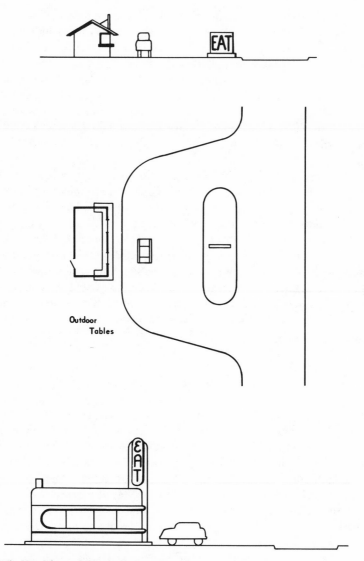

Fig. 7–5. Hypothetical Roadside Stand

sidering them "specialty buildings" not easily convertible to other uses should a business fail. Bankers still thought of restaurants in terms of multi-purpose "Main Street" storefronts.

Johnson's buildings were designed for visibility, instant recognition, and

Fig. 7–6. Roadside Stand in Hartford, Connecticut (1933)

brand identity. Unmistakably they were restaurant buildings. Originated in New England but spread through the Middle Atlantic states by World War II (with two outlying stores in Florida), the chain adopted a pseudo-colonial style. Called roadside "cathedrals," the buildings were thought to be reminiscent of New England town halls and churches. White stucco walls, turquoise cupolas, and orange roofs suggested modernity.

Gas rationing during World War II led to the closure of all but twelve of Johnson's restaurants, forcing him to rebuild his chain. Modern simplicity dominated postwar buildings. Food service contracts of the Pennsylvania Turnpike and other modern auto roads clearly linked the company with progressive road building. To the soda, shake, and sundae concoctions based on his twenty-eight flavors of ice cream, Johnson added hot dogs, hamburgers, chicken, steaks, and clams. As in other roadside eateries, food was fried in order to speed service. Stephen Kurtz noted that Johnson's food was consistent with his decor: "Nothing calls attention to itself; it is all remarkably unremarkable. The sense of *déjà vu*, so strange in other circumstances, is commonplace here."[13]

Drive-Ins

The American economy vigorously rebounded after World War II as pent-up buying power was channeled into new automobiles and new subur-

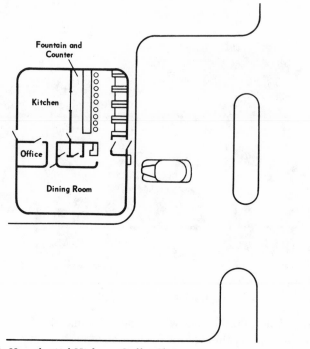

Fig. 7-7. Hypothetical Highway Coffee Shop

ban houses. The roadside restaurant came into its own in the form of the drive-in restaurant. Combining the attributes of the roadside stand with those of the highway coffee shop, the new drive-ins featured both indoor and outdoor service. Layout varied from drive-in to drive-in, but three principal spaces always emerged: a canopy-covered drive, an outdoor dining area, and a kitchen. Large electric signs dominated on-site advertising.[14]

Drive-ins varied in size. The thirty-nine Prince Ice Cream Castles of Illinois, Iowa, and Indiana were no larger than necessary for convenient placing of equipment and storage, with indoor seating kept to a minimum. Only six people were required to run each store. Casey's three drive-ins in Abilene, Texas, employed fourteen people at each location (seven carhops, two waitresses, two cooks, a dishwasher, a maintenance man, and a cashier). Casey's showed movies on small outdoor screens to boost business.[15] Atlanta's Varsity Drive-in (which claimed to be the "World's Largest" in the early 1950s) employed one hundred fifty people in three shifts. The parking lot held two hundred cars, all serviced under canopies; indoor seating accommodated an additional 100 people.[16] Al Green's Drive-in in Indianapolis was representative of the big city drive-ins. A large sign dominated the adjacent building that housed the kitchen and soda fountain. A covered canopy extended from the back of the building and away from the highway (Fig. 7–8).

Labor costs at drive-ins were high, averaging approximately 25 percent of sales through the early 1960s. Various devices were introduced to trim labor requirements. For example, the Track Drive-in in Los Angeles featured a cumbersome system of tracks and service boxes connecting the kitchen and adjacent parking stalls. Telephones and speaker boxes were more commonly used.[17] Orders, called directly to the kitchen by customers, were delivered by carhops. Many chains established central commissaries where food was prepared and then trucked to the roadside.

Outdoor Walk-Ups

Originally considered a fixed cost, labor came to be viewed as a variable cost to be reduced by further mechanizing the food preparation process and by eliminating carhops altogether.[18] New "walk-up" restaurants evolved when drive-ins were stripped to their bare essentials: small buildings with kitchen, service windows, and restrooms (Fig. 7–9). Served outside from

Fig. 7–8. Drive-in in Indianapolis, Indiana (1979)

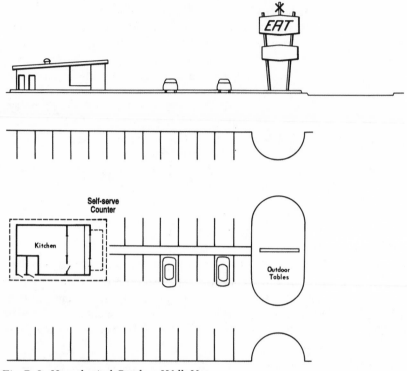

Fig. 7–9. Hypothetical Outdoor Walk-Up

windows, customers ate in their automobiles, sat at picnic tables, or took their food to eat elsewhere. Service windows were protected by glass vestibules erected during the winter months. Many buildings were prefabricated, flat-roofed, steel-frame structures covered with glass and porcelain enamel.

Although most drive-ins sported large electric signs, the buildings themselves, for their glitter, also served as a kind of sign.[19] Franchise chains sought distinctive architectural decoration to stimulate ready customer recognition through brand consciousness and brand loyalty. "Place-product-packaging," launched along the roadside by Howard Johnson, came of age. McDonald's was the most successful competitor for public attention. Each red-and-white McDonald's building sported a pair of golden arches easily recognized from the highway.

The history of McDonald's has been told and retold to the point of assuming mythic, even mystical, qualities. To some, Ray Kroc, the franchiser of the restaurants, stands as an entrepreneurial wizard in a league with the likes of Henry Ford. As Ford is believed to have mechanized automobile manufacture, so Kroc is thought to have put hamburger-making on assembly lines.[20] Time and motion studies produced a system capable of delivering a hamburger, fries, and a shake every fifty seconds.[21] At most drive-ins carhop service was slow and food was rarely delivered hot. At McDonald's carry-out windows, the food was not only hot, but the elimination of carhops substantially reduced labor costs. The McDonald's system, fueled by careful organization, a comprehensive training program (including the famous Hamburger University with degrees in Hamburgerology), and extensive advertising (especially on television), became the nation's largest restaurant chain. Over four thousand units were in operation when the company celebrated its twentieth birthday in 1975.[22]

But McDonald's was not alone. Many traditional drive-ins added "take home" departments in the early 1950s.[23] Numerous franchisers promoted chains of new walk-up restaurants. For example, Burger Chef developed a prototype building with a cantilevered gable-roof supported by an illuminated trapezoidal arch. Burger Chef's fast service featured a conveyorized infrared broiler that prepared hamburgers at a rate of eight hundred an hour.[24] At Burger King the process of hamburger manufacture was separated into discrete tasks. Buns of bread and patties of meat traveled at precise speeds on conveyors through the broiler to fall into small chutes, where they were sandwiched.[25] Burger Queen, Burger Jet, Whataburger, and numerous other chains developed variations on the automation theme.

Building prefabrication continued to enjoy popularity as a means of trimming construction costs. Salesmen emphasized that prefab units could be moved to new locations should highway relocation or other problems arise. The Biff-Burger system developed a Port-A-Unit that could be erected and furnished in less than a week, thus saving construction costs.[26] Ice cream vendors were more reliant on prefab units than the purveyors of hamburgers. Eskimo pies, ice cream cones, and popsicles had been joined shortly before World War II by "soft" ice cream or "frozen custard." Dairy Queen, Tastee Freeze, Carvel, and other chains grew rapidly, featuring the new specialty food.

Cheap labor was the key to fast-food profits. The entrepreneur substituted capital equipment for labor by mechanizing. The high degree of specialization through adoption of limited menus and the use of unskilled labor through job specialization allowed for greater use of part-time, minimum-wage employees. As a result, absenteeism and labor turnover are significant problems, with turnover as high as 300 percent per year for some chains.[27] Employees confront arbitrary shifts, long hours, and drudgery work, and most workers consider fast-food employment to be only temporary.

Indoor Walk-Ups

The earliest roadside restaurants had been attention getters. From the Dutch windmills and inverted ice cream cones to the turquoise and orange Howard Johnson's to the golden arches of McDonald's, entrepreneurs had sought to achieve maximum visibility. Bold forms, gaudy colors, and garish signs brightly illuminated at night had combined to sharply contrast restaurants with their surroundings. In the mid-1960s, negative public reaction to the excesses of roadside huckstering brought restraint. New designs sought to blend buildings with their surroundings.

The late 1960s was a period of relative affluence and Americans were spending approximately 4 percent of their incomes on restaurant food.[28] Franchisers sought to make their fast-food stores more attractive and more comfortable to better compete for the restaurant dollar. Enclosed dining rooms were added to renovated walk-up restaurants. Although dining rooms were included in the new units, customers continued to order at walk-up counters.

McDonald's led the new trend toward tasteful restraint and stylishness. After 1968, McDonald's red-and-white exteriors were replaced by dull brown brick and plate-glass facades. Roofs were capped by double-mansard shingle roofs. "The pulsing, exuberant Golden Arches were streamlined into the current subdued, nonbiodegradable yellow plastic logos that rear more gently from the road."[29] McDonald's decor changed inside as well as out. Called "restaurants" rather than "drive-ins," each McDonald's boasted plastic seats and tables, tile floors, and indirect lighting. Decoration varied from unit to unit. Local franchisees and managers were encouraged to adopt "escape" motifs appropriate to their localities. Again, McDonald's was not alone. Burger Chef introduced a new building type with eight alternative exterior "theme" motifs: Colonial, rustic wood, rustic stone, Granada, New Orleans, Monterrey, Tudor, and nautical.[30]

After 1970, "drive-through" windows were included in many fast-food restaurants. Orders placed at nearby call boxes were picked up at side windows protected by canopies.

Highway Coffee Shops: A Revival

Despite the rise of the drive-in and two generations of competitive walk-up restaurants (including those with drive-through service), the highway coffee shop survived to enjoy a revival in the 1960s. The new coffee shops were suburban manifestations located in commercial strips, often adjacent to shopping centers. They also appeared at interstate highway interchanges, often grouped with motels. Beyond the kitchen with its food preparation and storage spaces, the typical coffee shop was still evenly divided between an informal eating section containing fountain, counter, and booths and a more formal dining room with tables and chairs. Waitresses took all orders and served the food. Small regional chains dominated. For example, Bill Knapp's restaurants in Michigan were located at interstate highway interchanges close to cities of at least 50,000 population and close to industrial parks or office buildings to ensure larger luncheon trades.[31] Since food was distributed from a central commissary, the chain was restricted to a 200-mile radius around Battle Creek, the corporate headquarters.

Franchising

Early franchising focused either on the food product or the techniques of food preparation rather than on the restaurant itself. Roy Allen and Fred Wright, who registered the "A & W" brand name in 1925, had franchised 451 outlets by 1950 to handle their root beer syrup.[32] Originally, little effort was made to standardize A & W Root Beer stands beyond common signage. Through the 1960s the company's stores were located primarily in small towns that did not warrant full-scale drive-ins or highway coffee shops. Bob Wigan's "Big Boy" sandwiches originated at his ten-stool diner in Glendale, California. By 1975 rights to use the Big Boy logo had extended to more than sixteen companies, which varied in size from two restaurants in a single city (Bud's of Cheyenne, Wyoming) to 137 restaurants in a single state (Elias Brothers of Michigan) to 194 restaurants in a large region (Shoney's, headquartered at Nashville).[33] Harland Sanders franchised his fried chicken recipe and sold the equipment necessary to the special deep-frying process. Kentucky Fried Chicken's profits came from a small royalty charged on the gross chicken sales of each franchise. The Colonel, like most franchisers, extended exclusive rights to product and processes within clearly defined territories.[34]

Advantages accrue to both franchisers and franchisees. A developer of a new idea stands to make a more rapid penetration of the marketplace than otherwise possible, thus preempting competition. Franchisers use the capital or borrowing capacity of franchisees to expand rapidly toward market saturation. By tying in with a chain, inexperienced franchisees buy a head start on the learning curve of the food service business. Franchisees can spread the costs of promotion, advertising development, and national media purchase. Where centralized procurement is available, they can achieve purchasing leverage and thus lower food, paper, and other material costs. Above all, franchisees buy an image: place-product-packaging to tie them into an established market. Franchisees are given visibility along the roadside since logos are instantly recognized. Place meaning is clearly defined. Large signs not only declare a restaurant's wares but serve to dominate location even to redefining the character of surrounding neighborhood spaces. Signs and buildings communicate clear place meanings even across language and cultural boundaries.

Franchising also has its disadvantages. Careless or disreputable operators can quickly tarnish the image of an entire chain. Franchisers are forced to maintain costly supervisory personnel to identify and correct problems. As for franchisees, they are restricted in style of operation and in line of products sold because there is no room for experimentation and innovation. Chains exist to make a standardized product available in the same kind of setting everywhere. To deviate is to disrupt customer place expectations.

By 1979 an estimated 390 firms had franchised some 65,000 fast-food outlets, with over $25 billion in sales.[35] The 1960s were the boom years, with substantial corporate experimentation and overexpansion. Restaurants tended to conform to one of seven standardized menus.[36] Hamburger, hot-dog, and roast beef sandwich restaurants accounted for nearly half the total. Pizza, steak, and chicken restaurants accounted for approximately 13 percent each; Mexican, seafood, and pancake restaurants accounted for approximately 4 percent each. Most ice cream and root beer chains had converted to wider fast-food menus. Over two-thirds of all franchised firms operated self-service, drive-in, and/or drive-through facilities as opposed to sit-down restaurants with counter or table service. Many franchise operations represented chains within chains. Gino's of King of Prussia, Pennsylvania, for example, operated over 325 Kentucky Fried Chicken stores besides its own 150 Rustler Steak Houses. Chart House of Lafayette, Louisiana, operated 200 Burger King units and is now subfranchising Burger King stores.[37]

Success was pyramided toward the top. During the 1970s the seven largest fast-food franchisers accounted for 47 percent of all fast food outlets and 46 percent of industry sales.[38] Ownership patterns have changed in recent years as giant food corporations and conglomerates have taken advantage of a depressed stock market to acquire restaurant chains. Mergers have provided cash transfusions to companies strapped by rapid expansion. Burger Chef is now a General Foods subsidiary, whereas Pillsbury owns Burger King and Hublein owns Kentucky Fried Chicken.

The impact of fast-food franchising has varied regionally in the United States. Americans now spent nearly 32 percent of every restaurant dollar on fast food.[39] In 1977 fast-food restaurants were most successful in the small cities of the southeastern and southcentral United States (Fig. 7–10). These cities had depressed economies through the 1950s, but have subsequently boomed to become heavily influenced by the automobile. Fast-food restaurants are also more prevalent in Utah, Alabama, Georgia, and South Carolina, where the serving of alcoholic beverages is or has been widely prohibited in the restaurants, thus precluding traditional restaurant development. Fast-food sales are substantially below the national average in New York, New Jersey, and Vermont (Fig. 7–11). They are least significant in New York City, where older, traditional restaurants still predominate. During the 1960s substantial opposition developed in New York City to the locating of McDonald's and other fast-food outlets in inner-city neighborhoods, thus forcing McDonald's and other companies to develop storefront blend-in units.

Vending

Since the earliest days of automobile travel, food sales have been tied to a wide range of complementary travel services. In the 1920s small ice cream and cold drink counters were located in gasoline stations on an experimental basis. Vending machines were more practical and by the 1940s they had become universal not only in gasoline stations but in motels and other businesses. Totally automated restaurants, called vendiners, were introduced in the 1950s, but never on a large scale.[40] Using microwave ovens to prepare frozen foods, the automats were difficult for customers to operate, and the lack of human contact produced sterile settings.

Conclusions

The roadside restaurant has come of age as a distinctive kind of place important in the daily lives of many Americans. It is a place-type familiar to all. As the majority of Americans reside and work in automobile-convenient landscapes, roadside eateries provide the standards by which the food service industry abides. The popularity of roadside "fast food" is a function of many factors. Traditionally, roadside food has been prepared and consumed quickly and at relatively low prices. It has been attractive to people on the move in a society highly mobile geographically. The roadside, with its sense of informality, conveys an aura of glamor, especially the glamor of the traveler enjoying easy, free, and independent adventure. Place-product-packag-

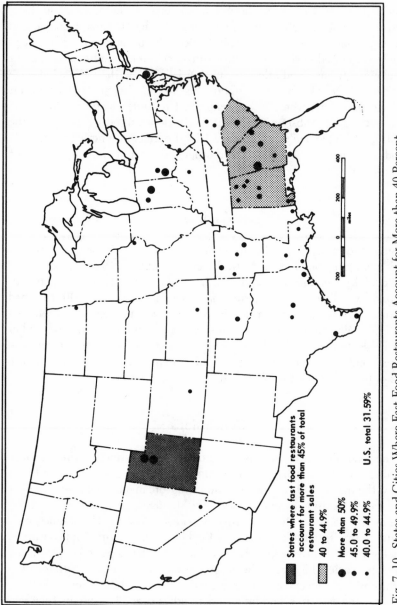

Fig. 7–10. States and Cities Where Fast-Food Restaurants Account for More than 40 Percent of the Total Restaurant Sales (1977)

States where fast food restaurants
account for more than 45% of total
restaurant sales

40 to 44.9%

● More than 50%

• 45.0 to 49.9%

· 40.0 to 44.9%

U.S. total 31.59%

200   0   200   400

miles

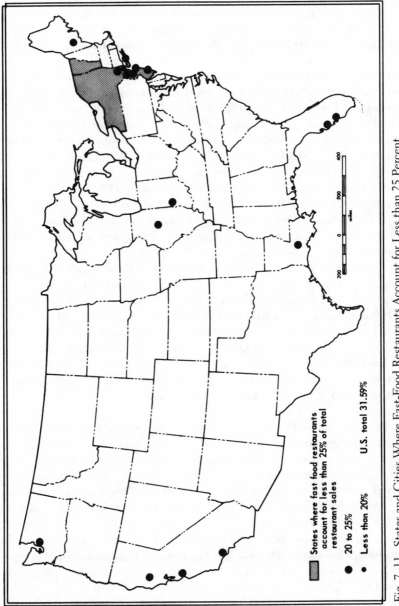

States where fast food restaurants account for less than 25% of total restaurant sales

20 to 25%

Less than 20%

U.S. total 31.59%

200   0   200   400

miles

ing has served well the needs of a highly mobile society. People find in roadside restaurants places of comfort where standardized environments, products, and services provide security as well as nourishment away from home. Anxiety from adventuring is contained by the familiar.

Place-product-packaging is a "total design" idea. As behavior settings, roadside restaurants are carefully contrived to attract and satisfy customers traveling by automobile. Little is left to chance, for customer expectations must be validated. Kind of location, opening and closing hours, menus, service, decor, and prices must be consistent as total place product. Restaurants must look like restaurants. Since 1920 a succession of standardized building types has evolved, with each type prevailing for a short period of time. Building types have changed primarily in response to new merchandising techniques intended to cut labor costs. Restaurant chains have sought to establish clear brand identities through both architectural styling and distinctive logos. Yet no chain willingly deviates too far from place-product-packaging norms for fear of alienating customers. Thus roadside restaurants have contributed to standardized highway landscapes where subtle changes in decoration and logos have been subordinated to less frequent and less dramatic changes of building type.

Rarely is the American motorist ever far from a familiar place to eat. The larger chains are everywhere. Logos not only symbolize products and services within establishments, but cue the nearby availability of complementary places such as gasoline stations and motels. Motorists in cities and small towns are alerted to general urban location. Thus the roadside restaurant serves as an important category of landmark. The corporate presence in the landscape has become a significant regional cue as lesser companies are known to predominate more in some areas and less in others. Indeed, the varying density of fast-food restaurants across the United States serves to distinguish regions.

Roadside restaurants contribute substantially to the sense of monotony many travelers experience today. The roadside looks and is very much the same from one part of the United States to another; the sense of déjà vu is strong everywhere. A "placeless" or "commonplace" quality pervades the travel experience reduced to the logistics of refueling, lodging, and eating by the roadside. The traveler sometimes finds places too familiar and his needs too well anticipated.

For being commonplace, restaurants, along with other elements of the roadside, have received relatively little attention from cultural geographers and other scholars. Traditionally geographers have not studied "places" defined at such large scales. Structures are usually studied in aggregate as they vary regionally or they are subsumed in the study of land use. As valuable as this research may be, geographers need also to study places as actual behavior settings. How do roadside restaurants function as places defined in location, temporal, structural, and behavioral terms? How are such settings symbolized in the landscape? How do they relate to other settings? How are behavioral expectations attached and validated? How do places change and how do place expectations change? Analysis of place-product-packaging would appear to be the most appropriate context upon which to focus research.

Notes

1. Bruce A. Lohof, "The Service Station in America: The Evolution of a Vernacular Form," *Industrial Archeology* 2 (Spring 1974), 1–13; John A. Jakle, "The American Gasoline Station 1920–1970," *Journal of American Culture* 1 (Fall 1978), 520–24; David I. Vieyra, *Fill 'Er Up: An Architectural History of America's Gasoline Stations* (New York: Macmillan, 1979).

2. Warren J. Belasco, *Americans on the Road: From Autocamp to Motel, 1910–1945* (Cambridge: MIT Press, 1979); John A. Jakle, "Motel by the Roadside: America's Room for the Night," *Journal of Cultural Geography* 1 (Fall/Winter 1980), 34–49.

3. Richard Oliver and Nancy Ferguson, "The Environment Is a Diary," *Architectural Forum* 131 (July 1978), 115–20.

4. C. H. Claudy, "Organizing the Wayside Tea House," *Country Life in America* 30 (June 1916), 55.

5. John Baeder, *Diners* (New York: Abrams, 1978); Richard J. S. Gutman and Elliot Kaufman, *The American Diner* (New York: Harper & Row, 1979); Paul Hirshorn and Steven Izenour, *White Towers* (Cambridge: MIT Press, 1979).

6. George H. Waltz Jr., "Roadside Riches," *Restaurant Digest*, n.v. (July 1954), 14.

7. Paul Dickson, *The Great American Ice Cream Book* (New York: Atheneum, 1973), 66.

8. Lawrence Witchel (ed.), "Drive-Ins: A Chronology," in *Drive-In Management Guidebook* (New York: Harcourt Brace, 1968), 9, 11.

9. "Roadside Refreshment Stands," *Printer's Ink* 135 (April 22, 1926), 127–28; Leslie Childs, " 'Hot Dog Kennels' as Nuisances to Adjoining Property Owners," *American City* 38 (February 1928), 137–38.

10. "Winning Designs in the Wayside Refreshment-Stand Competition," *American Builder* 45 (July 1928), 92–93.

11. Stephen A. Kurtz, "Howard Johnson's: Elevating the Host," in *Waste-*

116   John A. Jakle

land: Buying the American Dream (New York: Praeger, 1973), 19–25; Warren J. Belasco, "Toward the Culinary Common Denominator: The Rise of Howard Johnson's, 1925–1940," Journal of American Culture 2 (Fall 1979), 503–18.

12. "10,000,000 Motorists' Dollars Help Howard Johnson Build Up Chain of 130 Company-Owned Shops," Ice Cream Review 23 (July 1940), 25; "The Howard Johnson's Restaurants," Fortune 22 (September 1940), 94.

13. Kurtz, 23.

14. William C. Hoch Jr., "Lights that Invite," Restaurant Digest, n.v. (July 1954), 18.

15. "Free Movies Keep 'Em Comin' to Casey's Drive-In," Fountain Service 47 (November 1948), 26.

16. "World's Largest Drive-In," Restaurant Digest, n.v. (May 1953), 25.

17. "A Robot Takes the Car Hop Out of the Track's Service," Fountain Service 49 (November 1950), 30; "A Telephone Speeds Car Service," Fountain Service 49 (July 1950), 28.

18. D. Daryl Wyckoff and W. Earl Sasser, The Chain Restaurant Industry (Lexington, Mass.: Lexington Books, 1978), viii.

19. David G. Orr, "The Ethnography of Big Mac," in The World of Ronald McDonald, ed. Marshall Fishwick (Bowling Green, Ohio: Popular Press, 1978), 382.

20. Joseph F. Trimmer, "Enter the Wizard," in Fishwick, 349.

21. "Self-Service Works When There Is Money to Be Saved by Customers," Fast Food 63 (May 1964), 93.

22. Trimmer, 350, 352.

23. Ralph L. Blaikie, "Remodeling a Drive-In Around Its New Take-Home Department," Fountain and Fast Food 53 (March 1954), 44.

24. "How Burger Chef Speeds Service," Fast Food 58 (January 1959), 33.

25. Bruce A. Lohof, "Hamburger Stand: Industrialization and the American Fast Food Phenomena," Journal of American Culture 2 (Fall 1979), 528.

26. "Biff Burger Experimenting to Come up With 'The Best,'" Fast Food 63 (May 1964), 166.

27. Wyckoff and Sasser, lviii; E. Christine Jackson, "Ethnography of an Urban Burger King Franchise," Journal of American Culture 2 (Fall 1979), 534–39.

28. "The Growing American Appetite for Inexpensive Food," Restaurant Business 78 (May 1979), 159.

29. Max Boas and Steve Chain, Big Mac: The Unauthorized Story of McDonald's (New York: Mentor Books, 1976), 48.

30. Carol Lynn Tiegs, "Burger Chef Carving Out an Image," Restaurant Business 79 (March 1980), 162.

31. Richard Morehouse, "A Talent for Success," *Restaurant Management* 88 (March 1961), 63.

32. "Pay Your Money, Pick a Plan: A & W Offers One for Every Spot," *Fast Food* 64 (May 1965), 88.

33. "Meet the Big Boys from Your Big Boy," *Restaurant Business* 74 (June 1975), 68.

34. Roman G. Hiebing Jr., "Territorial Marketing and the Franchise System," *Fast Food* 68 (March 1969), 192–98; Jacob H. Bennison, "Franchising's Current Legal and Regulatory Issues," *Restaurant Business* 77 (March 1978), 152–60.

35. Department of Commerce, Industry and Trade Administration, *Franchising in the Economy, 1977–1979* (Washington, D.C.: Government Printing Office, 1979), 75.

36. Andrew Kostecka, "Restaurant Franchising in the Economy," *Restaurant Business* 79 (March 1980), 130.

37. Wyckoff and Sasser, lix.

38. Ibid.

39. Shelby D. Hunt, "The Trend Toward Company Owned Units," *Journal of Retailing* 49 (Summer 1973), 3.

40. James R. Meyers, "Cater to the Traveling Public," *Restaurant Digest*, n.v. (November 1957), 4.

8

The Burger Kingdom: Growth and Diffusion of McDonald's Restaurants in the United States, 1955–1978

Laurence W. Carstensen

The spread of the McDonald's restaurant chain throughout the United States represents the leading edge of the fast-food industry's impact on American cultural geography. Although other small chains operated before McDonald's, none have demonstrated the amazing success of Ray Kroc's hamburger business.

Statistics to support this claim are as numerous as are new McDonald's restaurants. For example, the 1978 Annual Report states:

> At year end 1978, the McDonald's worldwide system included 5,185 restaurants, 514 more than at the end of 1977. Among the year's new restaurants was the first McDonald's in Belgium. [A]t December 31, 1978 an additional 171 restaurants, including 45 in international markets, were under construction.[1]

The 1978 rate of growth represents a restaurant opening somewhere in the world every seventeen hours. Similarly, over the entire study period, the expansion from two restaurants in 1955 to 5,185 twenty-three years later is truly an American success story.

The major objective of this research is to focus on the geography of the remarkable growth of the McDonald's restaurant chain within the conti-

Reprinted by permission from *Geographical Perspectives* 58 (1986), 1–8.

nental United States between 1955 and 1978, and to describe the varied character of this growth in different regions of the country.

Diffusion Theory

The theories of spatial-temporal change known as spatial diffusion were first devised and explored by Torsten Hagerstrand over forty years ago. Simply stated, spatial diffusion is the study of the movement of new ideas, products, and services throughout geographic space with the passage of time. Many geographic models have been devised to explain existing patterns and to predict future trends. Hagerstrand's early studies of the acceptance of pasture improvement subsidies and the adoption of the automobile in southern Sweden have provided the basis for many later works with different foci.[2] William Bell studied the diffusion of radio and television broadcasting in the United States.[3] The findings that the innovation first spread throughout a hierarchy of populous places, followed by a distance-based expansion into smaller markets, were not unexpected, but illustrated the geographic component of an interesting phenomenon affecting many people. Many studies of spatial diffusion have demonstrated the applicability of Hagerstrand's theories regarding other widely divergent themes, such as the decision to irrigate crops in eastern Colorado, the growth of the urban ghetto in Seattle, and the erection of billboards in the State College, Pennsylvania area.[4] Each of these studies has described and explained a changing geographic surface over time, and each has been based on the original work of Hagerstrand.

More recent work dealing with diffusion processes has found that the individual choice models of Hagerstrand may not be effective and applicable for many special-interest cases in which *the innovation is propagated by an entity motivated to bring rapid and complete diffusion.*[5] Instead, a market and infrastructure perspective borrowed from the field of economics may be more relevant. In such a case, the evolution of an expansion diffusion process may be directed by a "centralized structure" that makes marketing decisions, or by a "decentralized structure" in which individual members of the innovation chain make independent decisions to locate. Either the centralized or decentralized system may operate in a profit-making or non-profit mode.[6]

This research describes the growth of the McDonald's hamburger chain from 1955 to 1978 through the construction and manipulation of a computerized geographic information system. The study of the evolving pattern of restaurants in the McDonald's chain was carried out in two stages: database construction and cartographic analysis.

The Database

Data on the location of McDonald's restaurants were collected from directories that listed all restaurants in the system at year's end: 1965, 1969, 1971, 1972, 1973, 1974, 1975, 1976, 1977, and 1978. (The McDonald's Corporation discontinued the printing of store directories after the 1979 annual report, thus this study was forced to end at that time.) In order to determine changes in the pattern of restaurant location over time, each store in the system had to be assigned a period of first service. Since not all years were represented in the available data, the restaurants were placed into one of ten categories according to their first appearance in a directory: 1965 or before, 1966–69, 1970–71, 1972, 1973, 1974, 1975, 1976, 1977, or 1978.

Census materials then were used to gather population counts for each town and city served. Next, each restaurant was located on a large U. S. basemap. In cases in which multiple restaurants were located in the same town, different sites were selected within the city limits. Finally, a Federal Information Processing Standard (FIPS) state code was assigned to each restaurant. The resulting data file contained over 4,400 records indicating, for each store: the place name, the year of opening, the population of the place, the coordinates of the location, and the FIPS code. A preliminary analysis of the data, using dot maps generated from the locational coordinates, indicated several interesting trends.

By 1965, the two sources of the innovation, Des Plaines, Illinois, and San Bernadino, California, had diffused McDonald's restaurants to the larger cities. Several fairly dense clusters appeared, one in Washington, D.C., another in Atlanta, Georgia; and others in the regional centers of St. Louis and Kansas City, Missouri; Columbus and Cleveland, Ohio; Detroit, Michigan; Seattle-Tacoma, Washington; Los Angeles, California; and Denver, Colorado. Such a pattern in the early period of expansion supported the hypothesis that the diffusion may be based on the population of the areas to be served.

By 1969, the major growth was in California. The state acquired 150 new McDonald's restaurants during the four-year period, one opening every 9.7 days. Texas, which had very few McDonald's locations in 1965, had shown limited growth, as had Florida. The New England area had just begun to be represented by 1969. In 1969, all forty-eight states had at least one McDonald's restaurant.

By 1971, the growth had been heavy in the New England states. The first surge of expansion in New York City was noted, and the number of outlets in the southeastern states increased.

By 1974, the pattern in the Southeast was noteworthy because the clusters found in 1971 had not intensified, but rather many new markets were penetrated. The trend in New York City was continued expansion, and the old Northwest (Ohio, Indiana, and Illinois) experienced substantive growth.

By 1978 the Southeast had experienced a substantial increase in the density of McDonald's. The Raleigh-to-Atlanta piedmont crescent was well served. In New York City, there were now 113 restaurants among all the boroughs. Overall, the pattern of McDonald's restaurants was similar to a population dot map of the United States. Heavy clusters were seen in the larger places, with lesser development found in less populated areas. Because the dot maps had implied that the distribution was related to the presence of population, one statistical relationship was established prior to a determination of the type of diffusion exhibited by the McDonald's Corporation. A Pearson product moment correlation was run to determine the strength of the relationship between population and the number of restaurants in a place. Over 90 percent of the variation in the number of restaurants per city was explained by the variation in the population of these towns and places.

Analysis by State

The dot maps in the preliminary analysis suggested that growth was uneven, so a state analysis was undertaken. A table cross-tabulating years of opening with the state FIPS codes was generated, and expected growth patterns were developed for each state. The expected number of restaurants built in a state in a given year was equal to that state's proportion of all restaurants nationally at the end of the study period (1978) multiplied by the total number of restaurants built nationwide in that given year. For example, if Iowa had 10 percent of all McDonald's restaurants in 1978, and there were 200 built nationally in 1972, then 10 percent of that 200, or 20 restaurants, should have been added in Iowa during 1972. By comparing the expected value with the actual rates of growth in each state for each time period, times of rapid or slow growth were traced. A map locating those states that had boom periods at differing times during the study showed areas of focused growth in the United States during the 1955–78 period (Fig. 8–1).

Prior to 1965 the states with the fastest growth stretched from Ohio to

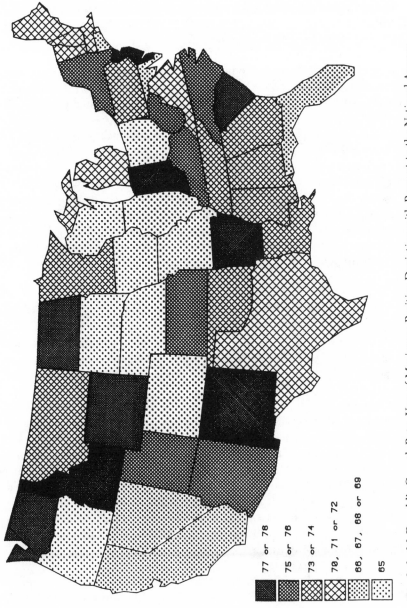

Fig. 8–1. McDonald's Growth Rate: Year of Maximum Positive Deviation with Respect to the National Average

77 or 78

75 or 76

73 or 74

70, 71 or 72

66, 67, 68 or 69

65

Colorado (except in Indiana which grew very rapidly then, but grew slightly faster in the last study period). Oregon was the one state with its fastest growth occurring in this period but that was not in the central cluster.

In the 1966–69 period, California dominated in the building of new Mc-Donald's restaurants. Nevada, Florida, Maryland, and Connecticut also had much higher than expected growth during this time.

Between 1970 and 1972, five of the six New England states had their maximum growth. Only in Connecticut, where restaurant expansion was noted during the last period, was the rate of growth not as a peak. Texas, virtually ignored until this time, gained restaurants very rapidly from 1970 to 1972.

The ascendancy of the Southeast characterized the next period, 1973–74. Tennessee, Mississippi, Alabama, Georgia, and Louisiana had their maximum growth rates during these years. North Carolina and South Carolina lagged behind with development occurring during the next two periods.

During the last two periods, 1975–76 and 1977–78, a clear regionalization of growth was far less evident. New York and New Jersey grew as did such disparate locales as New Mexico, North Dakota, and Arkansas. The only contiguity of any dimension was found in the Northwest (Wyoming, Idaho, and Washington).

Comparison with Diffusion Processes

The next question addressed is whether the process of diffusion in this case more closely matches the hierarchical or contagious models of Hagerstrand or the marketing and infrastructure models of Lawrence Brown and Kevin Cox.

Hierarchical diffusions follow a ranked list of population centers, with larger places adopting the new idea, service, or product sooner than smaller places. A contagious pattern is based on distance; therefore a location nearer to an adopted innovation is likely to receive that innovation sooner than one farther from the source.[7] The maps and statistics used thus far have not fully determined which process is more significant to the national expansion of the McDonald's chain. The statistical analysis implied movement along a hierarchy, as did the dot maps. However, the contiguous region of states centered on Illinois produced during the state-level analysis suggested that a few more tests were necessary before abandoning the contagious-diffusion model.

There are several possible means of determining the answer to this question, and the computerized database can provide many useful statistics.

First, a simple graph of the population of adopters of McDonald's over time was plotted (Graph 8–1). Populations where new McDonald's restaurants were located became markedly smaller during the study period, from an average of over 115,000 people in 1965 to under 10,000 in 1978. The shape of this curve is very similar to the rank-size curve found by Bell.[8] On average, larger places received McDonald's restaurants earlier than did smaller places.

Two final tests were made to be certain that there was no contagion involved at national or subnational scales. Because the definition of a contagious diffusion states that it must occur outward from a source position, if the mean distance of all restaurants from the original restaurant located in Des Plaines, Illinois, increased over time, some contagious component might be surmised. The distance from Des Plaines to each restaurant was calculated using the location coordinates. Distances were sorted into groups by year of opening, and averaged by group. To imply an expanding conta-

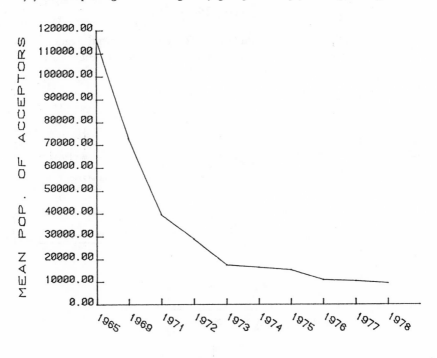

YEAR OF FIRST McDONALD'S

Graph 8–1. Population of Adopters of McDonald's (1965–78)

gious diffusion, a graph plotting the average distance of each restaurant from Des Plaines should show a positive slope from 1965 to 1978 (Graph 8–2). This effect is not apparent.

Because the 1965 data suggested a fairly well-defined set of regional centers, a test was run to determine whether the pattern appeared to follow that of radio broadcasting found by Bell.[9] The final test was to determine whether expansion into larger cities was followed by growth within their hinterlands governed by distance. Using Denver, Los Angeles, Atlanta, Washington, D.C, and Chicago as centroids, researchers sorted the restaurants into five groups according to the Thiessan polygon into which they fell. All restaurants were associated with the nearest regional center and the procedure searching for an increasing mean distance over time was repeated for each of the groups. Again no relationship between distance and the year of opening could be ascertained.

A Marketing Perspective

Because McDonald's restaurants are licensed by a central headquarters and because they operate under a profit-making motive, the location of

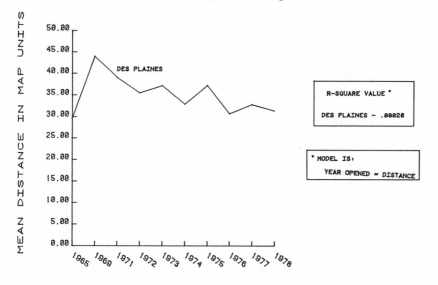

Graph 8–2. Average Distance of Each McDonald's Restaurant from Des Plaines, Illinois (1965–78)

a new McDonald's restaurant could be reasonably selected based on the anticipated profit expected in alternative sites. In this case, potential sites for restaurants would be ranked according to specific criteria perceived by the central office to be related to the probability for restaurant success. Markets then would be entered sequentially moving down the list.[10] The overall pattern of diffusion is created solely according to an economic assessment of potential markets. However, the case of McDonald's restaurants is a bit more complex. Most McDonald's restaurants are operated as franchises by individuals interested in managing their own businesses. The likelihood of a spatially uneven distribution of applicants could also affect the diffusion pattern for the system. But, because the central office is the sole decision maker in the system, the ranking process is still a valid model for McDonald's. The selection of a new town or city to be included in the chain would be determined by ranking all the sites that have applied for licenses. The top-ranked sites would be granted licenses, with those farther down the list denied the right to operate.

It cannot be the intent of research at a national scale to uncover the location secrets of the McDonald's Corporation. The statistical inquiry in this study determined that the presence of population was clearly involved in the ranking of potential sites. If the market and infrastructure model is the most applicable diffusion model, as would seem likely, and population is a key factor in the ranking process, the results of the diffusion would still appear hierarchical. The national scope of this study does not permit any further analysis. Such efforts would require more localized data.

Conclusions

The enormous success of the McDonald's hamburger chain is based on locating restaurants in areas with population to be served. While this finding is not surprising, it has led to better understanding of the pattern of diffusion for the system. From beginnings in larger cities, to stops along heavily traveled highways, to locations in resort areas with little permanent population, McDonald's restaurants have nearly always made inroads into the American lifestyle and diet.

Although growth has been rapid, it was spatially uneven from 1955 to 1978. Differing strategies must have been applied to penetrate different regions of the country at varying times during the system's evolution. This fact is exemplified by the widely varying rates of growth among the states.

Finally, there is no evidence that the locations selected for new restaurants are affected by their distance from previously existing restaurants.

McDonald's "Burger Kingdom" has been created in a hierarchical manner in the markets that could support it. By its growth and continued strength in the fast-food market, it is evident that decisions on location have been made and executed successfully.

Notes

1. McDonald's Corporation, *Annual Report 1978* (Oak Brook, Ill.: 1979); see also annual reports for 1965, 1969, 1971, 1972, 1973, 1974, 1975, 1976, 1977.

2. Torsten Hagerstrand, *The Propagation of Innovation Waves* (Lund, Sweden: Lund Series in Geography, Series B, Number 4, 1952).

3. William Bell, "The Diffusion of Radio and Television Broadcasting Stations in the United States" (unpublished Master's thesis, Pennsylvania State University, 1965).

4. Leonard W. Bowden, *Diffusion of the Decision to Irrigate* (Chicago: Department of Geography, University of Chicago Research Paper Number 97, 1965); Richard Morrill, "The Negro Ghetto: Problems and Alternatives," *Geographical Review* 55 (July 1965), 339–61; Robert Colenutt, "Linear Diffusion in an Urban Setting," *Geographical Analysis* 1 (1969), 106–14.

5. Lawrence A. Brown, *Innovation Diffusion: A New Perspective* (New York: Methuen, 1981).

6. Lawrence A. Brown and Kevin Cox, "Empirical Regularities in the Diffusion of Innovation," *Annals of the Association of American Geographers* 61 (September 1971), 551–59.

7. Peter Gould, *Spatial Diffusion* (Washington, D.C.: Association of American Geographers, Commission on College Geography, Resource Paper Number 4, 1969).

8. Bell, "The Diffusion of Radio and Television Broadcasting Systems in the United States."

9. Ibid.

10. Brown and Cox, "Empirical Regularities in the Diffusion of Innovation."

9

Selected Reading III

Chapters 7 and 8

American Heritage Cookbook and Illustrated History of American Eating and Drinking. New York: Simon & Schuster, 1984.

Belasco, Warren J. *Appetite for Change: How the Counterculture Took on the Food Industry, 1966–1988*. New York: Pantheon, 1989.

Brown, Linda Keller, and Mussell, Kay. "American Food and Foodways," *Journal of American Culture* 2 (1979), 392–570.

———. *Ethnic and Regional Foodways in the United States*. Knoxville: University of Tennessee Press, 1984.

Camp, Charles. "Foodways in Everyday Life," *American Quarterly* 34 (1982), 278–89.

Egerton, John. *Southern Food: At Home, on the Road, in History*. New York: Knopf, 1987.

Jones, Ewan. *American Food: The Gastronomic Story*. New York: Dutton, 1975.

Kroc, Ray. *Grinding It Out: The Making of McDonald's*. Chicago: Regnery, 1977.

Lasky, Michael S. *The Complete Junk Food Book*. New York: McGraw-Hill, 1977.

Levenstein, Harvey A. *Revolution at the Table: The Transformation of the American Diet*. New York: Oxford University Press, 1988.

Pillsbury, Richard. *From Boarding House to Bistro: The American Restaurant Then and Now*. Boston: Unwin Hyman, 1990.

Root, Waverly, and de Rochemont, Richard. *Eating in America: A History.* New York: Morrow, 1976.

Zelinsky, Wilbur. "The Roving Palate: North America's Ethnic Restaurant Cuisines," *Geoforum* 16 (1985), 51–72.

Part IV: Religion

Using a vernacular region description coined by H. L. Mencken more than seventy years ago, Steve Tweedie, my colleague at Oklahoma State since the early 1970s, gives a reinterpretation of the Bible Belt boundaries based on television ministry viewer data. The acknowledged leaders of the "religious right" movement, a post-World War II popular culture phenomenon, are experts in the art of television communication, or televangelism. No longer found on the camp meeting circuit, Christian ministers now use the "electric church" to reach the nation's living rooms on Sunday mornings. Although his article was originally published more than fifteen years ago, prime-time religion appears to have flourished into the 1990s. Tweedie's research remains the classic case study of the Bible Belt region as delimited by a cultural geographer. Finally, his analysis provides us with a previously unmapped dimension of popular religion in America.

Barbara Weightman of California State University-Fullerton presents an intriguing look at the changing religious landscapes of America's second largest urban center—Los Angeles. The population of Los Angeles has not only experienced phenomenal growth, but has become increasingly diverse. This has resulted in the construction of new sacred places as well as a restructuring of the old. Moreover, previously restricted religious events are now openly celebrated by the public. Ethnic group membership has modified established religious rituals, and multilingual services have been incorporated in mainline denominations. Finally, a new generation of religious clientele has prompted the development of market-oriented, full-service "megachurches" and drive-in religious facilities.

10

Viewing the Bible Belt

Stephen W. Tweedie

Where is the Bible Belt? The term has been used frequently, and loosely, ever since it was coined by H. L. Mencken about 1925 to "designate those parts of the country in which the literal accuracy of the Bible is credited and clergymen who preach it have public influence."[1] He generally used the term in a derogatory context, with such phrases as "the Bible and Hook-worm Belt,"[2] and "Jackson, Mississippi, in the heart of the Bible and Lynch-ing Belt."[3]

Mencken never bothered to give the Bible Belt a specific location, but his use of the term clearly associates it with areas dominated by rural Baptists and Methodists. His essays dealing with fundamentalist religion include references to rural Iowa and South Carolina, Georgia, Mississippi, Arkansas, Nebraska, and "darkest Tennessee." In an essay titled "Protestant-ism in the Republic" he states,

> In all those parts of the Republic where Beelzebub is still as real as Babe Ruth . . .—for example, in the rural sections of the Middle West and everywhere in the South save a few walled towns—the evangelical sects—declare a holy war upon every decency that civilized men cherish.[4]

The term Bible Belt has increased in popular usage ever since Mencken's time, and while still used as a term of derision by outsiders, it is now also used with pride by those who consider themselves to be part of it. For example, one article reported, "Oklahoma City has more than 200 churches

Reprinted by permission from the *Journal of Popular Culture* 11 (1978), 865–76.

and often calls itself, proudly, the Capital of the Bible Belt,"[5] and another referred to Bob Jones University in Greenville, South Carolina as "the Buckle of the Bible Belt."[6]

Scholarly usage of the term has been nearly as vague as popular usage. Edwin Gaustad, for example, in mapping the Church of Christ comments,

> From Tennessee across Arkansas and Oklahoma to Texas is a real belt— perhaps more a Bible Belt than any other region can offer.[7]

A 1952 survey based on nearly three thousand interviews concluded that if the term implies Bible readers, it should be applied primarily to the West South Central, East South Central, and South Atlantic census regions.[8]

While these studies represent an improvement over subjective impressions, they fall far short of a comprehensive mapping of the Bible Belt. Whatever, or wherever, the Bible Belt is, it is certainly not limited to one specific denomination, and a stratified sample of three thousand interviews is far too few to allow specific mapping of even state-to-state differences.

Neither church attendance records nor church membership statistics are valid indicators of fundamentalist religious orientation. Wilbur Zelinsky, in his 1961 paper on patterns of church membership in the United States, commented on the difficulty of using denominational affiliation as an indicator of religious or social identity because of the tremendous range in theological, social, and cultural attitudes found within each denomination.[9]

James Shortridge, using 1971 church membership data collected by the National Council of Churches, mapped the relative dominance of liberal versus conservative churches for each county in the United States.[10] The resulting map reveals a southern region, dominated by conservative churches, that extends from the Atlantic Coast through Texas into eastern New Mexico, and reaches as far as the northern boundaries of Virginia, Kentucky, Missouri, and Oklahoma, with an extension into southern Illinois. Conservative churches also dominated a large part of the northern plains centered on North Dakota, and the Mormon region centered on Utah.[11] Shortridge concludes,

> Jackson, Mississippi, could perhaps be called the "buckle" of the Bible Belt, but Oklahoma City is definitely marginal, and Kansas is not in it. Perhaps a Great Plains association with the term has been formed because this natural region connects two of the more religiously conservative portions of the country.[12]

Shortridge acknowledges several of the major problems in using church membership statistics. In his study, West Virginia is classified as a liberal

Protestant area with low church membership rates. Commenting on the low church affiliation rates reported for Appalachia, he states,

> Their low percentages may be simple functions of access, but another possibility exists in the frontier-like attitudes that remain to a degree in these areas. Local autonomy in religion and in other institutions is a jealously guarded tradition in Appalachia especially, leading to many dissociations of congregations and individuals from larger church units. Because such autonomous people would not be included in the religious survey data, these areas may be cases of large statistical error.[13]

It is also very possible that a high degree of latent fundamentalism exists even among nonmembers, a situation perhaps similar to that found by the frontier preachers of an earlier day. The classification of West Virginia as liberal Protestant is certainly suspect, and illustrates one of the problems involved in using church membership statistics as an indicator of religious orientation.

An ideal indicator would have to provide adequate spatial coverage and measure an ubiquitous activity that clearly reflects a fundamentalist religious orientation. Television audience estimates for religious programs meet these requirements.

The Television Ministry

In recent years the television ministry has become a major phenomenon on the American religious scene. In one survey week in February 1973, a total of 67 religious programs were offered, with a combined viewing audience of 14,313,000 households, 22 percent of the national total.[14] Of these programs only three were produced by the major commercial networks. The other 64 are classified as syndicated programs, sponsored by a large variety of Protestant groups representing both formal denominations and independent evangelical organizations, in addition to Jewish, Mormon, and Roman Catholic organizations. Formats include variations of traditional church services as well as children's cartoons, dramatic presentations, lectures, panel discussions, and sacred music (ranging from classical to country). While program orientations reflect the diverse viewpoints of these sponsors, the evangelical, fundamentalist Protestant position is the most heavily represented.

These syndicated programs are marketed through a distributor (frequently a subsidiary of the program producer) who buys time on local television stations. In a given television market area the programs may be carried by the local affiliate of any one of the three commercial networks. The networks themselves are not involved in this process.

Measured by the number of persons reached, the various television ministries are clearly major enterprises. Table 10–1 compares the 1971 membership statistics for some of the leading denominations with the audience estimates for the leading religious programs. Since audience estimates are given in number of households, the membership statistics have been adjusted accordingly. For example, using an estimate of two church members per household would result in approximately six million Southern Baptist households. If half of these households were in attendance on a given Sun-

Table 10–1. Sunday Morning Audience Estimates: Major Denomination and Leading Television Programs

Denominations	Membership 1971	Estimated Households	Estimated Sunday Attendance (in households)
Southern Baptist	12,000,000	6,000,000	3,000,000
Methodist	10,000,000	5,000,000	2,500,000
Lutherans (3 major groups)	6,000,000	3,000,000	1,500,000
United Presbyterian	3,000,000	1,500,000	750,000
United Church of Christ	2,000,000	1,000,000	500,000
Disciples of Christ	900,000	450,000	225,000

Television Program	February/March 1973 Sunday Audience Estimates (in households)
Oral Roberts	2,375,000
Cathedral of Tomorrow (Rex Humbard)	1,540,000
Day of Discovery	1,114,000
Gospel Singing Jubilee	970,000
This Is the Life	671,000
Jerry Falwell	580,000
Insight	480,000
Revival Fires	410,000

Sources: Douglas Johnson, Paul Picard, and Bernard Quinn, *Churches and Church Membership in the United States* (New York: National Council of Churches, 1974), 1–2, and Arbitron, *Television Syndicated Program Analysis*, February/March 1973.

day morning, the total number of households reached on an average Sunday morning by *all* Southern Baptist churches would be around three million. The results of similar calculations for the other major denominations are given in Table 10–1. If these estimates are at all representative,[15] then of the major American Protestant denominations only the Baptists and the Methodists reach more people on a Sunday morning than are reached by the television ministry of Oral Roberts. Other leading religious programs are clearly competitive in Sunday morning outreach with the major denominations.

The question of who watches such programs, and why, remains largely unanswered. Age and sex profiles of viewing audiences are available and reveal that for the top three programs 55 percent of the viewers are adult females, with only about 30 percent adult males, and the remaining 15 percent teenagers and children. Two-thirds of the adult viewers are over fifty years of age. There is no breakdown by race or religious affiliation. There is also no indication as to whether religious television programs complement or compete with traditional Sunday morning religious activities. People may find the television program more appealing than the local fare. Few local preachers have the charisma of Oral Roberts or can match a guest testimonial by Johnny Cash. On the other hand, the television message may be reaching an otherwise unchurched population, stimulating people to become more involved in local church activities. But while the exact role of the television ministry may be uncertain, there is no doubt that it is an activity of major proportions.

Methodology

Television audience estimates are available for area units known as "areas of dominant influence" (ADIs), defined as follows:

> ADI is an area that consists of all counties in which the home-market stations receive a preponderance of viewing. Each county in the United States is allocated exclusively to only one ADI.[16]

The 209 ADIs used as mapping units ranged in size from New York, with 6,161,000 households, to Glendive, Montana, with 4,100 households. One-third (69) of the ADIs had less than 100,000 households and are referred to as small markets. The 69 ADIs with over 256,000 households are classified as large ADIs, and the remaining 71 are termed medium.

The diversity of religious programming would make a map of total viewing virtually meaningless. Thus five of the leading programs were selected as representative of the evangelical, fundamentalist orientation.[17] These five programs all feature a combination of preaching and sacred music, and together account for 42 percent of the total households viewing religious programming. Since none of these programs has a formal denominational tie, the viewer response should indicate a basic fundamentalist orientation that cuts across denominational ties.

Television audience surveys were taken in November 1972, February/ March 1973, and May 1973. Audience estimates for the three separate survey periods were first averaged in order to reduce the possible effect of a single unrepresentative statistic. Estimates for the five programs were then summed, and the combined audiences were divided by total television households for each television market area to calculate a viewing rate. The results are mapped in Figure 10–1.

Findings

Although in general the total number of viewers of any television program bears a direct relationship to the number of television households in the market area, exceptions abound. In fact, six of the ten largest ADIs (Chicago, Philadelphia, Boston, Cleveland, Washington, and Pittsburgh) are not found in the top forty markets for these five religious programs. Mencken would undoubtably rejoice in the fact that his hometown, Baltimore, the nineteenth largest television market, with 708,200 households, provides a total of only 9,500 viewing households. On the other hand, Tampa-St. Petersburg, the twentieth largest ADI, places second only to Los Angeles in its response to these programs, and Johnstown, Pennsylvania, sixty-ninth in size with 269,500 households, places a close third, supplying more viewers than New York City, which has over twenty times as many potential viewing households. Of the twenty largest viewing markets for these programs, only five are among the twenty largest ADIs.

Market size affects the statistics in another way. Many small ADIs have only one or two home-market television stations, which reduces the number of programs that can be offered. For example, Tuscaloosa, Alabama, has only a local CBS station. The three leading religious programs are all carried by the NBC station in Birmingham, whose coverage includes Tuscaloosa. A distributor will not normally buy a small market separately when it is already covered from an adjacent large ADI. As a result viewers in Tuscaloosa watching such programs are counted as part of the Birmingham audience.[18] Anniston, Alabama, has a similar situation, which helps account for these

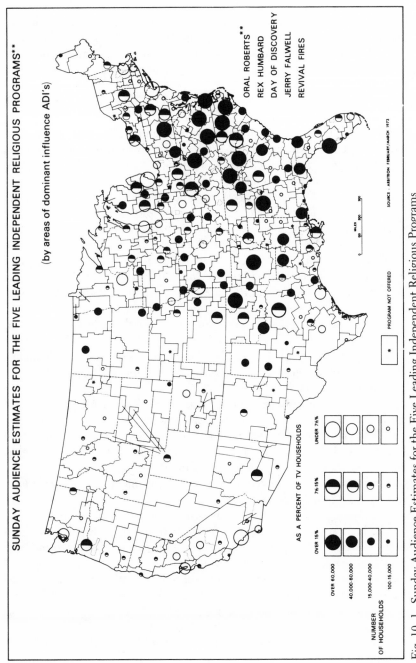

Fig. 10-1. Sunday Audience Estimates for the Five Leading Independent Religious Programs

low spots in what is otherwise a high-response area. Ten of the small markets did not carry any of the five programs, and an additional seven markets offered only one program, attracting fewer than a thousand households. Undoubtedly these statistics are not an accurate reflection of the true religious orientation in these areas.

Seventeen of the twenty largest ADIs also had low viewing rates. With the larger number of television channels available in these areas, to say nothing of the number of alternatives to watching television, it might be expected that the percentage of households viewing any particular program would be lower. However, except for these very large and very small ADIs, viewing rates were unrelated to market size.

Although the television market areas do not coincide neatly with state boundaries, the four standard census regions provide a useful basis for a preliminary look at regional variations. Both Figure 10–1 and Table 10–2 reveal that the West and the Northeast appear to be relatively uninterested in this type of programming. Of all cities in the West, only Cheyenne falls in the highest rate category; in the Northeast only Johnstown, Pennsylvania, Binghamton, New York, and Presque Isle, Maine have high viewing rates. About half of the cities in both regions fall in the low-rate category.

In the West this lack of response to fundamentalist television programming confirms the relative disinterest in traditional religion previously indicated by church attendance and membership statistics.[19] It also differentiates the unique religious orientation of the Mormon region from the conservative Protestant groups.

The low interest in the Northeast, and especially in Megalopolis, also comes as no surprise. Fundamentalist Protestant religious programming is not likely to attract the large numbers of the Jews, Catholics, and liberal Protestants that dominate the region. In addition, although the religious orientation is similar to that of black Protestant groups, the almost total lack of black personnel featured on the programs might reduce their appeal among those groups as well.

The South and North Central regions stand in sharp contrast. In the South, Mencken's "walled towns" have fallen! Nearly half of the southern ADIs have high viewing rates, with only six of the region's twenty-nine large television markets falling in the low-rate category. These six "exceptions" are all in peripheral locations with respect to the South—Baltimore, Washington, Louisville, San Antonio, Houston, and Miami. Of the six medium-sized markets with low viewing rates, three (El Paso and Waco, Texas, and Lafayette, Louisiana) are also on the fringe of the South. The other three (Columbia, South Carolina; Macon, Georgia; and Montgomery, Alabama) appear to be true "exceptions."

Table 10–2. Viewing Rates by Market Size and Region

| Region | Large ADIs (over 265,000 households) | | | |
	High (over 15%)	Medium (7.5-15%)	Low (under 7.5%)	Total
Northeast	1	6	6	13
North Central	0	9	9	18
South	13	10	6	29
West	0	3	6	9
TOTAL	14	28	27	69

| Region | Medium ADIs (100,000–265,000 households) | | | |
	High (over 15%)	Medium (7.5-15%)	Low (under 7.5%)	Total
Northeast	1	3	1	5
North Central	16	9	2	27
South	16	8	6	30
West	0	6	3	9
TOTAL	33	26	12	71

| Region | Small ADIs (under 100,000 households) | | | |
	High (over 15%)	Medium (7.5-15%)	Low (under 7.5%)	Total
Northeast	1	0	4	5
North Central	5	4	3	12
South	13	4	13	30
West	1	9	12	22
TOTAL	20	17	32	69

Source: Arbitron, February/March 1973.

The "walled towns," in fact, show up in the Middle West. *None* of eighteen large North Central markets has a high viewing rate, contrasted with thirteen of the twenty-nine southern markets. However, for the medium-sized ADIs the two regions are very similar. Sixteen of thirty southern markets and sixteen of twenty-seven in the North Central region have high viewing rates. Viewing tendencies for small ADIs are also fairly similar for the two regions. Thus the major difference between the regions appears to be the urban enclaves found within the Midwest.

Viewed as a whole, the Bible Belt appears as a broad zone stretching from

Virginia to northern Florida in the East and from the Dakotas to central Texas in the West. Within this area are two cores: eastern and western. Table 10–3 lists the top religious television markets defined on the basis of a combination of both absolute and relative responses. Group A consists of those ADIs with over 60,000 viewing households *and* at least a 15 percent viewing rate. Group B identifies those markets with either 60,000 viewers and a moderate rate (7.5 to 15 percent), or those with 40,000–60,000 viewers and a high rate (over 15 percent).

Eleven of the thirteen strongest markets (Group A) define the eastern core. It is centered on the five major markets in Virginia and North Carolina—Richmond, Roanoke, Norfolk, Raleigh, and Greenville—with its perimeter defined by five other major markets—Tampa, Birmingham, Knoxville, Charleston, and Johnstown. Greenville, South Carolina, home of Bob Jones University, is the remaining major market in this eastern core. Of the Group B markets, seven fall within or are adjacent to this region. Other smaller markets in the eastern core having high rates are listed in Group C.

This eastern core has two northern extensions of moderate response. One crosses central Pennsylvania and retains some strength in Upstate New York. The second extends through Ohio and into lower Michigan, with high rates recorded in Lima, Ft. Wayne, Lansing, and Traverse City-Cadillac.

The western core of the Bible Belt hinges on Little Rock and Tulsa, with the secondary centers of Dallas-Ft. Worth and Wichita Falls-Lawton to the southwest; Monroe, Louisiana, and Jackson, Mississippi, to the southeast; and Kansas City to the north. Other small, high-response centers associated with this core are listed in Group C.

Connecting these two cores lies a zone of moderate response. None of the cities in this zone satisfies the criteria for Group A and only Mobile-Pensacola qualifies for Group B. Nashville, Memphis, and New Orleans all fall short on the viewing rate criteria. Evansville and Terre Haute have high viewing rates but attract fewer than 40,000 households. The major cities of Indianapolis, Louisville, and St. Louis fail to meet either requirement.

Another break separates the western core from the northern plains. The major markets of Des Moines and Omaha show very little interest, and Davenport-Rock Island-Moline, Cedar Rapids-Waterloo, and Lincoln-Hastings-Kearney manage only a moderate response.

Conclusion

The television audience estimates for these evangelical, fundamentalist religious programs do reveal a previously unmapped dimension of religion

Table 10–3. Leading Television Markets for Religious Programs

Group A (over 60,000 viewing households and over 15% viewing rate)		
Eastern Core	Western Core	Other
Birmingham, Ala.	Little Rock, Ark.	
Charleston-Huntington, W.Va.	Tulsa, Okla.	
Greenville-New Bern- Washington, N.C.		
Greenville-Spartanburg- Asheville, S.C.-N.C.		
Johnstown-Altoona, Pa.		
Knoxville, Tenn.		
Norfolk-Portsmouth-Newport News-Hampton, Va.		
Raleigh-Durham, N.C.		
Richmond, Va.		
Roanoke-Lynchburg, Va.		
Tampa-St. Petersburg, Fla.		

Group B (either 60,000 viewing households and moderate [7–15%] viewing rate or 40,000–60,000 households and high [over 15%] viewing rate)		
Eastern Core	Western Core	Other
Augusta, Ga.	Dallas-Ft. Worth, Tex.	Mobile-Pensacola,
Charlotte, N.C.	Kansas City, Mo.-Kans.	Ala.-Fla.
Chattanooga, Tenn.	Jackson, Miss.	
Cincinnati, Ohio	Monroe-El Dorado, La.-Ark.	
Jacksonville, Fla.	Wichita Falls-Lawton, Tex.-Okla.	
Tallahassee, Fla.		
Wheeling-Steubenville, W.Va.-Ohio		

Group C (smaller markets with high [over 15%] viewing rates)		
Eastern Core	Western Core	Northern Plains
Salisbury, Md.	St. Joseph, Mo.	Minot-Bismarck, N.Dak.
Harrisonburg, Va.	Topeka, Kans.	Fargo, N.Dak.
Clarksburg-Weston, W.Va.	Ottumwa-Kirksville, Iowa-Mo.	Pembina, N.Dak.
Bluefield-Beckley-Oak Hill, W.Va.	Quincy-Hannibal, Ill.-Mo.	Sioux Falls-Mitchell,
Lexington, Ky.	Peoria, Ill.	S.Dak.
Wilmington, N.C.	Columbia-Jefferson City, Mo.	Sioux City, Iowa
Florence, S.C.	Springfield, Mo.	Mankato, Minn.
Charleston, S.C.	Joplin-Pittsburg, Kans.-Mo.	Rochester-Mason City-
Savannah, Ga.	Ft. Smith, Ark.	Austin, Minn.-Iowa
Albany, Ga.	Tyler, Tex.	
Columbus, Ga.	Abilene-Sweetwater, Tex.	
Panama City, Fla.	Lubbock, Tex.	
Ft. Myers, Fla.	Amarillo, Tex.	
	Beaumont-Port Arthur, Tex.	

in America, a basic fundamentalist orientation that cuts across denominational lines and is perhaps impossible to isolate on the basis of any other available data. Clearly the areas of strong response cut across religious regions based on denominational patterns, as identified by David Sopher and Zelinsky.[20] The Baptist South certainly is a major part of this Bible Belt, but areas of strength also include parts of the Methodist-dominated Midwest as well as portions of the predominantly Lutheran Dakotas.

While the extensions into Pennsylvania, Michigan, and the central and northern Great Plains have long been recognized by scholars familiar with the basic cultural composition of those areas, a common indicator that allows its extent and intensity to be compared with other regions has been lacking. The completely voluntary act of turning the television dial provides such a measure, and affords us our best view yet of the elusive Bible Belt.

The strength and location of this Bible Belt would come as no surprise to H. L. Mencken. In an essay on Puritanism he commented:

> Today, save in its remoter villages, New England is no more Puritan than, say, Maryland or Missouri. There is scarcely a clergyman in the entire region who, if the Mathers could come back to life, would not be condemned by them instantly as a heretic, and even as an atheist. The dominant theology is mild, skeptical and wholly lacking in passion. The evangelical spirit has completely disappeared. . . . The old heat is gone. Where it lingers in America is in far places—on the Methodist prairies of the Middle West, in the Baptist backwaters of the South. There, I believe, it still retains not a little of its old vitality. There Puritanism survives, not merely as a system of theology, but also as a way of life. It colors every human activity.[21]

Notes

1. Mitford M. Mathews (ed.), *Dictionary of Americanisms* (Chicago: University of Chicago Press, 1951), I, 110.

2. H. L. Mencken, *Prejudices: Sixth Series* (New York: Knopf, 1927), 92.

3. James D. Bernard, "The Baptists," *American Mercury* 7 (January 1926), 136–46. Although Mencken did not author this article his editing certainly would have encouraged the use of this phrase, and may have originated it.

4. H. L. Mencken, *Prejudices: Fifth Series* (New York: Knopf, 1926), 111.

5. Milton MacKaye, "The Cities of America: Oklahoma City," *Saturday Evening Post* 220 (June 5, 1948), 21.

6. Larry L. King, "Bob Jones University: The Buckle on the Bible Belt," *Harper's Magazine* 232 (June 1966), 51–58.

7. Edwin S. Gaustad, "Religious Demography of the South," in *Religion and the Solid South*, ed. Samuel S. Hill Jr. (Nashville: Abingdon, 1972), 155.

8. John L. Thomas, *Religion and the American People* (Westminster, Md.: Newman Press, 1963), 126.

9. Wilbur Zelinsky, "An Approach to the Religious Geography of the United States: Patterns of Church Membership in 1952," *Annals of the Association of American Geographers* 51 (June 1961), 165–66. See also Charles Y. Glock and Rodney Stark, *Religion and Society in Tension* (Chicago: Rand McNally, 1965), 86–122.

10. James R. Shortridge, "Patterns of Religion in the United States," *Geographical Review* 66 (October 1976), 420–34.

11. Ibid., 426. Shortridge classified the Church of Jesus Christ of the Latter-day Saints as conservative Protestant.

12. Ibid., 427.

13. Ibid., 433.

14. Arbitron: *Television Syndicated Program Analysis*, February/March 1973. These figures include only regularly scheduled Sunday programs. Audience estimates for prime-time specials, such as the Oral Roberts Easter Special, or the various Billy Graham crusades, which preempt regular programs, are generally unavailable. Locally produced programs, such as a locally televised church service, are also excluded from these statistics.

15. In fact, these church attendance estimates are probably too high. The attendance rate for Protestants in 1971 was about 37 percent, and the average size of household in 1970 was 3.1 persons.

16. Arbitron: *1972–73 Exclusive Television Market Areas of Dominant Influence in the United States*, 2.

17. The five programs selected are Oral Roberts, Cathedral of Tomorrow (Rex Humbard), Day of Discovery, Jerry Falwell (Old Time Gospel Hour), and Revival Fires. Each was carried in over 100 ADIs with a nationwide distribution.

18. If the Tuscaloosa station did carry the program, then the viewer would be counted as part of the Tuscaloosa audience even if he was watching the program on the Birmingham channel.

19. Zelinsky, 150; Shortridge, 432.

20. David E. Sopher, *Geography of Religions* (Englewood Cliffs, N.J.: Prentice-Hall, 1967), 84–85. See also Zelinsky, 162–64 and 193.

21. Mencken, *Prejudices: Fifth Series*, 253.

11

Changing Religious Landscapes in Los Angeles

Barbara A. Weightman

Landscapes of religion derive from interrelationships between religions and extant cultural contexts.[1] Numerous geographers, while addressing the character of sacred phenomena in rural and urban settings, have clarified spatial patterns and processes inherent in the emergence of religious landscapes.[2] Such studies reveal the interplay of societal change and these landscapes. However, none are specifically concerned with religious landscapes in a postmodern metropolitan area.

Postmodern places, undergoing restructuring in virtually all aspects, are marked by pluralism and comprise fluctuating coalitions of changing interests conceived in light of deindustrialization, large-scale immigration, and demand for instant gratification in an information era. Religion, in response, thrives through intensified ingenuity in meeting the needs of increasing numbers of diverse interest groups.[3] These postmodern trends are epitomized in the evolving cultural landscapes of the Los Angeles metropolitan area.[4]

Los Angeles, the City of Angels, has always been a magnet for both migrants and immigrants. As the keystone of a major Pacific Rim conurbation, it continues to draw a broad spectrum of people from around the world, and the consequential human dynamic is reflected in rapidly changing cultural landscapes. Change is particularly apparent in the metropolitan area's religious landscapes.

Reprinted by permission from the *Journal of Cultural Geography* 14 (1993), 1–20.

California has long had a pluralistic religious environment. It not only had early encounters with Asian religions but also engendered a more experimental and secular atmosphere for different spiritual experiences than existed elsewhere in the nation.[5] A major migration destination in the latter part of the nineteenth century, Los Angeles evolved as an assemblage of relocatees—a diverse mix of individuals and groups seeking comfortable niches in the existing spiritual milieu. As historian James Gregory notes, Southern California's "Xanadu dimension" encouraged all of increased secularity, religious innovation, and extreme pluralism.[6] These are ongoing processes which can be understood in the modern context of "restructuring."

Sociologist Robert Wuthnow purports that American religion has undergone a major restructuring, molded by an array of larger social forces. For example, he argues that while society might appear to be more secular, it is not really, because human spiritual needs as well as what constitutes "religion" and "religious" have changed. Wuthnow goes on to discuss alterations in modes of identification, interaction, moral obligation, and discourse appropriate to defining religious communities in current social, economic, and political contexts.[7] However, he does not address visual landscape expression of religious restructuring.

This study explores some of the ways in which restructuring of religion has impacted the Los Angeles metropolitan area (Fig. 11-1). It will show that landscape transformation is derived not only from population dynamics, including the influx of people of different faiths, but also from the response of various religions and belief systems to increasing permutations in population composition and religious identity. The intent here is not to identify all or even a broad sampling of religious landscape expression. Rather it is to clarify, by example, the means by which religious landscapes are created or modified in a metropolitan crucible of social flux.

New Religious Landscapes

Los Angeles is a microcosm of California's ethnic mosaic. Today, the Los Angeles metropolitan area is home to people from more than 140 countries. With its rampant multiculturalism, Los Angeles is viewed by writer David Rieff as the "Capital of the Third World" and precursor of this nation's future.[8] Institutional presence is critical to the creation and sustenance of collective and individual ethnic identity.[9] Consequently, the establishment of a religious site can be seen as a landscape validation of institutional

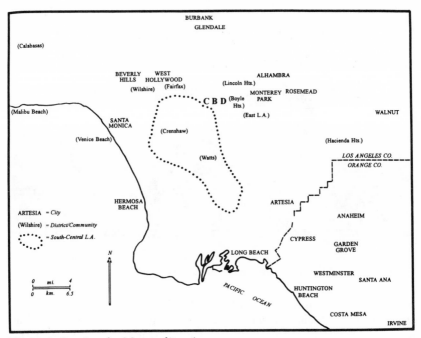

Fig. 11–1. Los Angeles Metropolitan Area

presence. The most obvious response to increasingly diverse religious needs is the production of entirely new religious landscapes.

In 1985, a new Zoroastrian worship center opened in the suburb of Westminster (Fig. 11-2). Of the some six thousand Zoroastrians in the United States, approximately fifteen hundred reside in Southern California.[10] The temple, with its roof supported by four pillars topped with bulls' heads, is modeled after one built in Persia by King Darius. This worship center exemplifies the collective aspirations of a people wanting to preserve their identity in a new environmental context.

An estimated 250,000 Muslims in Southern California are accommodated by five Islamic centers and 82 mosques—symbols of continuity of Islam in North America and connectivity with religious authorities of the Middle East as well as the international Muslim community.[11] These religious buildings have fostered the emergence of ancillary activities such as food markets offering *halal* (ritually prepared foods), restaurants, and Islamic bookstores.

Education and proselytization are important tools for faith maintenance and expansion, and mosques traditionally have been centers of learning

Fig. 11–2. The California Zoroastrian Center in Westminster (1992)

and communication. In Garden Grove, the Orange Crescent School was established in 1983 in association with an Islamic center and mosque. Catering to a spate of nationalities, most of its students were born in the United States of immigrant parents. The construction of the Masjid Umar Ibn Al-Khattab in south central Los Angeles reflects increasing numbers of Muslim immigrants in addition to acquisition of new converts through proselytization in adjacent African American communities.

The presence of Hindus is revealed by the construction of the Sree Venkateshwara Temple at Calabasas in the hills just north of Malibu. It is the largest Hindu shrine of the Chola style in the Western Hemisphere. While the Hindu Temple Society of Southern California was formed in 1977, the 1981 act of bringing in expert temple builders from India to create the temple according to tenth-century religious documents signified the permanence and importance of Southern California's 10,000 Hindus.[12]

Sree Venkateshwara, with its hilltop site, rural setting, and east-west orientation, exemplifies the Hindu transformation of space as described by geographer Carolyn Prorok in her discussion of Prabhupada's Palace of Gold Krishna Temple in West Virginia.[13] In similar fashion, this temple, with its resident priests and cycle of celebrations and events, establishes spiritual links to India's sacred places and validates Hindu identity in an essentially non-Hindu realm. It exemplifies requisite functional adaptations in the North American culture realm. Hindus reside throughout the Los Angeles area with significant concentrations around Artesia and Walnut, both 40 miles from Malibu. This patterns the North American spatial arrangement where devotees typically travel great distances to engage in religious obligations. In response to secular work schedules and driving times, the temple has devised a regular timetable of activities. It also functions as a social center and facilitates Hindus in adapting to California culture. This structured organization is not characteristic of temples in India but is typical of those in North America.[14]

Buddhism is becoming increasingly evident in California's landscapes; today's array of temples represents numerous schools of thought, especially Pure Land, which arrived with Chinese and Japanese immigrants in the nineteenth century. The most dramatic landmark testifying to the significance of the Buddhist community is the Fo Kuang Shan Hsi Lai Temple in Hacienda Heights, an emerging Asian suburban area in the San Gabriel Valley (Fig. 11-3). Hsi Lai means "coming to the west" and the temple is an architectural replica of Fo Kuang Shan in Taiwan. Of the Pure Land persuasion, Hsi Lai caters to devotees from Taiwan, but it also has a broad range of outreach programs for Asians and non-Asians alike.

Hsi Lai's massive ten-building complex is implicitly and explicitly international. Constructed of materials from Korea, Japan, Taiwan, Thailand, Italy, and the United States, it houses statuary and artifacts from most Buddhist regions of the world. Both monks and nuns are trained here and the complex serves, too, as the headquarters of the International Buddhist Progress Society. And, in 1988, the World Fellowship of Buddhists met for the first time outside Asia, at this site. The Hsi Lai Temple symbolizes not only intensification of the region's Asian presence but also the paramountcy

Fig. 11-3. Buddha Hall of the Hsi Lai Temple in Hacienda Heights (1992)

of Southern California as a center of Buddhism in the Western Hemisphere.

Another new religious landscape unfolding within the urban fabric focuses on the more than 800,000 Jews in the Los Angeles area. In Hollywood alone, three new edifices, a Museum of Tolerance, Martyrs Memorial and Museum of the Holocaust, and Los Angeles Holocaust Monument memorializing the Holocaust, have opened since 1991 in a sea of controversy. Yet large numbers of Jews are walking away from Judaism—affiliation with synagogues or other Jewish organizations in Southern California is down to between 15 and 25 percent of the population. Some would argue that the "Holocaust is killing America's Jews," and that droves are being turned off by the "specter of endless victimization and suffering."[15] However, there are signs of rejuvenation in light of Jewish immigration from the former Soviet Union.

West Hollywood and the Fairfax district of Los Angeles are now home to an estimated 40,000 to 80,000 Russian Jews. A collage of institutions, including Russian food stores and storefront synagogues, has emerged in response to their presence. In Plummer Park, where Russian Jews gather in the afternoon to play dominoes, chess, and cards, a monument to the infamous Babi Yar in Ukraine was unveiled in 1991. In that same year, hundreds gathered in the park to celebrate Hanukkah. Even for those many Russian Jews who are not particularly religious and unaware of the tradition of Hanukkah, these festivities were of special significance because they symbolized a newfound freedom to practice religion.[16]

Adaptive Reuse of Structures

Not all landscape transformations are so dramatic because few recent immigrant groups can garner the economic and political support requisite to creating such levels of complexity. More often, feasibility confines change to adaptive reuse of ready-made buildings. With only a few modifications, a single-family dwelling becomes a Vietnamese Buddhist temple or a strip-mall shop is turned into a synagogue for Russian Jews. Through religiously imbued appropriation, former secular residential and commercial spaces become sacred entities. Examples proliferate throughout the Los Angeles metropolis.

The most prominent example of appropriation of space is the storefront church. In the first half of this century, "white" Pentecostal and Adventist storefronts lined the main streets of Long Beach, landscape manifestations of fundamentalist Protestant individualism delivered by in-migrants from across the nation.[17] Today, storefronts are a landscape staple in the African American community appealing to those on the socioeconomic margins of urban life (Fig. 11-4). For example, the New Beginnings Missionary Baptist Church in Watts is flanked by the B & B Cafe and Alonso's Wrought Iron. The New Testament Church of God was founded to offer services in Creole to recent immigrants from Belize, Jamaica, and Haiti. Another houses an Islamic outreach center. Storefront churches are landscape indicators of the urban black religious experience. Charismatic in nature, they emphasize preaching ability, which is central to the black church, and offer hope to the most desperate and needy. Frequently, a storefront is a step up from a former location in a home and only one step away from the dream of a church edifice—the ultimate goal of storefront congregations.[18]

A relatively recent phenomenon is the widespread emergence of storefronts in many conventionally Roman Catholic Latino communities continually impacted by immigrants from Mexico and Central America. Signs such as "Templo Calvario" and "Iglesia de Dios Nueva Jerusalem" are commonplace along commercial thoroughfares and in strip malls. These are visual evidence of the success of evangelical Protestantism among Latinos in the Americas.

African American and Latino neighborhoods are frequently in spatial jux-

Fig. 11–4. African American Storefront Churches in the Crenshaw District (1992)

taposition and landscape change becomes even more apparent as neighborhood turnover ensues. For example, one south-central Los Angeles neighborhood was 5 percent Latino and 93 percent black in 1970. According to the 1990 census, it is now 48 percent Latino and 51 percent black. African American businesses have given way to a host of Latino churches, mostly evangelical storefronts. Iglesia de Dios/Monte Sinai, for example, occupies a former black beauty parlor and holds services six nights a week.

While storefronts proliferate, they also tend toward impermanence. Serving essentially poor and transient populations means financial uncertainty, frequent closure, and relocation. Moreover, while intense religiosity is apparent during services, the storefront stands empty for much of the week, a vacant reminder of the extant socioeconomic malaise of its surroundings. A storefront is unlike a conventional church that is, by definition, never without spiritual content.[19] It is like a shell to be filled with spirituality only at designated times. Considered singularly, a storefront church is potentially an intermittently sacred landscape phenomenon. Collectively, however, storefront churches are salient and enduring attributes of the religious landscapes of the Los Angeles metropolitan area.

Sometimes existing religious structures fall prey to adaptive reuse and acquire new identities in context of demographic change. From the 1920s through the 1940s, an area known as Boyle Heights had the largest Jewish population west of Chicago and more than twenty synagogues served the community. Today, the area is predominantly Latino, with an influx of Koreans and other Asian groups. A synagogue on the fringe of the Los Angeles expanding Koreatown is illustrative of the adaptive reuse process.

According to the Hebrew cornerstone, the Sinai Congregation was founded in 1906 and the synagogue constructed in 1925. Today an English and Korean sign announces that this is the Korean Philadelphia Presbyterian Church (Fig. 11-5). While two menorahs and biblical tablets remain on the face of the (former) synagogue, five crosses have been added, one replacing a Star of David. Alterations of exterior signs and symbols provide a cloak of transition from one sacred realm to another. By means of adaptive reuse, what is perceived as profane space is intentionally appropriated as sacred place. In the end, the resanctification of a sacred landscape entity symbolized a secular process—neighborhood transition.

Diffusion of Sacred Practices and Symbolism

Another impact of immigration is the diffusion of sacred practices and symbolism. Evidence that diversification within black and Latino popula-

Fig. 11–5. Adaptive Reuse of a Synagogue by a Korean Presbyterian Congregation (1992)

tions is challenging traditional religious constructs is apparent through the appearance of more than a hundred *botánicas* (shops catering to adherents of Afro-Caribbean belief systems) throughout the Los Angeles metropolitan area. There are an estimated 50,000 to 100,000 adherents of *Santería* in Southern California, making it the third largest American concentration after New York and Miami. However, here the clientele is not Cuban or Puerto Rican but rather an eclectic mix of African Americans, Latinos, Asians, and Anglos. Many are new converts. For some, *Santeria* is seen as a New Age phenomenon; for others it symbolizes the relevance of an ancient African heritage. *Botánicas* represent both the resurgence and the perceived legitimacy of ethnic belief systems.[20]

In many Latino communities, wall murals, depicting historic and sacred personages and events, are significant in fusing place-environment identity.[21] A favorite is the *Virgen de Guadalupe*, the Nahuatl-speaking Mary, paramount saint in Mexico. On one *botánica* wall in the urban core, the Virgin shares space with the Yoruba *orixa* (god) Schango, a chance juxtaposition illustrating both competition and syncretism of Afro-Caribbean belief systems and Roman Catholicism (Fig. 11-6).

The Nativity Catholic Church in south-central Los Angeles illustrates the dynamics of neighborhood transition. Built by an all-white congregation in 1925, by the mid-1970s the congregation was primarily black. In 1988, the all-Latino congregation placed a *Virgen de Guadalupe* within the sanctuary.

Public Celebration of Religious Events

In the Los Angeles area, every calendar month is marked by one or more religious events. While most are held in immediate ethnic areas, there is a

Fig. 11–6. A *Botánica* in a Primarily Latino Area of South Los Angeles (1992)

noticeable trend for some events to be celebrated in the larger public sphere. For example, in 1992 Los Angeles residents witnessed the first Chinese New Year parade and festival held beyond the confines of Chinatown. Billed as Chinatown's "suburban alternative," the festivities were sponsored by the San Gabriel Valley cities of Monterey Park and Alhambra, which, according to the 1990 census, are 57 and 33 percent Asian respectively.

Numerous homes in the surrounding streets exhibit a variety of sacred phenomena. There are "good luck" signs, mirrors over doors to ward off evil spirits, and all sorts of religious paraphernalia, such as door guardians, joss urns, and statues of the goddess Kuan Yin. In a sense, the parade's public display is a landscape metaphor for more personal belief systems evidenced in less obvious ways in quieter, private realms. These landscape symbols reveal the significance of Asian immigration, the continual process of Asian suburbanization, the growth of ethnic enclaves and establishment as identifiable communities, and the perpetuation of folk beliefs.

In 1993, the Vietnamese New Year celebration of Tet was observed as public events at four different locations in Orange County: on the grounds of a community college in Huntington Beach, in a public stadium in Westminster, in a commercial complex known as "Asian Village" in Santa Ana, and in an area known as "Little Saigon" in Westminster and Garden Grove. Orange County is home to more than eighty thousand Vietnamese who, like many Chinese, function in a solar calendar time-frame on a secular level but in a lunar calendar time-frame on a sacred level. Both Chinese and Vietnamese date the new year according to the arrival of the new moon in the Far East.

One longstanding public event is the *Jagannatha Ratha-Yatra*, or Lord of the Universe Festival of the Chariots, held since 1977 in Venice Beach by the International Society for Krishna Consciousness. The largest in America, the festival draws crowds of more than fifty thousand people. However, this elaborate celebration of Lord Krishna attacks the sensitivities of some Christians who perceive such rituals as anti-Christian and essentially blasphemous.[22]

These events are momentary displays of longstanding tradition. Each celebration replicates the previous one, thereby sustaining sacred and precious memories through the process of recreation. The fact that the host culture infringes on or even alters tradition is of little consequence because ethnic groups in modern settings are always revamping their identities in context of the dominant society and its other ethnic constituents.

Nature of Christian Churches

Christians are avid church builders; the church in the sense of "community" soon becomes the church established as real estate. As demographic change ensues, congregations move on, but the building remains. How have Christian churches responded to community ethnic changes? Declining congregations and increasing multiculturalism have provoked many denominations to reach out into their potential service areas with relevant appeal.

In the Roman Catholic Diocese of Los Angeles, cultural adaptations of both liturgy and ritual are made to fulfill the needs of 93 different ethnic groups. For example, St. Brigid's, a traditionally Irish Catholic church with a dwindling congregation in south-central Los Angeles, began to promote an African orientation in 1979. Now its congregation of more than a thousand families is 85 percent black. Red, green, and black freedom flags hang beside the altar, a portrait of Martin Luther King hangs under stained glass windows, and African music is played at services.[23]

Countless formerly English-speaking congregations now reflect the ethnic diversity of the entire metropolitan area and ministries have found it essential to offer other-language services in order to survive. For instance, according to the *Ethnic Services Directory* of the Roman Catholic Diocese of Los Angeles, mass is spoken in 42 languages.

The venerated United Methodist Church in the mid-Wilshire district east of Beverly Hills has survived only through adaptation to the new reality of ethnic complexity, as revealed by its sign announcing services in English, Filipino, Korean, and Spanish. In fact, the Los Angeles area is replete with Protestant churches offering services in Korean.

During the 1980s, according to the 1990 census, the Korean population of Los Angeles and Orange counties increased 140 and 217 percent respectively to a total of close to 200,000. The successful inroads of Christianity both in South Korea and in the United States are indicated by the existence of more than six hundred Korean Protestant churches in the two counties. Many Korean congregations are housed in formerly non-Asian churches and many simply share churches with non-Asian parishioners.

But what about second-, third-, or older-generation Christian ethnic groups? In the city of Rosemead, where Asian and Asian American populations increased by 371 percent in the recent census decade, the Evergreen Baptist Church provides an example. The majority of this 900-member congregation is American born and represents seven different Asian groups. However, services are in English. According to the Reverend Ken Fong, this church "appeals to the most Americanized Asians who wouldn't set foot in the immigrant-influenced churches."

The True Light Chinese Presbyterian Church in Lincoln Heights specifically targets those English-speaking Chinese who want to preserve their cultural identity but who prefer Americanized services and programs. True

Light prospers via the intraurban migration process. When members move to a different location in the Los Angeles metropolitan area, a new church is founded. While the "mother church" offers one service in Cantonese and two in English, the "daughter churches" provide services in English only.[24]

Various ethnic groups are perceived by some expansionist denominations as ripe for missionizing. Latinos, for instance, are targeted by the Church of Jesus Christ of Latter-day Saints and are the fastest-growing ethnic group in the Mormon community. The number of Latino Mormons in Southern California has tripled since 1981 to 24,000, inducing the creation of new administrative wards and stakes. In 1992, the California Anaheim Mission formed the second stake in the country made up entirely of Spanish-speaking members. The other is in East Los Angeles.[25]

Response to General Societal Change

In view of general societal transformation, it is generally agreed that mainline Christian institutions have failed to meet the diverse needs of communities at large. How can religious organizations captivate increasing numbers of baby-boomers who are returning to religion, sampling various creeds and modes of religious expression, and seeking a "custom-made God"?

Temporal change is one way to meet the challenge of variant work schedules and leisure pursuits. Roman Catholics were the first to provide options to Sunday services in 1970 when the Vatican gave permission for Saturday masses. Burbank's St. Finbar is half full with five hundred parishioners for Saturday's 5:00 p.m. mass in English and full for the 6:30 p.m. mass in Vietnamese. A Protestant pioneer was Hope Chapel in Hermosa Beach, which offered Friday night services in 1977 and added Saturday night services in 1980. Numerous other churches have successfully followed suit, attracting hundreds to non-Sunday services.

Recognizing that church growth is fostered by community involvement, another institutional response is to provide a variety of social services targeted to particular community concerns. For instance, the Vietnamese Christian Pentecostal Church of Santa Ana holds Saturday night and Sunday services in a rented building. Sunday school classes are taught in English by Vietnamese teachers and the church offers classes in driving, apartment renting, and welfare application. Many churches go even further, offering substance-abuse programs, day care, summer camps, sporting and entertainment activities, and trips abroad.

This proliferation of social services has come to be known as the full-service concept. In his investigation of the 12,000-member evangelical Calvary Chapel of Santa Ana, religion scholar Randall Balmer counted 51 events scheduled in a single week. The intensity of providing services is largely related to sizes of congregations. Those organizations with the broadest range of services are described as "megachurches."[26]

According to the 1991–92 *Almanac of the Christian World*, California has 25 of the 100 largest congregations in the United States and 17 of these are in Los Angeles and Orange counties. The Crenshaw District's West Angeles Church of God in Christ, for example, is one of the two fastest-growing Protestant churches in America. Catering to African Americans, it addresses more than eight thousand people at its four Sunday services, one of which is in Spanish in response to the changing demographics of its immediate area. Offering social and educational services and a Skid Row ministry, West Angeles demonstrates the positive relationship between spiraling church growth and community relief efforts.

A recent poll of churchgoers in Orange County found that three in ten belong to congregations of two thousand or more members. The county's megachurches are epitomized by South Coast Community Church in Irvine and Crystal Cathedral in Garden Grove. South Coast Community has a membership of 10,000, a staff of 68, and a 2,500-seat sanctuary. Its myriad services include post-football game parties for 2,000 young people on Friday nights, shuttle buses from satellite parking areas, and shopping boutiques catering to demographically targeted groups. Born as a drive-in church, the now impressive steel and glass Crystal Cathedral still ministers to people in their cars via closed-circuit TV (Fig. 11-7). One of its endless list of services is the provision of a shuttle bus from the church to an adjacent shopping mall. It even has its own on-site cemetery and columbarium.[27]

Megachurches are situated and designed as recipients of auto-era congregants. Apparently, people who have long daily commutes do not mind driving a fair distance to a church with plenty of parking space as long as the trip is shorter than their work commute. Conversely, people with a short work commute do not object to driving farther to a church with plenty to offer including off-street parking. Joel Garreau describes such auto-centered, freeway-accessible churches as "spiritual shopping malls."[28]

Megachurches, because they epitomize the restructuring of religion in context of societal change, have drawn the attention of scholars worldwide.[29] A church becomes "mega" through tried-and-true marketing techniques. Analysis of demographics and data from telephone and mail surveys plays a critical role in contemporary church growth and private consulting firms have emerged to serve growth-oriented religious organizations. But smart development alone does not ensure perpetuity.

Fig. 11–7. Crystal Cathedral in Garden Grove (1992)

Advertising and public relations gimmicks aside, megachurches thrive for several reasons. Congregants not only feel comfortable in large institutions and increasingly typify modern society, but they also enjoy the many available options for social interaction and style of worship and ministry. Megachurches also have the requisite resources to address the multiple concerns of diverse members of a society in flux.

The United States is experiencing a historic transition from a predominantly white society rooted in Western culture to a global society incorporating increasingly disparate racial and ethnic minorities of all income levels concentrated primarily in urban areas.[30] The socioeconomic consequences of this postmodern metamorphosis are presenting perplexing challenges to religious and other groups and institutions. As William Swatos observes, "In the move from premodern, to modern, to postmodern cultures, the relevant cultural forms of religion have necessarily shifted. Religions that address the culture of the emotions within the complexity of postmodernity draw comparably more converts from the populace at large."[31]

Conclusion

Clearly, the landscapes of religion and belief systems in the Los Angeles metropolitan area are in transition with change being more apparent than continuity. Ongoing population dynamics have given rise to entirely new religious landscapes and thoroughly transformed older ones. The drama of spiritual quest is played out in numerous forms, ranging from new and modified architectural sites to vibrant urban art and gala events. These are public displays capable of enrapturing adherents and assaulting disbelievers. As the region's historical Christian foundation crumbles in the wake of demographic change and social upheaval, various Christian organizations are literally reshaping, repackaging, and marketing their product. All told, the evolving religious landscape mosaic of the Los Angeles metropolitan area reflects the multifarious needs and aspirations of its diverse and changing inhabitants.

Visible landscapes are expressions of societal change and every landscape is both an historic accumulation and a code to be interpreted and deciphered.[32] While postmodernism generates pluralistic landscapes within culturally heterogeneous metropolitan areas, there is potential for cultural convergence among major metropolises undergoing similar demographic and economic transformations. Processes of creation, alteration, and adaptation shaping the religious landscapes of Los Angeles may be paralleled elsewhere, presenting opportunities for further research.

Notes

1. Lily Kong, "Geography and Religion: Trends and Prospects," *Progress in Human Geography* 14 (September 1990), 367; David Sopher, "Geography and Religions," *Progress in Human Geography* 5 (December 1981), 510–24; Roger W. Stump, "Introduction," *Journal of Cultural Geography* 7 (Fall/Winter 1986), 1–3.

2. See for example: Alice Andrews, "Religious Geography of Union County, Georgia," *Journal of Cultural Geography* 10 (Spring/Summer 1990), 1–19; Charles Heatwole, "Sectarian Ideology and Church Architecture," *Geographical Review* 79 (January 1989), 63–78; Gisbert Rinchede, "The Pilgrimage Town of Lourdes," *Journal of Cultural Geography* 7 (Fall/Winter 1986), 21–34.

3. David Griffin, "Creativity and Postmodern Religion," in *The Post-Modern Reader*, ed. Charles Jencks (New York: St. Martin's Press, 1992), 373–82; Charles Jencks, "The Post-Modern Agenda," in *The Post-Modern Reader*, 10–39.

4. Edward Soja, "Taking Los Angeles Apart: Towards a Postmodern Geography," in *The Post-Modern Reader*, ed. Charles Jencks (New York: St. Martin's Press, 1992), 227–98; Edward Soja, *Postmodern Geographies* (New York: Verso, 1989), 190–248.

5. Edwin Gaustad, *A Religious History of America* (San Francisco: HarperCollins, 1990), 161–63.

6. James Gregory, *American Exodus: The Dust Bowl Migrations and Okie Culture in California* (New York: Oxford, 1989), 193–98.

7. Robert Wuthnow, *The Restructuring of American Religion* (Princeton: Princeton University Press, 1989), 5–10.

8. David Rieff, *Los Angeles: Capital of the Third World* (New York: Touchstone, 1991).

9. Peter Kivisto, "Religion and the New Immigrants," in *A Future For Religion? New Paradigms for Social Analysis*, ed. William Swatos Jr. (Newbury Park, Calif.: Sage, 1993), 103.

10. Russell Chandler, "Zoroastrians: Ancient, Tolerant Faith Flourishing in the Southland," *Los Angeles Times* (August 24, 1985), Section 2, 16.

11. Tony Marcano, "Ways of the Islamics," *Los Angeles Times* (Orange County Edition, December 7, 1990), Section T, 1–2; Allen Richardson, *East Comes West* (New York: Pilgrim Press, 1985), 171–75.

12. Kenneth Garcia, "Sight to Behold: Ornate Hindu Temple in Malibu Is Shrine Where East Meets West," *Los Angeles Times* (March 25, 1988), Section 2, 10.

13. Carolyn Prorok, "The Hare Krishna's Transformation of Space in

West Virginia," *Journal of Cultural Geography* 7 (Fall/Winter 1986), 129–40.

14. Richardson, 31.

15. Anthony Day, "Troubling Times for U.S. Jews," *Los Angeles Times* (January 23, 1992), Section A, 26; Ephraim Buchwald, "The Holocaust Is Killing America's Jews," *Los Angeles Times* (April 28, 1992), Section B, 7.

16. Steven Gold, "Russian Jews in California," *Society* 29 (November/December 1991), 77; Amy Kazmin, "Hanukkah Lights the Hearts of Immigrants," *Los Angeles Times* (September 2, 1991), Section B, 7.

17. David Reid, "The Possessed," in *Sex, Death and God in L.A.*, ed. David Reid (New York: Pantheon, 1992), 200.

18. Kathleen Hendrix, "Ministering on the Front Line," (Black Church Life in Southern California), *Los Angeles Times* (March 11, 1993), Section E, 1; Eric Lincoln and Lawrence Mamiya, *The Black Church in the African American Experience* (Durham, N.C.: Duke University Press, 1990), 136.

19. Robert Sack, *Human Territoriality: Its Theory and History* (London: Cambridge University Press, 1986), 126.

20. Edward Humes, "They Kill Chickens Don't They?" *Buzz* 2 (September/October 1991), 65; Robert Voeks, "African Medicine in the Americas," *Geographical Review* 83 (January 1993), 76. For an account of Afro-Cuban religion in Miami, see James Curtis, "Miami's Little Havana: Yard Shrines, Cult Religions and Landscape," *Journal of Cultural Geography* 1 (Fall/Winter 1980), 1–15.

21. Daniel Arreola, "Mexican American Exterior Wall Murals," *Geographical Review* 74 (October 1984), 409–24.

22. International Society for Krishna Consciousness, "Celebrating the 15th Annual Jagannatha Ratha-Yatra Festival of the Chariots" (Los Angeles: International Society for Krishna Consciousness, 1991).

23. Msgn. Soto, Minister for Hispanic Programs, Roman Catholic Diocese of Orange, California, interview by author, March 1992; Kathleen Hendrix, "Gospel of St. Brigid's," *Los Angeles Times* (February 23, 1992), Section E, 1.

24. Letitia O'Connor, *Exploring Cultural Resources in Los Angeles* (Los Angeles: *Los Angeles Times*, 1990), 49; Russell Chandler, "Churches Reach Out to Asian Americans," *Los Angeles Times* (August 11, 1991), Section B, 1, 3.

25. Tammerlin Drummond, "Mormons Reach Out for Latino Converts," *Los Angeles Times* (March 3, 1992), Section A, 3.

26. Randall Balmer, "Catholic Church in America Fails to Keep Pace with the Changes," *Los Angeles Times* (February 29, 1992), Section F, 19; Randall Balmer, *Mine Eyes Have Seen the Glory* (New York: Oxford Univer-

sity Press, 1989), 17; John Dart, "Church is Growing on Saturday," *Los Angeles Times* (September 21, 1991), Section F, 15–16; Richard Ostling, "The Church Search," *Time* 141 (April 5, 1993), 45.

27. John Dart, "Pastors, Music Help Black Protestant Churches Thrive," *Los Angeles Times* (May 10, 1991), Section A, 3; Tammerlin Drummond, "O.C.'s Faith Is Strong, Ties to Churches Weak," *Los Angeles Times* (December 15, 1991), Section A, 18; Joel Garreau, *Edge City: Life on the New Frontier* (New York: Doubleday, 1991), 65, 293.

28. Garreau, 65; Lyle Schaller, "Megachurch!" *Christianity Today* 34 (March 5, 1990), 20–24.

29. *Religion Watch* 8 (December 1992), 1–2.

30. William O'Hare, "Diversity Trend: More Minorities Looking Less Alike," *Population Today* 21 (April 1993), 1–2.

31. Schaller, 21; William Swatos Jr., "Introduction," in *A Future For Religion: New Paradigms for Social Analysis*, xi.

32. Donald Meinig, "Introduction," in *The Interpretation of Ordinary Landscapes*, ed. Donald Meinig (New York: Oxford University Press, 1979), 1–7; Peirce Lewis, "Axioms for Reading the Landscape," in *The Interpretation of Ordinary Landscapes*, 11–32.

12

Selected Reading IV

Chapters 10 and 11

Albanese, Catherine A. *America, Religions and Religion.* Belmont, Calif.: Wadsworth, 1981.

Capps, Walter H. *The New Religious Right: Piety, Patriotism, and Politics.* Columbia: University of South Carolina Press, 1994.

Egbert, Donald Shaw. "Religious Expression in American Architecture" in *Religious Perspectives in American Culture,* eds. Ward Smith and A. Leland Jamison. Princeton: Princeton University Press, 1961.

Fishwick, Marshall W. *Great Awakenings: Popular Religion and Popular Culture.* Binghamton, N.Y.: Haworth Press, 1994.

Gaustad, Edwin S. *Historical Atlas of Religion in America.* New York: Harper & Row, 1976.

Hill, Samuel S. "Religion and Region in America," *Annals of the American Academy of Political and Social Science* 480 (1985), 132–41.

Isaac, Erich. "Religion, Landscape, and Space," *Landscape* 9 (1959–60), 14–18.

Kennedy, Roger G. *American Churches.* New York: Stewart, Tabori and Chang, 1982.

Newman, William M., and Halvorson, Peter L. *Atlas of Religious Change in America, 1952–1971.* Washington, D.C.: Glenmary Research Center, 1978.

——. *Patterns in Pluralism: A Portrait of American Religion.* Washington, D.C.: Glenmary Research Center, 1988.

Shortridge, James R. "Patterns of Religion in the United States," *Geographical Review* 66 (1976), 420–34.

————. "A New Regionalization of American Religion," *Journal for the Scientific Study of Religion* 16 (1977), 143–53.

Stump, Roger W. (ed.). "The Geography of Religion," *Journal of Cultural Geography* 7 (1986), 1–140 (Special Issue).

Zelinsky, Wilbur. "An Approach to the Religious Geography of the United States: Patterns of Church Membership in 1952," *Annals of the Association of American Geographers* 51 (1961), 139–93.

Part V: Architecture

Architecture is the most conspicuous element of popular culture. One can be turned off by the music of Madonna or abhor the taste of a Big Mac, but unless you live in the mythical cave, the built environment permeates our lives each day. Architecture provides buildings and structures that serve us while we work, play, eat, or sleep. It is a mirror of our culture, a tangible expression of a way of life.

Popular architecture, sometimes called modern vernacular, accounts for about 95 percent of our built environment, according to Richard Wilson, an authority on popular culture and architecture. He emphasizes that popular architecture should not be restricted only to the fast-food palace or strip development, but must also encompass such structures as diners, gas stations, shopping malls, and a host of additional buildings that surround us.

Cultural geographers have written extensively on architecture; however, a vast majority of the literature deals with folk buildings and structures located in a rural context. In contrast, the two articles by cultural geographers included here focus on popular architectural forms that are urban-oriented and emerged in the twentieth century.

John Jakle, professor of geography at the University of Illinois-Urbana, discusses a type of modern vernacular architecture associated with the automobile and America's highways—the motel. He examines its origin and evolution from the early tourist homes and auto camps to the present-day downtown motels.

Over the years, the architectural plans and designs of these highway-oriented facilities became standardized because of influence from trade associations, chains, and franchises. The outcome was an architectural uniformity found throughout the country in terms of interior arrangement, exterior design, and signage (e.g., Holiday Inns). Jakle concludes that the motel and hotel have borrowed from each other, thereby resulting in significant changes in each. This is reflected in the decreased formality in today's downtown high-rise hotel brought on by the motel's traditional informality, while the motel has taken on hotel-like qualities such as location near airports and in downtowns as well as an expansion of services.

Jim Curtis, geographer at California State University-Long Beach, presents a thorough analysis of the historic forces that shaped the Art Deco style of architecture in Miami Beach. Located in a one-square-mile section of the southern end of the city, the Art Deco district contains three hundred certified residential and commercial properties recognized by the National Register of Historic Places. It is one of the best representations and largest concentrations of this style in the United States. Art Deco peaked in Miami Beach from the late 1920s to the early 1940s because of a combination of economic and social conditions. It flourished during the Depression because of a promotional campaign by city leaders to attract middle-class tourists who, as a form of escapism from hard times, vacationed in this seaside resort community. Additionally, Art Deco was popular because of a fascination of the American people with machine-age technology, and it appealed to those who sought modernistic and futuristic architecture. Curtis concludes that the Art Deco district conveys a cohesiveness of style, scale, and design features that has contributed to the place identity of Miami Beach.

13

Motel by the Roadside:
America's Room for the Night

John A. Jakle

The history of the American motel is rooted in the 1920s. Unpretentious of form, the motel grew from obscurity out of other vernacular features of the American roadside, especially the auto camp and the tourist home. This study discusses the phases by which motels evolved on the American scene: from the cabin camp to the cottage and motor court and beyond to the motor inn and highway hotel. It focuses on changing motel morphology in order to describe the special role that motels have come to play in the United States as purveyors of geographical mobility.[1]

A motel, as everyone knows, is a roadside establishment providing public lodging. Howard Morgan in 1964 maintained that a motel differed from a hotel in that "guests travel by automobile and park adjacent to their rooms; the structure is not over three floors in height; a restaurant is not commonly found on the premises; and services such as valet, laundry, barber and travel arrangements are not usually provided."[2] Clearly this definition, once acceptable, begs revision, as the differences between hotels and motels have been substantially blurred in the recent decade.

Hotels

Downtown hotels dominated the lodging industry in the early 1900s. Oriented to railroad and public transit focused in central business districts, few

Reprinted by permission from the *Journal of Cultural Geography* 1 (1980), 34–49.

hotels were automobile convenient (Fig. 13–1). Garages, where they existed, were usually located at some distance, with valet attendants responsible for parking automobiles for a fee. Hotel design emphasized public space: large entrance lobbies (Fig. 13–2), lounges, and expensive corridors as well as restaurant, coffee shop, bar, banquet, ballroom, and meeting room facilities. Private spaces were cramped. Except where a special tariff was paid for a suite of rooms, the standard accommodation comprised a bed, a chair, a desk, and enough space to reach a tiny closet and small bathroom. This emphasis on public rather than private space reflected the hotel industry's peculiar profit mix. Only 50 percent of hotel profits have come traditionally from room rentals. This compares to about 8 percent for motels since World War II.[3]

Auto Camps

Auto camps evolved in the western United States as an alternative to hotels (Fig. 13–3). They appealed to the migratory transient and to the seasonal tourist. Partly out of civic pride and partly from a sense of self-protection, towns along migratory routes took to roping off spaces for campers. Water, fuel wood, privies and sometimes flush toilets, showers, and

Fig. 13–1. Hotel in Medford, Massachusetts (c. 1940)

Fig. 13–2. Lobby of the Hotel Deming in Terre Haute, Indiana (c. 1920)

Fig. 13–3. Auto Camp Near Sacramento, California (c. 1920)

laundry facilities were provided free of charge much to the disgust of hotel owners, who considered such civic action unfair competition (Fig. 13–4).

By 1920 private operators had entered the auto-camp business nation-wide. The typical camp comprised a central service building and tent sites variously defined by picnic benches and the trodden ground of previous campers. In the 1930s hotel owners attempted to legislate them out of existence under Title One of the National Recovery Act. They defined as "unfair competition": "The selling or offering for sale of sleeping or other hotel accommodations, at farm houses, tourist accommodation houses, seasonal automobile or tourist camps, cabins, highway roadhouses, and all other places . . . which provide taxes in small amounts in contrast with hotels."[4]

Tourist Homes

In the eastern United States the tourist home filled many of the western auto camp's functions.[5] The typical tourist home was a private house, usually located on a major thoroughfare near downtown, where one or more bedrooms were "let for the night" (Fig. 13–5). A sign with "Transients Accommodated" or some such message adorned the front lawn. Off-street parking in the rear was usually available. Tourist home operators were ste-

Fig. 13–4. Auto Camp Near Pierre, South Dakota (c. 1920)

Fig. 13–5. Tourist Home at Lewisburg, Ohio (c. 1945)

reotyped either as widows struggling to make ends meet or as businessmen bankrupt in previous endeavors struggling to regain business composure.

Cabin Camps

An understanding of evolving motel morphology requires (1) a concern with building types, and (2) a concern with the arrangement of buildings in a complex of structures. Changing building types are illustrated in Figure 13–6. For example, the first motels, the cabin camps, emerged from the auto camp and tourist home heritage. As shown, three varieties of the cabin camp evolved: the auto camp with cabins added, the cabin camp built from scratch without tent camping or tourist home facility, and the tourist home with cabins added. Various patterns of spatial arrangement typified motels over the past fifty years: row, row-on-row, L, narrow U, wide U, crescent, clustered, and cruciform (Fig. 13–7). These basic arrangements applied variously to detached, integrated, center-core and high-rise buildings. Cabin camps tended to be arranged in row, row-on-row, L, crescent, and clustered patterns (Fig. 13–8).

The first recorded cabin camp was opened in Douglas, Arizona, in 1913.[6] By the late 1920s some six hundred camps, some improved as cottage

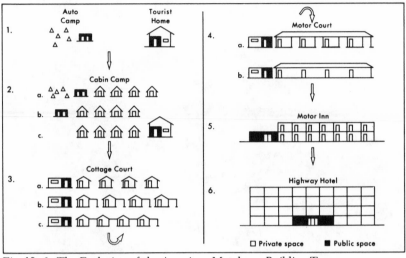

Fig. 13–6. The Evolution of the American Motel as a Building Type

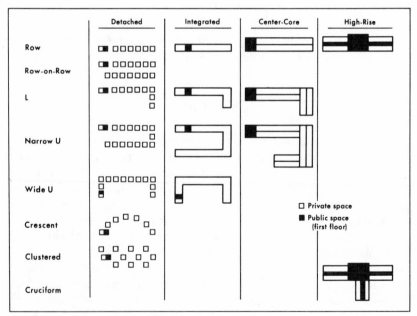

Fig. 13–7. Dominant Variations in Motel Spatial Organization

Fig. 13–8. A Cabin Camp Row Arrangement in Baraboo, Wisconsin (c. 1930)

courts, had been opened in the United States.[7] Cabin camps offered attractions not generally available in downtown hotels. They were situated in peripheral highway locations where land was cheap, and those with less than a dozen cabins could be operated by two people, usually a husband and wife who lived on the premises. Building and operating costs were low and room prices could be kept to a minimum. Few hotels could compete with their rates, and those that did were usually run-down and derelict establishments. Cabin camps intercepted travelers at the city's edge. Travelers did not have to fight evening traffic congestion to reach a downtown hotel. Parking space was readily available next to each cabin. Above all, the cabin camp offered informality. Guests, who could be informally dressed, were not required to traverse a public lobby to register or tip bellboys. Once registered they could come and go at will without intensive public scrutiny.

Cabin camps developed an unsavory reputation in the popular media. Courtney Cooper, ghostwriting under J. Edgar Hoover's name in *The American Magazine*, published an article entitled "Camps of Crime."[8] The article was subtitled: "Behind many alluring roadside signs are dens of vice and corruption, says America's head G-Man. . . . He points out the menace to the public from hundreds of unsupervised tourist camps, 1940-style hideaways for public enemies." Not only did criminals take refuge in cabin camps, according to Hoover, but these early motels were also used as places of illicit assignation: "hot-pillow joints" in the parlance of the period.

Favorably situated cabin camps flourished without illicit trade. For example, the U-Smile Cabin Camp at Kansas City, Missouri, began in 1922 as twelve cabins and a bathhouse with public restrooms.[9] Arriving guests signed the registry book and paid their money. A cabin without a mattress rented for $1.00. A mattress for two people cost an extra 25 cents, and blankets, sheets, and pillows another 50 cents. The manager rode the running boards to show guests to their cabins. Each guest was given a bucket of water from an outside hydrant, and in the winter a scuttle of fuel wood. Such cabin camps required little investment, the business attracting people with little capital who were willing to work long hours. *Fortune* magazine commented: "There was a time when the sailor home from the sea went to chicken farming. Nowadays he buys a motel by the side of the road."[10]

Many cabin camps were combined with gasoline stations and other businesses. In 1935 the *Census of Business* counted 9,848 "tourist camps" of which 20 percent sold gasoline.[11] The petroleum industry encouraged jobbers and agents to invest in cabin camps. A *National Petroleum News* editorial advised: "The lower the cost of touring the farther down the economic scale touring is made possible, and as sleeping and eating costs less the tourist can cover more territory consuming [more] gasoline and oil."[12] A camp might sell groceries and offer roadside entertainment, as at the Red Hat Tourist Camp in Baxley, Georgia. The camp's menagerie featured a black bear, a monkey, an alligator, and some peacocks. "The bear imbibes about 40 cold drinks a day . . . and the proprietor of the place frequently sells as much as fifteen cases of drinks on Sunday."[13]

Cottage Courts

As cabin camps became more substantial, the word "cottage" crept increasingly into their naming (Fig. 13–9). Cottages were not only of more permanent construction, they were also larger and more winterized for year-round business. Each unit contained a private bathroom. Norman Hayner, a sociologist, described a typical cottage in his 1930 study of motels in Oregon and Washington:

> The main room was equipped with a good bed (bedding could be rented for 50 cents if desired), chairs, mirror, and clothes closet. The kitchen was a separate room with an excellent wood cook stove, running hot and cold water, sink, cupboards, table, chairs, dishes, cutlery, cooking utensils, and even a line for hanging up dish towels. The bath was also a separate room and included a flush toilet, wash bowl, mirror, hot and cold shower. The walls were plastered, the windows attractively curtained, and there was linoleum on the floor.[14]

Fig. 13–9. Cottage Court Near Lincoln City, Oregon

After 1930 the word "court" crept into the language descriptive of motels. Cabins and cottages were increasingly arranged geometrically centered on open spaces or courts. U-shaped courts were narrow or wide depending on the depth of the lot and the extent of highway frontage (Fig. 13–7). Cottage complexes came in three basic forms (Fig. 13–6). In the 1920s cottages were usually arrayed as individual units with open spaces between the units. Attached garages were popular after 1930, and after 1940 it was common to find cottage/garage combinations linked wall to wall to form continuous facades. Although a facade might be continuous, the integrity of each building was preserved in individual roof lines. A separate building housed a small reception desk, the only pretense to interior public space. Public space was relegated outdoors to the interior of courtyards or crescents or to the front yards of row and L-shaped complexes. Space not given to automobile parking was often landscaped to give the motel a gentrified aspect. Architecturally, cottages were made to look like up-to-date suburban housing, thus to appeal more to the middle-class tourist and traveling businessman and less to the migratory transient.

Motor Courts

Motor courts evolved copying the form of cottage courts except that room units were totally integrated under a single roof line often in one building (Fig. 13–10). Motor courts were single-story structures with or without garage facilities (Fig. 13–6). Many courts contained coffee shops

Fig. 13–10. Motor Court in St. Joseph, Michigan (c. 1940)

as part of the integrated design. In 1948 there were approximately thirty thousand motels in operation; the average size was twenty units.[15] Eighteen percent contained coffee shops or restaurant facilities and 25 percent operated gasoline stations.[16]

Motor courts varied from converted cabin and cottage courts ("upgraded" to conform with the new integrated style) to elaborate complexes such as the Danish Village completed in 1929 near Portland, Maine (Fig. 13–11).[17] Although a range of architectural styles characterized the more substantial motor courts, "Western" themes were most popular. Motor courts with their facades integrated around interior courtyards were reminiscent of Spanish missions and haciendas, especially when constructed of stucco to simulate adobe. Motel names such as El Rancho and Casa Grande appeared coast to coast.

After World War II the word "motel" came rapidly into fashion to describe the new motor courts. Various terminologies had been devised. For example the word "autel" had a limited popularity.[18] The word "motel" (originally Mo-Tel) had been coined by a California architect as early as 1925.

Motel construction boomed in the late 1950s and early 1960s to a high of over 61,000 establishments by 1964.[19] Many factors fostered this rapid growth. Motels benefited from the general decentralization of cities and towns that followed in the wake of increased automobile ownership. The federal interstate highway program begun in 1956 was an important part of this decentralization process. More important, however, were factors internal to the motel industry. The motel business was characterized by a higher cash flow than most other types of real estate investment. Thus interest and principal on loans could be easily amortized. New motel properties in

Fig. 13–11. The Danish Village on U.S. 1 at Scarboro, Maine (c. 1930)

growth areas appreciated rapidly, producing substantial capital gains when sold, thus inviting speculation. Banks and insurance companies looked favorably on motel investments and required small cash down payments. Such leverage produced higher rates of cash return on initial investments, enabling investors to gain more appreciated value when motels were sold.[20]

The 1954 Tax Code not only stimulated new construction, but tended to limit the life expectancy of motel buildings, thus precipitating short-term ownership and cyclical renovation and modernization. The Tax Code remains a built-in mechanism for change today. Equity is sheltered through accelerated depreciation in the early life of a purchase. But in eight to ten years, when amortization payments become greater than depreciation allowances, it is time for the purchaser to sell and take his long-term capital gain. The investor is now ready to reinvest in another motel and repeat the process.[21] Owners take part of their profits by disinvesting their buildings: by providing minimum maintenance and repair. Buildings deteriorate until a change in ownership brings total renovation, usually embracing the latest fads and fashions in construction and styling. Architectural integrity in motel buildings is thus short-lived. The Tax Code has encouraged a brisk trade in second-, third-, and even fourth-hand motels, many of which would otherwise have been abandoned.[22] It has also encouraged builders to put up junky, flimsy construction and to otherwise seek impermanence on the roadside. In 1960 the average life of a motel building was nine years.[23]

Motor Inns

Motor inns appeared in the 1950s (Fig. 13–6). They were substantially larger and more luxurious than motor courts, often comprising a complex of two-story buildings organized around a courtyard (Fig. 13–7). The typical motor inn featured an elaborate outdoor area focused on a swimming pool and expanded public space indoors (Fig. 13–12). The coffee shop became a full-fledged dining room with adjacent cocktail lounge and banquet and meeting rooms. The registration desk expanded into a small lobby with magazine counter and gift shop. Guest rooms were large: the typical room containing two double beds, a night table with telephone, baggage rack, several lounge chairs, and a table as well as a dressing and bath area with sink and vanity separated from shower and toilet. Rooms were air-conditioned and no decor was complete without a television set. Motor inns tended to be built back to back with utilities placed down a center core (Fig. 13–7). The center-core buildings were noisier, but they were cheaper to heat and cool, and construction costs were lower.[24] Inns with 150 to 300

Fig. 13–12. Motor Inn at Hot Springs, Arkansas

rooms could be accommodated on sites where only 50 to 60 rooms had been possible before.

The small businessman dominated the motel industry until the 1950s, when motor inn construction came to require vast capital outlays. Although investment money was readily available, lenders wanted assurances that new motels would indeed profit by the roadside. The motel chain in various forms provided added security. Motel chains were not new. The idea had been applied in the 1920s to both primitive cabin camps and luxurious highway hotels, early predecessors of today's motel-like hotel complexes. In 1929, for example, the Pierce Petroleum Corporation opened five forty-room highway hotels along U.S. 66 in Missouri and Oklahoma.[25] Facilities included an emergency hospital with a nurse on duty and a restaurant equipped with an "electrola radiola."

Motel chains come in at least four different varieties: franchise chains, referral chains, one-operator chains, and co-owner chains.[26] Franchise chains license owners to use a standard name and operate in conformity with set standards of operation. Some architectural conformity is usually required. The oldest franchise chains, Treadway Inns founded in 1912 and Alamo Plaza founded in 1933 (Fig. 13–13), did not actually emphasize franchising until the 1950s. Today's dominant franchises (Downtowner, Holiday Inns, Howard Johnson's, Quality Inns, Ramada Inns, Rodeway Inns, and

Fig. 13–13. Alamo Plaza Motel Near Biloxi, Mississippi

Sheraton Inns) were all organized in the 1950s or early 1960s. Recent franchises oriented to budget accommodations include Days Inns and Regal 8 Inns.[27]

Referral chains are comprised of independently owned motels whose owners adhere to set standards and aid one another by supporting national advertising and a reservation and referral system. One-operator chains are totally owned by a single parent company. Examples include Hilton Inns and Charterhouse Motor Hotels. Co-owner chains are owned in partnership, a local investor-manager and a parent company. Examples include Travelodge and Imperial 400 motels.

Brand identity through standardized signage and standardized buildings long characterized industries dominated by relatively few corporations as, for example, the petroleum industry's development of the gasoline station.[28] But motels with their localized ownership were late in seeking the benefits of brand recognition. Motel chains provide this benefit by bringing substantial regimentation to architecture and signage especially in the franchise systems.

Motels not only have to look like motels, but, ideally, motels within a given chain should look alike.[29] The Howard Johnson motor inns of the 1960s shared the following features. Guests arrived at a gatehouse where the registration desk was located. Once registered, guests drove to their assigned room. On entering their room, guests faced a partition composed of built-in luggage rack and coat closet where bags would be conveniently dropped: the partition allowing only a partial view of the room, its furnishings, and large patio window beyond. A dressing area with a large mirror, counter, and lavatory came next. Thus a specific traffic flow was planned to heighten first impressions: from car to luggage rack to bathroom to bed and sitting area to view over patio and landscaped grounds. A company restaurant was erected immediately adjacent at many facilities.

Highway Hotels

The highway hotel, an unsuccessful experiment in the 1920s and 1930s, reappeared in the 1960s as an assemblage of rooms, floor upon floor (Fig. 13–14). Traditional motel designs that had favored row, L, and court building arrangements gave way to the cruciform (Fig. 13–7) and other unusual designs, including round and curvilinear structures.[30] Today the typical highway hotel includes a high-rise unit with the bulk of the public space on the first floor and the majority of the private rooms above, and one or more low-rise wings also containing rental rooms. Rooms are entered from central

Fig. 13–14. Plan for a highway hotel

hallways as in traditional hotels. The restaurants, cocktail lounge, and meet-ing rooms are large as in motor inns, although the emphasis in design luxury is still focused on large private guest rooms. Most highway hotels serve a general traveling public along suburban highways, near airports, and even in downtown areas, especially in the redeveloped peripheries of central busi-ness districts.

Conclusion

The development of the American motel has come full circle in approxi-mately fifty years. Initially conceived in contrast if not in direct opposition to hotel interests, the motel has become hotel-like. Not only has the motel penetrated the heart of the city, but it has expanded its services and now seeks increased profits from enlarged public spaces like traditional hotels. In the large highway hotels parking is not necessarily adjacent to or even near most private rooms. In most high-rise motel corridors and elevators focus at a central lobby and a registration desk. No longer do guests escape public scrutiny. Public space has become formal. Informality survives pri-marily at poolside. Hotels have become motel-like, with parking garages, large atriums simulating the informality of outdoors, and swimming and other recreational facilities. Traditional hotels differ from motels primarily by their larger size and their orientation to convention and packaged tour clientele. They also continue to derive a larger proportion of their profits from restaurants, banquet rooms, and other public facilities.

Until the motor chains matured in the 1960s the large corporation did not exert a standardizing influence on motel architecture. Nonetheless, a tyranny of taste and fashion managed to be exerted, bringing a surprising degree of uniformity from one part of the country to another. Uniformity manifested itself in the general structuring of motels: the size and furnishing of individual rooms as well as their arrangement within detached, center-core, and high-rise arrangements. The primitive cabin camp gave way to the more substantial cottage court. From the cottage court came the motor court, the motor inn, and finally, the luxurious highway hotel. Motel owners watched and copied one another, a process intensified with the creation of referral chains in the 1940s and the adoption of operating standards.

Changing motel morphology was characterized by evolution rather than revolution until the 1960s. The growth of automobile travel and the demand for new automobile-convenient lodging facilities along the American roadside prompted steady growth: the trend toward larger, more luxurious facilities to capture more and more of the traditional hotel trade. Older, obsolete motels continued to serve less affluent travelers through a trickle-down mechanism, or lent themselves to ready recycling as low-cost apartments or cottage rentals. The revised Tax Code of 1954 and the Highway Act of 1956 combined to jolt the motel industry as never before.

Accelerated depreciation as a tax option greatly stimulated new construction while older motels received new life with each sale cycle. Compared to other features of the American roadside, like gasoline stations and drive-in restaurants, motels tend to hold to their original function longer although not necessarily to their design integrity. The Tax Code invites cyclical disinvestment, resale, and remodeling, usually at intervals of eight to ten years. The motel is at once a stabilizing influence, given the fluid use of land along the nation's highways, and at the same time a symbol of change through the superficialities of facelifting and remodeling.

The motel survives on the American roadside and has invaded the new turf of airport and downtown locations because it serves a vital function for travelers. The motel is an interface with the private automobile, further cocooning and protecting the traveler away from home. It provides privacy. The motel has tended to depreciate formality to provide a homelike atmosphere. The motel is America's home away from home: a travel refinement in a society of high geographical mobility.

Notes

1. For an introduction to the motel as a feature of the American roadside, see John B. Jackson, "Other-Directed Houses," *Landscape* 6 (Winter

1956–57), 19–25, and "Design for Travel," *Landscape* 11 (Spring 1962), 6–8.

2. Howard E. Morgan, *The Motel Industry in the United States: Small Business in Transition* (Tucson: University of Arizona, Bureau of Business and Public Research, 1964), 1.

3. Ibid., 15.

4. "Hotel Code Has Passed Public Hearing Stage," *Hotel Monthly* 41 (October 1933), 41.

5. Alderson Molz, "Tourist Houses," *Hotel Monthly* 41 (January 1933), 15.

6. "A Hotel-Operated Tourist Camp That Creates Business," *Hotel Monthly* 44 (July 1936), 24.

7. Wallace W. True, "Significant Trends in the Motel Industry," *Appraisal Journal* 27 (April 1959), 229.

8. J. Edgar Hoover with Courtney Ryley Cooper, "Camps of Crime," *American Magazine* 160 (February 1940), 14–15, 130–32.

9. Betty Herman, "Travel and Motel Memories," *Tourist Court Journal* 32 (March 1969), 28.

10. "Money on the Roadside," *Fortune* 27 (August 1951), 80.

11. U.S. Bureau of the Census, *Census of Business 1935. Tourist Camps* (Washington, D.C.: U.S. Department of Commerce, 1937); E. L. Barringer, "Uncle Sam Takes Census of Tourist Camps," *National Petroleum News* 29 (December 15, 1937), 44–45.

12. Ward K. Halbert, "Tourist Camps Pay Southern Jobbers as Rented Dealers Outlets," *National Petroleum News* 21 (March 1929), 164.

13. E. L. Barringer, "Highway Cabin Camps," *National Petroleum News* 27 (October 9, 1935), 33.

14. Norman Hayner, "Auto Camps in the Evergreen Playground," *Social Forces* 9 (December 1930), 256–66.

15. True, 229.

16. *Motels, Hotels, Restaurants and Bars: An Architectural Record Book* (New York: Dodge, 1953), 25.

17. "Danish Village Is Outstanding Highway Camp," *National Petroleum News* 43 (October 23, 1935), 49.

18. "Operates a Hotel and Two Autels," *Hotel Monthly* 48 (September 1940), 28.

19. Ray Sawyer, "A Survey of Motel Chain Organizations, Part One: Referral Chains," *Motel/Motor Inn Journal* 38 (December 1974), 65.

20. C. Joseph Molinaro, "Ten Reasons Why People Buy Motels," *Motel/Motor Inn Journal* 37 (May 1974), 49.

21. Ibid.

22. Seymour Freedgood, "The Motel Free-For-All," *Fortune* 35 (June 1959), 171.

23. David B. Carlson, "New Hotel vs. Old Code," *Architectural Forum* 113 (November 1960), 208.

24. Carleton Whiting, "Gas Stations Grow to Motorists Hotels Under Pierce Terminal System," *National Petroleum News* 22 (March 1930), 153.

25. Bob Gresham, "Anatomy of Chain and Referral Motels," *Tourist Court Journal* 30 (August 1967), 59–70.

26. In 1960 a Holiday Inn franchise cost $10,000 plus a charge of $4.50 per month per room or 2.5 percent of the gross, whichever was larger. For a comparison of various franchise chains see Arthur W. Baum, "The New American Roadside," *Saturday Evening Post* 233 (July 30, 1960), 32–36, 48–49, and Gresham, 59–70.

27. John A. Jakle, "The American Gasoline Station, 1920 to 1970," *Journal of American Culture* 1 (Spring 1976), 520–42.

28. Rufus Nims, quoted in *Interiors Book of Hotel and Motor Hotels*, ed. Henry End (New York: Whitney Library, 1963), 118.

29. Carol Koch, "Design for a Franchise Chain," *Motels, Hotels, Restaurants and Bars* (New York: Dodge, 1960), 48.

30. "Motel/Hotel Architecture: The State of the Art; Part Two," *Motel/Motor Inn Journal* 38 (May 1975), 42–48; "Travelodge Opens First Tri-Arc," *Tourist Court Journal* 33 (June 1970), 88–89.

14

Art Deco Architecture in Miami Beach

James R. Curtis

A distinctive architectural style, both as artifact and symbol, is often the most enduring and expressive manifestation of the spirit of an age. There are cultural landscapes where the elements of time and architectural style have become inseparable; the style has come to represent the era, just as the era once found expression in the style. If the architectural legacy is memorable, sufficiently concentrated, and left essentially unaltered, it may greatly contribute to that elusive sense of place and enable one to experience—through the style—a reflection of time past. One of the more outstanding examples of this spontaneous melding of time past and architectural styles in the urban landscape is the Art Deco District in Miami Beach.

In 1979 a one-square-mile section at the extreme southern end of Miami Beach was officially recognized as a federal historic district and placed in the National Register of Historic Places (Fig. 14–1). It became the youngest and second largest district among the fifteen hundred entered in the register.[1] Its overriding significance lies in the fact that it houses the nation's greatest concentration of both Art Deco and Streamlined architecture, which are collectively known as Style Moderne, although in the common vernacular the term "Art Deco" has come to subsume both styles.[2]

The district is more than a collection of isolated showcase structures scattered at random in a loosely defined area. Rather, building after building, block after block, the concentration of representative architecture is overwhelming and clearly bounded by natural barriers, abrupt changes in prevailing architectural style, and patterns of land use. There are in fact

Reprinted by permission from the *Journal of Cultural Geography* 3 (1982), 51–63.

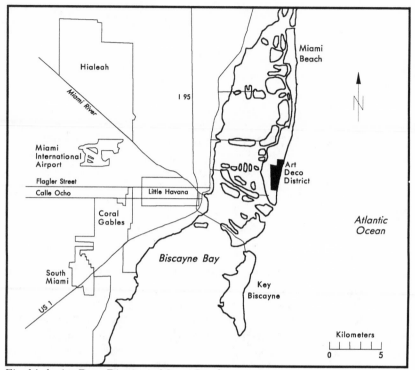

Fig. 14–1. Art Deco District in Miami Beach

over three hundred certified Art Deco buildings within the district, including both residential and commercial structures, especially small three- and four-story hotels.[3] It is the sum, the totality, not the individual parts per se, that merits attention and distinguishes this historic district.

The buildings themselves are as stylistically consistent and compatible as they are concentrated. Their extraordinary homogeneity and cohesiveness in style, scale, proportions, materials, and specific design features reflect a combination of social, economic, and historic forces during their brief period of construction, dating from the mid-1920s to the early 1940s. They may be considered an artistic response to, and have become a distinctive material symbol of, the unusual sense of place and spirit of Miami Beach in the Depression years. Moreover, at a less provincial level, the style was strongly influenced by and clearly mirrored national and international artistic trends of the period.[4]

The characteristic design features of this upbeat, almost whimsical style and the factors responsible for its emergence in Miami Beach in the Depression era are examined in this study.

Pre-Deco Miami Beach

The emergence of Art Deco architecture in Miami Beach during the Depression was in sharp contrast to the style it replaced. From its incorporation in 1915 through the early 1930s the dominant "style of choice" could be classified as Mediterranean Revival, an eclectic mixture of Venetian Gothic, Tuscan Villa, and especially Spanish Colonial.[5] It was a richly ornate and opulent style with common features that included rough stucco facades painted in soft pastel colors, low-pitched red barrel-tiled roofs, extensive use of wrought iron, cornice moldings, arched openings, balconies, interior courtyards, terraces and open loggias. As a reflection of the indulgent spirit of the Jazz Age this style seemed appropriate to the pervasive sense of prosperity and exclusiveness that characterized Miami Beach, which fashioned itself in the 1920s an American "Riviera" or Atlantic City south.[6]

Land where only a decade or two earlier stood dense stands of tangled mangrove in miry swamps had by the 1920s become a favored winter playground for the wealthy and the social elite. Many of the nation's leading captains of industry and commerce, such as Harvey Firestone, J. C. Penney, Harvey Stutz, and Albert Champion, had taken up seasonal residence in newly built Spanish-style mansions, creating an instant "Millionaire's Row" along Collins Avenue bordering the Atlantic shore. A majority of the affluent visitors, however, found suitable accommodations in a number of elegant, well-appointed hotels built by the town's principal promoters and land speculators, most notably Carl Graham Fisher, the Prest-O-Lite battery magnate. Replete with golf courses, tennis lawns, polo fields, beach and "bath" clubs, and yachting facilities, these grand hotels—such as the Flamingo, Nautilus, Boulevard, Fleetwood, and Roney Plaza (Fig. 14–2)—offered their well-heeled patrons a full complement of services and leisure activities. Hotel guests could even sail the canalways in gondolas manned by Bahamian oarsmen resplendent in colorful, if not traditional Venetian attire.[7]

The glamor of the resort hotels and the subtropical winter charms of southern Florida were complimented by other amenities. The availability of bootleg liquor and gambling in plush nightclubs all contributed an element of excitement and enhanced the prevailing sense of well-being. Rumors of quick profits through land speculation ran wild, further adding to the festive spirit and serving to lure additional investors and tourists. Over two hundred "smart" shops lined Lincoln Road, which was considered the "Fifth Avenue of the South." By 1925 Miami Beach had a year-round population of nearly eight thousand, yet sported twice as many polo fields as churches and had more casinos than schools.[8] It was a gay and carefree

Fig. 14–2. The Roney Plaza Hotel

time and conformed fully to the image of the period as voiced by F. Scott Fitzgerald, who wrote of the 1920s, "It was an age of miracles, it was an age of art, it was an age of excess. . . ."[9]

Suddenly events took a sharp turn for the worse in late 1926 when a hurricane struck Miami Beach full force, inundating the town and causing widespread property damage. Literally overnight the image of Miami Beach as a "paradise under the sun," which had been so closely nurtured and promoted, lost a considerable bit of its luster.[10] Investment money quickly evaporated and the land boom came to a rather abrupt halt. An economic malaise soon gripped the community as the winter tourist trade suffered through its worst season. Yet, to prove its resilience and optimism, in 1927 the city fathers elected to build an impressive nine-story City Hall constructed in classic Beaux Arts style. Recovery, however, was temporarily crippled when only two years later the nation slumped into the depths of the Great Depression.

Depression Prosperity

Early in the Depression years Miami Beach suffered like most other American cities, perhaps even more than some since its economic base, namely, winter tourism, had already been seriously undermined. Yet by 1933 the first signs of revitalization were clearly visible and the subsequent rate of growth during the remainder of the Depression was startling, far surpassing the initial spurt of prosperity enjoyed a decade earlier. By the mid-1930s, for example, it ranked during certain periods among the top ten cities in the country in terms of the value of building construction. Overall, in excess of $75 million was spent on construction between 1933 and 1940.[11]

The major thrust of development focused on the construction of relatively small hotels, ranging in size from two to seven stories and averaging considerably less than a hundred rooms. From 1935 to 1940 nearly two hundred of these modest hotels were erected, including 88 in 1939 and 1940.[12] By contrast there were only 77 hotels in all of Miami Beach in 1933. The permanent population of the city also grew correspondingly, increasing from 6,500 in 1930 to just over 28,000 in 1940. This growth in itself prompted the construction of over four hundred small apartment complexes during the period.[13] The new area of construction was a tightly compacted, roughly 75-block area of south Miami Beach, known locally as "South Beach" (which would subsequently become the Art Deco District). So successful was the economic recovery that *Time* magazine in February 1940 declared that Miami Beach was a "booming, catholic pleasure dome . . . like no other city in the U.S., or in the World."[14]

There were many reasons for Miami Beach's unprecedented expansion during the Depression. As a glamorous seaside resort it symbolically represented freshness, vitality, excitement, and of course the fantasy of escape. To a beleaguered nation the theme of escapism held tremendous appeal and was actively pursued (as record-setting attendance at movie theaters likewise suggests). Miami Beach was one of the fortunate places that managed to capitalize on this fascination. Importantly, there was space available for expansion since the area had not been overdeveloped in the 1920s. The municipal government also responded in a positive fashion by offering tax breaks to developers and by implementing an austere fiscal policy. The major reason, however, was related to a shift in the tourist trade. Unlike the 1920s, when tourism catered primarily to the moneyed elite, during the Depression middle-income tourists were enthusiastically welcomed. Modest yet comfortable and ideally located accommodations for the budget-minded tourist were erected in the South Beach area. This change was accomplished in large part through a lavish promotional advertising campaign in magazines such as *Vanity Fair* that promised, for example, "a utopia of pleasure and health . . . for the wallet-weary."[15] By any measure it was successful (Fig. 14–3). Again, as reported in *Time*, "Swarming thousands of

Fig. 14–3. Miami Beach in the 1930s

thrifty folk stretch a year's saving in 'South Beach' where there are many small, relatively cheap ($5 to $7) hotels, the dog-track, drug-store lunch counters, and the only public beach space."[16] In 1940 over 75,000 tourists visited Miami Beach in the winter season, including both the middle class and the wealthy, who had returned to stay at the still-elegant hotels built in the 1920s.[17]

The spirit of the 1930s involved more than the grim realities of the Depression, or the counterpoint offered by Miami Beach. In almost all aspects of American life and culture, it was an age that was self-consciously modern, optimistic, forward-looking, and utterly intrigued by science, technology, and industry. Machines, especially machines of transport, were revered. The art of the day, including architecture, was strongly influenced by both the functionalism and the aesthetics of the machine. Art Deco was a visual form born of that fascination and perspective.[18] Nowhere was it better manifested architecturally than in Miami Beach.

Art Deco and Streamlined

Technically Art Deco and Streamlined are substyles or phases of Style Moderne, a twentieth-century invention with roots firmly planted in Art

Nouveau, Cubism, Futurism, Bauhaus, and the Dutch de Stijl. It emerged as an artistic reaction against and stood in sharp contrast to the classical revival modes (e.g., revival Gothic, Renaissance, Baroque) characteristic of the Beaux Arts that dominated the Victorian era. Though complex, if not confused in form and meaning as it evolved over the first two decades of this century, the style made its formal debut and was clearly articulated in the 1925 *L'Exposition Internationale des Arts Décoratifs et Industriels Modernes* held in Paris.[19] The exposition brought together the work not only of architects but also industrial and textile designers, glass and metal sculptors, and furniture craftsmen, among others. As the style further crystalized and gained acceptance, it was widely applied in a variety of design forms ranging from fashion to industry to art. It was, as Bevis Hillier has correctly stated, "the last of the total styles."[20]

Although Art Deco and Streamlined architecture share many common design features, there remain significant differences. Distinctions are worth drawing since both substyles were employed (and mixed) in Miami Beach during the Depression years.

True Art Deco, or Zig Zag Modern as it is also known, is the early phase of Style Moderne, which exerted its greatest influence from the mid-1920s through the mid-1930s. In shape the style is characterized by a sharp-edged, linear angularity that may be thought to reflect "the dominance of the triangle and the T-square."[21] Often the shape tended to give the illusion of soaring verticality. In respect to these straight lines and sharp angles, Paul Frankl in 1928 opined,

> Simple lines are modern. They are restful to the eye and dignify and tend to cover up the complexity of the machine age. If they do not completely do this, they at least divert our attention and allow us to feel ourselves master of the machine.[22]

Extensive decoration is another typical aspect of Art Deco, although its function is strictly ornamental and not integral to building design. The decorative motifs were usually geometric in form and often theme oriented. Eclectic "revival" such as Aztec, Egyptian, Persian, and American Indian was common.[23] Specific decorative features often included classical patterns of flowers, leaves, shells, animals, and human forms. Tropical subjects such as flamingos, palm trees, sunbursts, and ocean scenes were extremely popular in Miami Beach, particularly as displayed in etched glass windows. Although richly ornamental, design patterns were typically executed close to the surface.

Bold use of color is another common Art Deco characteristic.[24] Exterior facades were painted in bright hues of green, orange, pink, and blue against white or beige backgrounds. Extravagant colorism was also evident in the tinted keystone, patterned terrazzo, and neon electrographics.

One of the unifying architectural aspects of Style Moderne was that both Art Deco and Streamlined relied on a common set of machine-made building materials. They represented a distinct departure from preceding construction material modes. Virtually a physical checklist of modern materials, these products include concrete, Vitrolite, Bakelite, aluminum, porcelain-enameled steel, chromed tubular metal, glass blocks, and plastic.[25] The use of these materials was frequently highlighted by fluorescent and neon cove lighting.

Art Deco architecture in its purest form was not nearly as prevalent as Streamlined in Miami Beach. This is largely because the building boom of the Depression occurred there after Art Deco had enjoyed its greatest popularity in the late 1920s and the early 1930s. Still, there are outstanding examples and many specific design elements mixed with Streamlined extant throughout the district, such as the old Miami Public Library (now the Bass Museum) and the Hotel Savoy Plaza (Fig. 14–4).

By the early 1930s and with the Depression a harsh, undeniable reality, a transformation occurred in Style Moderne; Streamlined succeeded Art Deco as the style's prevailing form.[26] (This transition was clearly evident in and perhaps further accelerated by the 1933 "Century of Progress" World's

Fig. 14–4. The Hotel Savoy Plaza

Fair held in Chicago.[27]) Whereas Art Deco fully utilized machine-made products, Streamlined went a logical step forward and made the machine its focal design symbol. The stylistic changes mirror the essential differences between the 1920s and the 1930s.

"Today, speed is the cry of our era," wrote Norman Bel Geddes, one of the foremost advocates of Streamlined, in 1932.[28] This concern for speed, as well as efficiency and functionalism, exemplifies the machine aesthetic of the 1930s. It is without question reflected in the shape of Streamlined, which is based on "the French curve and the compass."[29] The sharp angular edges and straight lines of Art Deco gave way, as Aldous Huxley noted, "wherever circumstances demand a less puritanical treatment, to undulations and to curves."[30] This curvilinear form stresses horizontality, which tends to convey an organic feeling of smooth, continuous, machinelike movement. Certainly Miami Beach was one place in the Depression that demanded a "less puritanical treatment." There are literally hundreds of representative examples of the curvilinear form, including the Surrey Hotel (Fig. 14–5).

Unlike the richly ornamented surfaces characteristic of Art Deco, Streamlined surfaces are light, smooth, and either completely undecorated or only sparingly so. Where decoration was desired, the most common form was repetitive geometric patterns, such as circles or stripes, often in groups of three or four. Many of the hotels, such as the Commodore (Fig. 14–6),

Fig. 14–5. The Surrey Hotel

Fig. 14–6. The Commodore Hotel

sought to evoke a jaunty nautical theme with decorative design features that typically included portholes, pipe railings, hatches, roof decks, and even a ship's mast. These features were true both to the machine as the style's design symbol and to the spirit of Miami Beach as a special place during the Depression. Leicester Hemingway, author of *My Brother, Ernest Hemingway*, and resident of Miami Beach in the 1930s, commented on the style and its impression on him.

> They [the architects] were determined not to use any older styles like the Spanish. . . . They didn't quite know where they were headed; but they wanted something modern, so they smoothed the balconies, they smoothed everything until you got the feeling that life was smooth. The buildings made you feel all clean and new and excited and happy to be here.[31]

The Streamlined style did not remain static throughout the Depression; it evolved in response to changing economic conditions and social forces. It is perhaps not surprising that as the Depression dragged on and hope waned, an intense collective interest in the future emerged. This fascination was dramatically reflected in and fostered by elements of popular culture.[32] Hollywood fantasy films and futuristic comic strips were particularly influential, both visually and philosophically. In respect to comic strips, for example, the immense popularity of "Buck Rogers, 25th Century, A.D.,"

Fig. 14–7. The Plymouth Hotel

created in 1929, led to "Flash Gordon" in 1934 and to "Superman" in 1938; film versions, of course, were subsequently produced. In similar fashion, the spectacular and well-attended 1939 New York World's Fair greatly expressed and boostered the theme of futurism, especially the Trylon and Perisphere exhibits, which became the futuristic symbols of the fair.[33]

The influence of futurism on Streamlined architecture in Miami Beach was profound. Two reasons in particular stand out. Certainly as a resort community "less serious" architectural modes were not only condoned, but encouraged; buildings done in a "playful" style helped create an ambience conducive to enjoyment, relaxation, and escape. For their part, the relatively small number of local architects responsible for most of the buildings (e.g., fewer than twenty designed over three-fourths of all the structures) were thoroughly modern and eager to experiment.[34] One of the more dramatic examples of the futuristic Streamlined style is the Plymouth Hotel with its tall central spire, vertical ribbon windows, and simple unadorned

Fig. 14–8. The Tiffany Hotel

surface; it is a clean, sleek, sculptural style (Fig. 14–7). Another typical futuristic design feature is a towering finial, such as one atop the Tiffany Hotel (Fig. 14–8). In many cases a needle-thin spire was employed to give the impression of a Buck Rogers-like rocket.

Conclusion

Although the Art Deco buildings in Miami Beach are distinctive, it would be incorrect to conclude that they represent a radical departure from preceding architectural traditions, that they are altogether "unique." In this respect, Harris Sobin has astutely observed that these structures,

> with their axially-arranged plans and symmetrical elevations, were firmly grounded on Classical principles. A consistent use of the Classical language of the "orders" also becomes apparent: base, shaft, capital and cornice are all there in disguise.[35]

Though perhaps based on Classical traditions in terms of structural design, through clever and imaginative use of "disguise" the style was simultaneously "modern" and "futuristic." Any architectural style that combines in the present elements of the past and the future, that looks back as it looks forward, has achieved a remarkable dual goal. Art Deco not only accomplished this, but in Miami Beach also managed to fit the sense of place and the spirit of the time.

World War II brought an abrupt end to Art Deco architecture in Miami Beach; the relatively short-lived style was not revived after the conflict. One can only speculate why. Perhaps the war itself was the fundamental reason, as it demonstrated beyond imagination the terrifying and vulgar application of technology and machines to destructive, inhumane purposes. The image of the machine was suddenly tainted and the appeal of futuristic worlds paled in the unreal light of a world at war. In addition, the prosperity and renewed national vigor of the postwar period surely contributed to the demise of Art Deco. In short, it was a new day, born of bitter memories of the past and fresh dreams for the future, and it demanded change. Art Deco thus gave way to the International style in Miami Beach. Yet the style lives on in the Art Deco District and it still echoes the spirit of the 1930s.

Notes

1. The Art Deco District was officially entered in the National Register on May 14, 1979.

2. Anderson Notter Finegold, Inc., *Miami Beach Art Deco District: Preservation and Development Plan* (Miami: Miami Design Preservation League, 1981), 7.

3. In 1978 the Dade County Historical Survey documented over 500 "buildings of significance," including both Art Deco and Spanish styles, in an area only slightly overlapping the present boundaries of the historic district.

4. Bevis Hillier, *Art Deco* (London: Studio Vista, 1968); Giulia Veronese, *Style and Design, 1909–1929* (New York: George Braziller, 1968); Theodore Menten, *The Art Deco Style* (New York: Dover, 1972); Thomas Walters, *Art Deco* (New York: St. Martin's Press, 1973); Yvonne Brynhammer, *The Nineteen Twenties Style* (London: Paul Hamlyn, 1966).

5. Arlene R. Olson, *A Guide to the Architecture of Miami Beach* (Miami: Dade Heritage Trust, 1978), 8.

6. Kenneth Ballinger, *Miami Millions* (Miami: Frankline Press, 1936); Polly Redford, *Billion Dollar Sandbar* (New York: Dutton, 1970); Charles Edgar Nash, *The Magic of Miami Beach* (Philadelphia: David McKay, 1938).

7. David B. Longbrake and Woodrow W. Nichols Jr., *Sunshine and Shadows in Metropolitan Miami* (Cambridge: Ballinger, 1976), 29–30.

8. Olson, 9.

9. F. Scott Fitzgerald, "Echoes of the Jazz Age," in *The Crack-Up* (New York: New Directions, 1945), 14.

10. J. N. Lummus, *The Miracle of Miami Beach* (Miami: Miami Post Publishing, 1940).

11. Carl J. Weinhardt Jr., "Art Deco in Perspective," in *Portfolio: Art Deco Historic District*, ed. Barbara Baer Capitman (Miami: Miami Design Preservation League, 1980), 32.

12. Arlene Olson, "Miami Beach: Resort Style Moderne," *Florida Architect* 27 (January/February 1977), 19–21.

13. Ibid.

14. "Pleasure Dome," *Time* 35 (February 19, 1940), 18.

15. Mark A. Bernheim, "Dos Passos and *Vanity Fair*: The Novel and the Ad," in *Time Present, Time Past*, ed. Barbara B. Capitman (Miami: Miami Design Preservation League, 1980), 7–9.

16. *Time*, 19.

17. Olson, A *Guide to the Architecture of Miami Beach*, 10.

18. Sheldon Cheney, *Art and the Machine* (New York: McGraw-Hill, 1936); Reyner Banham, *Theory and Design in the First Machine Age* (London: Architectural Press, 1960); Klaus-Jürgen Sembach, *Style 1930* (New York: Universe Books, 1971) and "Design Decade," *Architectural Forum 73* (October 1940), 217–320.

19. *Encyclopédie des Arts Décoratifs et Industriels Modernes au XXeme Siecle* (New York: Garland, 1977) is a 12-volume work in French documenting the exhibition. Mary K. Grimes and Georgiann Gersell in *The Impact of Art Deco: 1925–1940* (Indianapolis: Indianapolis Museum of Art, 1976), 5, argue that the 1925 exhibition "was not the beginning of the style, but rather its peak."

20. Hillier, 9; Alain Lesieutre, *The Spirit and Splendour of Art Deco* (New York: Paddington Press, 1974).

21. David Gebhard and Harriette von Breton, *Kem Weber: The Moderne in Southern California* (Santa Barbara, Calif.: Peregrine Smith, 1975), 11.

22. Paul T. Frankl, *New Dimensions* (New York: Payson and Clark, 1928), 17.

23. Hillier, 10–13; Laura Cerwinske, *Tropical Deco: The Architecture and Design of Old Miami Beach* (New York: Rizzoli International, 1980).

24. Cervin Robinson and Rosemarie H. Bletter, *Skyscraper Style: Art Deco New York* (New York: Oxford University Press, 1975), 36–40; Ely Jacques Kahn, "On the Use of Color," in *Ely Jacques Kahn*, ed. Arthur Tappan North, Contemporary American Architects Series (New York: McGraw-Hill, 1931), 21–24.

25. Don Vlack, *Art Deco Architecture in New York, 1920 to 1940* (New York: Harper and Row, 1974), 92–117; Robinson and Bletter, 67–69.

26. Judith Applegate in "What Is Art Deco?" *Art News* 69 (December 1970), 42, describes the shift in fanciful terms: "The fat, turgid stylizations of the 'teens, the cautious *bon gout francais* or the giddy Scheherezade fantasies of the '20s finally succumbed to an apotheosis (usually rhapsodic) of the machine . . . speed and dynamism."

27. Gebhard and von Breton, 21; *Official Pictures of a Century of Progress Exhibition* (Chicago: Donnelley, 1933).

28. Norman Bel Geddes, *Horizons* (Boston: Little, Brown, 1932), 24.

29. Gebhard and von Breton, 11.

30. Aldous Huxley, "Notes on Decoration," *Creative Art* 7 (October 1930), 240.

31. Robert Liss, "Upbeat Architecture Was Their Answer to Depression," *Miami Herald* (September 10, 1978), Section A, 17.

32. Kathleen C. Plummer, "The Streamlined Moderne," *Art in America* 62 (January/February 1974), 46–54; Robinson and Bletter, 64–67.

33. Donald Bush, *The Streamlined Decade* (New York: George Braziller, 1975), 169.

34. Barbara B. Capitman, "Re-Discovery of Art Deco," *American Preservation* 1 (August-September 1978), 35–36; Olson, *Florida Architect*, 21.

35. Harris J. Sobin, "Miami Deco: Roots and Meanings," in Capitman, *Time Present, Time Past*, 15.

15

Selected Reading V

Chapters 13 and 14

Baeder, John. *Diners*. New York: Harry N. Abrams, 1978.

———. *Gas, Food, and Lodging*. New York: Abbeville Press, 1982.

Belasco, Warren James. *Americans on the Road: From Autocamp to Motel, 1910–1945*. Cambridge: MIT Press, 1979.

Cerwinske, Laura. *Tropical Deco: The Architecture and Design of Old Miami Beach*. New York: Rizzoli International, 1981.

Clay, Grady. *Close-up: How to Read the American City*. New York: Praeger, 1973.

Gowans, Alan. *Learning to See: Historical Perspectives on Modern Popular/ Commercial Arts*. Bowling Green, Ohio: Popular Press, 1981.

Headley, Gwyn. *Architectural Follies in America*. Washington, D.C.: Preservation Press, 1995.

Hillier, Bevis. *Art Deco*. London: Studio Vista, 1965.

Huxtable, Ada Louise. *Goodbye History, Hello Hamburger: An Anthology of Architectural Delights and Disasters*. Washington, D.C.: Preservation Press, 1986.

Junior League of Tulsa. *Tulsa Art Deco: An Architectural Era, 1925–1942*. Tulsa, Okla.: Junior League of Tulsa Publications, 1980.

Maddex, Diane (ed.). *Built in the U.S.A.: American Buildings From Airports to Zoos*. Washington, D.C.: Preservation Press, 1985.

Margolis, John. *The End of the Road: Vanishing Highway Architecture in America*. New York: Penguin Books, 1981.

McAlester, Virginia, and McAlester, Lee. A *Field Guide to American Houses*. New York: Knopf, 1984.

Minneapolis Institute of Art. *The World of Art Deco*. New York: Dutton, 1971.

Part VI: Politics

Even though popular culture seems at first glance nonpolitical, this does not mean it is apolitical. We usually think of politics as the election of officeholders, deliberations by government officials, and decisions by the Supreme Court. Additional relationships between politics and popular culture, however, can be identified. Many political ideas, attitudes, and images are manifested as a part of our popular experience and may be communicated to the mass population through various forms. The two subsequent articles represent communication about political ideas that are often overlooked in our contemporary society: symbols and maps, both tangible expressions of popular culture.

Wilbur Zelinsky, professor emeritus at Pennsylvania State University and an eminent American cultural geographer, traces the historical background of the nation-state concept in the United States. A nation is a group of people bound together by a set of cultural factors (e.g., language, race, and religion), and nationalism is the expression of collective behavior and shared values. Statism is based on a political community occupying a definite territory possessing an organized government and external/internal sovereignty. Zelinsky examines these forces and their effect on the political motifs and traditions that pervade our everyday existence. He identifies numerous examples of nationalism that dot the American scene, including monuments dedicated to political and military heroes; government-owned buildings and land such as post offices, courthouses, and national parks; and the ubiquitous interstate highway network. Moreover, he notes that the popular American icons of the bald eagle and national flag are exhibited in a vast array of phenomena ranging from doghouse adornments to gigantic displays in used car lots. Thus, Zelinsky concludes that much can be learned by exploring the elements of nationalism and statism—those powerful ideologies that help shape the political landscape of American popular culture.

Richard Francaviglia, director of the Center for Greater Southwestern Studies at the University of Texas-Arlington and a cultural geographer, offers a thought-provoking essay on popular cartography. He contends that the outline of a map can become an icon for a political unit such as Texas. Francaviglia emphasizes that the Texas map is one of the most recognizable of the fifty states and has capitalized on its geopolitical outline. It has aggressively promoted the state's shape in a variety of Texas-made goods as well as displayed it on a myriad of objects ranging from billboards to jewelry. The design characteristics of the Texas map, according to Francaviglia, have contributed to its use as a symbol resulting in the emergence of Tex-map mania in the state. His final analysis is that the map of Texas has become an effective promotional tool and has given the residents a sense of identity as Texans as well as attachment to a place.

16

The Changing Face of Nationalism in the American Landscape

Wilbur Zelinsky

When Europeans conquered and settled overseas territories they considered empty or temporarily encumbered by mere heathens hardly worth fussing over, they set about fashioning new settlement landscapes in short order. In such countries as Canada, Argentina, Brazil, South Africa, Australia, and New Zealand, the newcomers redesigned their surroundings, wittingly or not, in imitation of the models provided by the homeland.[1] But novel conditions, along with the sheer rapidity of the process, brought distinctly novel patterns, only partially mimicking the familiar European scene.

The case of the United States, at least from 1776 onward, represents an even greater departure from traditional landscape models than is observable in other neo-European lands. The swift advance of settlement frontiers over a continental expanse, the fiery nationalism of the young republic, and ultimately, the enormous power and prestige of a triumphant American nation-state have imparted to its human-made landscapes a brace of nationalistic motifs that are remarkable in their pervasiveness. My working hypothesis is that in the United States, as in virtually all countries of the modern world, two sets of ideological and institutional forces—nationalism and statism—have been at work molding the collective existence and, among other effects, the visible landscape.

Nationalism is a complex of emotions and attitudes rooted in what are

Reprinted by permission from the *Canadian Geographer* 30 (1986), 171–75.

perceived to be singular cultural attributes, myths, and traditions, and perhaps also the distinctive political and social values, of the "ethnie," the national community. As lobbied for, perhaps even fabricated by, an intellectual and political elite, nationalism is a creed that logically leads to the cry for political autonomy by its adherents. Statism is, in essence, a quite separate entity. For the believers in statism—a considerable majority of the world's population today—that mighty, faceless, all-embracing embodiment of the state-idea, the state (but not necessarily its inconvenient expression, the government) is regarded as the ultimate social reality, the repository of all that is fine and noble in life.[2] Indeed it is more precious than life itself when other states menace its safety or well-being. While the sociocultural differences among nations are striking and unbridgeable, the conditions of statehood are becoming more and more alike among the nation-states of our world. In some instances, the state has preceded the birth of the nation, and indeed found it necessary to serve as its midwife; in others, the two modes of thought evolved simultaneously. In the United States, as in modern Israel, Ireland, Poland, or India, the nation crystallized first. By examining the history and historical geography of the symbolic dimensions of nationalism and statism as expressed in the landscape and other aspects of American life, we can discern the distinctiveness of these two forces and their quite different trajectories over time.

It is convenient to recognize three epochs in the chronicles of American nationhood and statehood.[3] The earliest encompasses the years of struggle for independence and identity, the extraordinary blossoming of the conviction of providential chosenness, of being the Almighty's very special people, a period extending roughly from 1763 to 1850 when the Founders and Framers were alive or their memory was still bright and immediate. The *nation* was supreme, and the emotional fervor fueled by its fresh ideas blazed with an intense heat. The weak, emerging state was honored or tolerated only to the degree that it embodied the lofty national principles. A deeply internalized faith called for few tangible expressions in the landscape. The creation, virtually overnight, of a large pantheon of political and military heroes, the naming after them of numerous places, persons, and other entities, the initiation of national holidays—most notably July 4 and Washington's Birthday—the universal popularity of patriotic art, literature, and music (high, low, and in between), and a swelling chorus of high-flown, self-congratulatory oratory could well have sufficed.

True enough, there was the occasional Liberty Pole and the even more occasional triumphal arch to be glimpsed in the early American outdoors. If America's national totem, the bald eagle, could be found on tavern signs and ship's sterns, indoors it proliferated by the hundreds of thousands or millions on domestic articles and walls of dwellings. But the most visible landscape evidence of nationhood was an architectural style, one that has persisted to this day, though enfeebled in form and meaning: the Classic Revival.[4] Americans were building not only the New Jerusalem as their "City upon a Hill," but a New Athens and New Rome as well. Thus we find columned porticoes, triangular pediments, the obligatory white paint, and other stylistic elements, fondly believed to echo the classical world, gracing countless private homes as well as public buildings.

Signs of the fledgling central state were, of course, not totally absent. Like every other sovereign country, the young United States established customhouses at its major international ports and, eventually, along its inland borders, and also, in the absence of local will or resources, a series of lighthouses along the coast. From the 1780s onward, the impress of federal authority was manifested in newly created interstate boundaries and, most ubiquitously, in the rectangular land survey that framed properties, roads, and fields, and via mimesis, many city street plans throughout a national domain that ultimately accounted for at least three-quarters of all American real estate. But perhaps it was in the minuscule District of Columbia, where the federal establishment took up residence in 1800, that one can perceive most meaningfully, if only in utero, the statefulness that later was to crowd out all other claimants for the collective soul of America. If, for all its paper pretensions to imperial grandeur, the city of Washington remained a mostly vacant, pestilential backwater for its first several decades, it has certainly amply realized its destiny during the present century. Yet, despite the genesis of the new capital city and the manifestations of a federal presence in a few larger towns, visual signs of central authority were difficult to locate anywhere within those portions of the original thirteen states settled before the Revolution.

The second epoch began to materialize in the 1850s. By this time the early heroes, events, and ideals that initially inspired such an intense spasm of nationhood had receded into remoter emotional space. An increasingly muscular central state, which achieved unquestioned domination by 1865, began to assert its grip over the hearts and minds of Americans. As one of the most effective devices to jog the communal memory and cement the bonds between nation and state, monuments dedicated to national and regional notables or to historic events and ideals—objects utterly absent in the early American outdoors—began to appear in considerable numbers within the ceremonial spaces of towns large and small. The vogue for these sculptures, obelisks, and other erections, most of which paid homage to the American Revolution and the stalwarts of the Civil War, flourished most vigorously during the last third of the nineteenth century, then subsequently declined, so that after the 1920s the dedication of a new monument had become a rare happening.

Incredible as it may seem today, when uncountable legions of flags confront Americans everywhere, Old Glory was seldom seen outdoors in early America except on merchantships or the infrequent federal buildings and military and naval installations. It was only after the Mexican War and, even more emphatically, in the wake of the Civil War that the flag began to be a conspicuous item in the landscape. Its import was clear: a content-free emblem declaring loyalty to, and heartfelt identification with, an overarching state.

One other notable development during this transitional second period, when statism was beginning to overpower the pristine forms of nationhood, was the staging of the world's fairs within the United States.[5] This extreme form of international one-upmanship, which began tentatively enough in New York City in 1853, scored smashing successes in Philadelphia in 1876 and Chicago in 1893. There and elsewhere, these glorious entertainments have left their residue on the urban landscape not just in the form of surviving structures but especially, as in the case of Chicago's Columbian Exposition, through their impact on city planning and the design of public buildings.

During the present period, whose origins are detectable as early as the 1880s, we have a full-fledged nation-state, but, it must be repeated, one in which the state, or statism, is firmly in the saddle. The proof is obvious enough in the ubiquity of the physical apparatus of a centralized state. Federal courthouses and office buildings are core elements in the central business districts (CBDs) of major cities; and post offices, often constructed in accordance with a standard style, are centrally situated in towns of all sizes and occasionally, in the smallest, provide the only central-place function. Also widespread are the recruiting offices and armories of the military, U. S. Department of Agriculture and Social Security offices, and standardized Veterans Administration hospitals. Since the 1930s, instantly recognizable federal housing projects have materialized in the inner-city neighborhoods of major metropolises.

The federal government owns and administers a vast amount of land, most of it visually distinct from other properties. Thus the national park system (an American first), national forests, and huge hydroelectric power projects remind Americans of the power or benevolence of the state, as do the many military facilities and veterans' cemeteries throughout the land. Moreover, virtually every town of any consequence has one or more halls or centers of the American Legion or the Veterans of Foreign Wars. Although their architecture is highly varied, these are conspicuous places and house institutions that are virtual surrogates of the state.

Since the 1950s, the Interstate Highway System, of uniform federal design as well as funding, has begun to criss-cross the country, channeling and hastening its social and economic transformation. Along lesser roads Americans frequently meet billboards exhorting them to buy United States Savings Bonds, to enlist in the armed forces, or to aid in some campaign (e.g., support for Olympic athletes) that has been spawned or blessed by a federal government agency. A nationalized railroad system, so common elsewhere, may be missing in the United States, as is any government-owned airline or telecommunications system, but other landscape elements more than make up for their absence. But clearly the most highly concentrated, overwhelming landscape expression of American statism today is to be seen in Washington, D.C., where symbolic objects and activities abound in stunning profusion. And to good effect, for they are witnessed each year by millions of tourists, veritable pilgrims.

What makes the current American landscape peculiarly fascinating is not simply the visible hand of the state and the many tangible tokens of statism imposed from above, for these are discernible in greater or lesser degree in other countries. The distinctiveness of this particular landscape derives from a spontaneous, unforced expression of loyalty to the state by the citizenry at large. Thus we observe an incredible multitude of national flags flying on or next to private dwellings, on office buildings, factories, retail establishments, schools, and churches, or affixed to vehicles, clothing, advertising signs, and every variety of object. All this, of course, is in addition to any obligatory official display.

Even more remarkable in my opinion is the inescapability of the red-white-and-blue motif. This triad of hues, which constitutes the national colors and obviously alludes to the flag, shows up in the unlikeliest of contexts as well as in officially appropriate spots; and the impulse to choose this specific color combination may as often be subconscious as calculated. Thus we see it in the logos of numerous corporations and, consequently, in their outdoor advertising; and in an incalculably large array of other signs, bunting, and tinted articles of every description, the red-white-and-blue formula saturates the land to such an extent that it becomes part of the normal visual background, and the observer ceases to be aware of it.

Rivaling the flag in quantity and variety of settings is the eagle, another symbol the American masses have taken to their bosom. Although this formidable fowl has played a major role in patriotic iconography since its debut in the Great Seal in 1785, my investigations suggest that it is only within recent times that the eagle has attained maximum popularity and also that its message has altered over the years. What was once a declaration of the uniquely American versions of liberty, freedom, and pride therein has, like the flag, become an identification tag, a statement of devout obeisance to the state. In any event, one encounters great flocks of eagles on homes, mailboxes, flagpoles, signs, trademarks, and manufactured items of many kinds as well as on public buildings and monuments.

In an age when the serious nationalistic monument has evolved into the purely geometric and abstract, as, for example, the breathtaking arch in St. Louis, the Vietnam War Memorial on the Washington Mall, or the Kennedy memorial in Dallas, what of the historic, heroic past? The short answer is that nostalgia has supplanted memory, and as Robert Nisbet has commented bitingly, "Nostalgia is the rust of memory."[6] For whatever reasons, the overwhelming majority of present-day Americans do not cohabit with their past; at best they visit it occasionally, tourist-fashion. The landscape outcome of what has become the vestigial shell of early nationhood is a series of roadside attractions, many of them heavily commercialized. Historic preservation, or really the recycling of old places and their remaking into what Americans think they should have been, has become a growth industry. Drivers catch freshly installed historical plaques out of the corner of their eye as they whiz by along the highways, or patronize increasing numbers of restored battlefields, quaint museum villages, the birthplaces and homes of heroes, and an astounding profusion of new historical museums, not to mention the occasional patriotic exhibits at theme parks. On the domestic front, a synthetic Colonial style in single-family homes has won universal acceptance as a major vernacular house type since its introduction in the 1880s—and in retail chains as well (e.g., Howard Johnson's hotels, the A & P, and Ethan Allen Galleries). The result of all this is a romanticized, sentimentalized vision of the past, its "museumization."[7] What has survived from an early age of American self-discovery and its phenomenal political and intellectual ferment is merely the outwardly picturesque, while Americans have systematically neglected the ideological content, the genuine core of national existence.

The foregoing is only a sketch of the potentialities awaiting exploration by the historical or cultural geographer. There is much more to be learned about nationalistic elements in the landscapes of America, and we still await meaningful analyses of, and thus the possibility of cross-cultural approaches involving, landscape expressions of nationalism in countries outside North America. How exceptional is the American case? Is it simply representative of the perfected modern nation-state, but amid historical circumstances that render the phenomenon especially transparent? Or is the United States an aberration? What is certain is that careful, critical study of the historical geography of nationalism and statism in both their material and nonmaterial forms can educate us abundantly as to the essential meaning of these extraordinarily powerful forces.

Notes

1. For discussion of this phenomenon, see Louis Hartz, *The Founding of New Societies* (New York: Harcourt, Brace & World, 1964), and R. Cole Harris, "The Simplification of Europe Overseas," *Annals of the Association of American Geographers* 67 (December 1977), 469–83.

2. Among the more useful general treatments of nationalism and, at least implicitly, statism are Benedict Anderson, *Imagined Communities: Reflection on the Origin and Spread of Nationalism* (London: Verso, 1983); Carlton J. H. Hayes, *The Historical Evolution of Modern Nationalism* (New York: Richard R. Smith, 1931) and *Nationalism: A Religion* (New York: Macmillan, 1960); Harold R. Isaacs, *Idols of the Tribe: Group Identity and Political Change* (New York: Harper & Row, 1975); Boyd C. Shafer, *Faces of Nationalism: New Realities and Old Myths* (New York: Harcourt Brace Jovanovich, 1972); Anthony D. Smith, *Nationalist Movements* (New York: St. Martin's Press, 1977) and *Nationalism in the Twentieth Century* (New York: New York University Press, 1979).

3. I have derived this three-stage model of the sequential development of American nationalism/statism from a very wide range of documentary and other types of evidence and have it set forth in somewhat greater detail in "O Say, Can You See? Nationalistic Emblems in the Landscape," *Winterthur Portfolio* 19 (1985), 277–86.

4. Howard Mumford Jones, *O Strange New World. American Culture: The Formative Years* (New York: Viking, 1964), 227–72; Alan Gowans, *Images of American Living: Four Centuries of Architecture and Furniture as Cultural Expression* (Philadelphia: Lippincott, 1964), 243–84; Wilbur Zelinsky, "Classical Town Names in the United States: The Historical Geography of an American Idea," *Geographical Review* 57 (October 1967), 463–95.

5. J. Allwood, *The Great Exhibitions* (London: Studio Vista, 1977); Merle Curti, "America at World's Fairs: 1851–1893," *American Historical Review* 55 (July 1950), 833–56.

6. Robert Nisbet, *Twilight of Authority* (New York: Oxford University Press, 1975), 90.

7. David Lowenthal, "The American Way of History," *Columbia University Forum* 9 (1966), 27–32, and "The Bicentennial Landscape: A Mirror Held Up to the Past," *Geographical Review* 67 (July 1977), 253–67.

17

Tex-Map Mania: The Outline of Texas as a Popular Symbol

Richard V. Francaviglia

No state exploits its geopolitical outline more aggressively, and effectively, than Texas. The map of Texas is used to advertise thousands of Texas-owned and -operated businesses, Texas products, and Texas services. The average Texan sees daily the map outline on license plates, billboards, food products advertisements, and jewelry. The map complements and supplements "traditional" Texas popular imagery, such as the Lone Star, armadillos, oil wells, ten-gallon hats, and longhorn cattle.

This commentary explores the issue of popular cartography—especially the use of a map as an iconic symbol. In the case of Texas, the map outline helps to integrate time (history) and place (geography) in the popular mind. In an episode of *The Simpsons* on April 25, 1991, substitute teacher Mr. Bergstrom pretends to be a Great Plains cowboy from the 1830s, and challenges the students to tell him what is wrong with his cowboy outfit. Lisa Simpson quickly reels off the answers. One pertains to Bergstrom's Texas-shaped belt buckle, which Lisa tells him "can't be correct, because Texas didn't become a state until 1845." Lisa Simpson is something of a child genius, but historical cartographers will have to correct her, for the current shape of Texas dates from 1850: It took the Mexican War (and the Compromise of 1850) to yield the present outline.[1]

Thanks to aggressive promotion, that resulting outline has become one of America's most recognizable state maps. At the height of the Persian

---

Reprinted by permission from the *Journal of Cultural Geography* 12 (1991), 69–77.

Gulf crisis in 1991 an episode of *Saturday Night Live* used the outline to advantage by showing a map of Texas as the Middle East, to roars of laughter—perhaps an oblique reference to President George Bush's "line in the sand" statement that has subtle connections to the Battle of the Alamo. Generally, the public instantly recognizes the outline and many Texas college students can actually draw the map (or approximations of it) from memory.

Certainly, the prevalence of the map symbol in advertising graphics—from neon beer signs to the Texas Rangers logo—has conditioned people in unprecedented numbers to recognize the geographic outline of Texas. As a historical geographer interested in cartographic perceptions, however, I find the use of the state's outline on Texana (from earrings and T-shirts to bookmarks, ice cubes, and cookie cutters) to be intriguing, perhaps even predictable, because the outline of Texas possesses certain design characteristics that encourage its use as a symbol.

Putting aside for a moment the fact that it depicts a specific geographic area, the state's outline is associative, bringing certain abstract images to mind. Subconsciously, the Texas map outline may be viewed as a utilitarian shape: respondents have mentioned that, like a tool, perhaps a knife or dagger, it has a "handle" (Panhandle) at the "top" and a curving tip or point at the "bottom." It is also stereotypically geographical. As a cartographic representation, the outline of Texas is somewhat evocative of the larger countries or larger landmasses on the world map. With its bulging central section and its distorted, triangular base, the abstract proportions of Texas are eminently continental, perhaps basically subcontinental, vaguely reminding one of South America, Africa, or especially, the Indian subcontinent. Subconsciously, the shape or outline of Texas helps to reaffirm the state's size and geographic position, and to brand Texans as a particular people.

Even viewed by itself, the Texas map is subconsciously remembered in its position in the U.S. map. Texas is a major interlocking point in the perceptual morphology of the entire country. Viewed in geographic context, the outline of Texas is a crucial structural link, or keystone, holding the entire southern tier of states—and consequently the entire country itself—together. Texas intimately interlocks with other states, and it unites two major sections or regions (east and west). It is a crucial element that defines the southern and southwestern perimeter of the nation. Consider the dilemma faced by film characters Thelma and Louise as they attempted to reach Mexico from Oklahoma without traveling through Texas: An otherwise linear and direct journey became an epic circuitous odyssey.

A combination of several factors, including peripheral form and the proportions or "massing" of the image, help to make the map of Texas highly recognizable. Texas may *seem* to stretch interminably east and west, but in terms of its basic design, the map fits almost perfectly into a circle or square (Fig. 17–1). Squinting at a map of Texas makes one more aware of an important aspect of its morphology. Texas is, without question, the most "expansive" state in shape/outline—a distorted cross consisting of vertical and horizontal elements that intersect at a point somewhat off center. When viewed abstractly, its image is roughly cruciform—a combination of points (south and west) and blocks (north and east) protruding from a solid mass. And yet, the outline is also vaguely shaped like a star in that its perimeter has five (possibly six) "points." The integration of the map and the star is seen in a 1950s Humble Oil decal (Fig. 17–2). Somewhat significantly, the most acute or sharpest elements of the Texas outline are those at the south and west of the image; a visual thrust that may (subconsciously) reaffirm

Fig. 17–1. The Outline Map of Texas

Fig. 17–2. A Humble Oil Company Decal from the 1950s

both the "southern" and "southwestern" position of the state in the overall Sunbelt-oriented perceptual geography of the nation.

Although the roughly cruciform or stellar outline of Texas fits into either a square or a circle, it is not symmetrical. Internally, one finds a large block of space in what is (coincidentally) the most populous part of the state: south central and northeast Texas. This "bulge" invites the placement of visual information inside the outline, reaffirming Texas ownership or affiliation and/or validating a product or service placed within it. Common Texas maps contain the words "Texas-Made," and "Made in Texas," or "Made by Texans" inside the outline. Many businesses use the map to pinpoint their locations (most often with a star). Significantly, the map of Texas is associated with two seemingly opposing design forces: centrifugal, whereby the form encourages us to look at, or beyond, the edges or boundaries; and centripetal, wherein our attention is focused to the inside of the form as our eye is drawn inward toward the center. Thus, the outline of Texas makes an exciting, contradictory graphic in that it simultaneously encourages us to look toward both the core (reaffirming that anything placed within it is undeniably Texan) and the periphery. "Deep in the Heart of Texas" refers to a state of mind as well as a vaguely mythical place safely situated well within the state's rambling borders. The map of Texas defends or shelters a way of life by emphasizing a central nucleus. Graphically, the heart—like the center of a starfish or the converging axes of a cross—is the focus of centripetal energy: there is no better way to advertise a Texas product or service than to place it within the map boundaries. Small wonder, then, that many companies use the outline map to identify what they sell and to mark the location of their business enterprises.

Because the shape or outline of Texas is also centrifugal (or radiant), it has come to symbolize expansion, or expansiveness. As Texas has become the second most populous state, the map serves well as a territorial symbol of growth. Its outline is so easily recognized that up to half of it can be eliminated and the remaining half still says "Texas." The now familiar logo of Texas Instruments, introduced in the early 1950s, may mark the first international use of the Texas map as a symbol. Its design reaffirms the company's own identity, its Texas origins, and very importantly, the expansiveness of the company and the state.

In one truly ingenious packaging technique, the simulated leather cases of Texas Instruments ("TI") products often bear an embossed TI/Texas map logo, reminding one, perhaps, of a cattle brand. Some logos use only a portion of the state outline, for example, the Panhandle and Rio Grande, to convey Texas. Such map outlines may be termed dis-integrated or deconstructed, and they reaffirm the "recognizability" of certain portions of the Texas map outlines. Furthermore, the association between Texas and cattle reaffirms the expansive "Wild West" image. Significantly, the Texas map *is* used in about forty registered cattle brands, most of which are recent.[2] This supports my general observation that the use of the Texas map to symbolize "Texas" is a relatively recent phenomenon.

How, and when, did Tex-map mania begin? The state outline map may have been used first as an official border marker ("Welcome to Texas") during the 1936 Centennial. Today one sees many official uses of the outline, from a subtle background image on car titles, to a sobering outline for the numerous "DWI—You Can't Afford It" signs alongside roads and highways. By the 1950s the outline was being used on the Texas Historical Commission's historic markers.[3] Over the years since the 1930s, the map of Texas found its way into postcards, logos, and gift shop kitsch. By the 1950s, one could find Texas-shaped signs used in highway and main street advertising, as for example, a sign marking the Arlington State Bank.

By the Texas Sesquicentennial in 1986, *Espirit—The Magazine of the Mid-Cities* could illustrate "Deep in the Shape of Texas," a panoply of products shaped like the state.[4] Certainly, Tex-map mania is strongly associated with commerce and trade—especially services, food, and leisure products. Texas-shaped interlocking patio stones, hot tubs, and small adhesive-backed maps intended to shield the skin while sun tanning (when removed, these leave untanned areas in the shape of Texas on the body) underscore the fact that Tex-map mania affects Texans at leisure as well as at work. Many Texans immersed in the map fad report being "so used to seeing the map" that they are surprised to learn that the Texas map as icon is relatively recent, i.e., a mid- to late-twentieth-century phenomenon. It appears to be a product of mobility made possible by the automobile era, which in turn involves exposure to road maps. Texans are increasingly aware that their huge state is shrinking as a consequence of improved highways, commuter airlines, and the anticipated high-speed rail service that may link the state's largest cities.

Is the map of Texas used more frequently in some parts, or regions, of the state than others? Its appearance in Yellow Pages across the state suggests that it is very common throughout Texas, but it is used very heavily in tourist-conscious San Antonio and in metropolitan northeast Texas. Despite a growing sense of regionalism on the part of Texans who may also consider themselves residents of the "Hill Country," "West Texas," or "The Metroplex," the Texas map reinforces one's attachment to Texas as home.[5] The map outline can be found from border to border advertising all types of Texas products. One sees the Texas map symbol in urban, suburban, and rural settings—in all of the state's cultural regions.

Increasingly, a wide range of exported products (including groceries such as Texas okra, Texas beers, Tex-Mex foods, and Texas-style beans) has been actively marketed using the Texas map. These may reinforce the popular image of Texas as a colorful, vaguely ethnic, and somewhat trendy part of a much larger perceptual region—the Sunbelt.

Texas maps range in size depending on their intended use: jewelry, billboards, or earthworks. The smallest Texas outline is found on a small pin for an association of Texas science teachers, though diminutive earrings are close in size. The biggest Texas images are best seen from the air. Rumor has it that the Main Library at the University of Texas at Austin is shaped like the state, and a glimpse of the building from the air confirms that it could be creatively interpreted as such by those who see "Texas" in distorted cruciform shapes. The largest outline map of Texas is attributed to a farmer northeast of Rockfall, who recently excavated a large map-shaped farm pond "almost 250 feet long . . . to let folks know he's fond of living in

Texas."[6] One can only imagine the reaction that this vernacular earthwork gets from air travelers flying into and out of the Dallas-Fort Worth Metroplex.

Has the state outline reached its apex of popularity in recent years (that is, has it become so well known or predictable that it will soon lose its impact or novelty?), or will it continue to flourish as a symbol of identity and patriotism? If the outline map has not reached its zenith of iconic utility/popularity, will it become so popular that it will endanger or replace the premier state symbol—the Lone Star? (If this seems impossible, recall that this recently happened in license plates.)

The Lone Star was the first widely used Texas symbol: in the nineteenth century it was used in the logo of the Houston & Texas Central Railroad, and it symbolized Texas to those who saw its freight cars rolling across the United States. Since the 1930s, Texaco (Texas Oil Company) has made very effective use of the Lone Star as an advertising symbol—"You can trust your car to the man who wears the star . . . "—and many businesses continued the tradition in the 1940s and '50s. Today, however, fewer and fewer businesses use the star as their primary identity, while many more are using the Texas map. In fact, many businesses named "Lone Star . . ." have adopted the map outline as their logo, with the star appearing to mark location.

As the map identity has become stronger, one now occasionally sees the Texas map outline actually substituting for (i.e., replacing) the Lone Star in some clever version of the Texas flag, or quite commonly, the rectangular shape of the Texas flag replaced by the Texas map outline so that the map actually becomes a flag. Rather than being iconoclastic, these modifications to the Texas flag appear to confirm, and perhaps further encourage, Texans' nearly legendary pride in their state. Whereas the Lone Star is a highly abstract image that connotes independence, the map outline of Texas is a tangible symbol of place. Unlike the star, the map is never confused with any other symbol; thus, it is now probably more functional than the Lone Star image in advertising "Texas."

Conclusion

Studying Tex-map mania can help us understand more about the state's changing identity, which may actually transcend national identity. Many Texans consider themselves residents of a country (Texas) as well as residents of a nation (the United States). I am reminded of the time pro-choice demonstrators at an international rally in Washington, D.C., were asked to march in appropriate columns—one for the states and the other for countries: The Texas flag-bearing contingent immediately walked over to the international section!

Being rooted in a brief but romanticized republican past, Texas offers a geographic identity that is unique in the history of the United States. In other words, the power of "Imperial Texas," as geographer D. W. Meinig identified it, is still an operative memory today.[7] Texans will always remind visitors and newcomers that they stood alone in their fight for independence and held a sprawling frontier empire peripheral to both the United States and Mexico. Thus, the state map helps Texans reaffirm a historical/ mystical sense of place as their state has become more and more international in its orientation.

In the late twentieth century, Tex-map mania helps us understand that a map can serve many purposes and, in its most elementary form—the outline, become an icon or symbol of identity. When a geographic outline is truly distinctive, and can substitute for other more abstract symbols, it can effectively symbolize history, identity, and attachment to place.

Notes

1. A discussion of the changing borders of Texas is provided in Robert S. Martin and James C. Martin, *Contours of Discovery: Printed Maps Delineating the Texas and Southwestern Chapters in the Cartographic History of North America, 1513–1930. A User's Guide* (Austin: Texas State Historical Association, 1982).

2. Personal communication, Carol Williams, curator of the Cattlemen's Museum, Fort Worth, February 14, 1992.

3. James Steely, "THC Medallion Dates to 1961," *Medallion* 25 (October 1989), 1.

4. Erin O'Donnell, "Deep in the Shape of Texas," *Espirit, The Magazine of the Mid-Cities* 3 (March 1986), 40–41.

5. Terry Jordan, with John L. Bean Jr. and William M. Holmes, *Texas: A Geography* (Boulder, Colo.: Westview Press, 1984); Terry Jordan, "Perceptual Regions of Texas." *Geographical Review* 68 (1978), 293–307.

6. Marilyn Schwartz, "Feelings Go Deep for the Great State," *Dallas Morning News* (October 15, 1992), Section C 1.

7. D. W. Meinig, *Imperial Texas: An Interpretive Essay in Cultural Geography* (Austin: University of Texas Press, 1969).

18

Selected Reading VI

Chapters 16 and 17

Archer, J. C., and Shelley, F. M. *American Electoral Mosaics.* Washington, D.C.: Association of American Geographers, 1986.

Brunn, Stanley D. *Geography and Politics in America.* New York: Harper & Row, 1974.

Combs, James. *Polpop 2: Politics and Popular Culture in America Today.* Bowling Green, Ohio: Popular Press, 1991.

Elazar, Daniel J. *American Federalism: The View from the States.* New York: Harper & Row, 1984 (3rd ed.).

————. *The American Mosaic: The Impact of Space, Time, and Culture on American Politics.* Boulder, Colo.: Westview Press, 1994.

Francaviglia, Richard V. *The Shape of Texas: Maps as Metaphors.* College Station: Texas A&M University Press, 1995.

Johnston, R. J. *The Geography of Federal Spending in the United States.* London: Wiley, 1981.

Kodras, J. E., and Jones, J. P., III (eds.). *Geographic Dimensions of United States Social Policy.* London: Edward Arnold, 1990.

Martis, Kenneth C. *The Historical Atlas of United States Congressional Districts.* New York: Macmillan, 1982.

————. *The Historical Atlas of Political Parties in the United States Congress, 1789–1989.* New York: Macmillan, 1989.

Pearcy, G. Etzel. *A Thirty-Eight State USA.* Fullerton, Calif.: Plycon Press, 1973.

Zelinsky, Wilbur. *Nation into State: The Shifting Symbolic Foundations of American Nationalism.* Chapel Hill: University of North Carolina Press, 1988.

Part VII: Sports

Whether we call it "sports," "athletics," "games," or "play," this aspect of popular culture has become ubiquitous in America. The influence of sports on societies ranging from the bloody Roman spectacles to the staged demonstrations of the modern Olympiad and the Super Bowl is simply overwhelming. Sports, as one observer has claimed, is the new opiate of the masses.

According to Paul Weiss, a sports philosopher, sports and games are irrevocably divided from the workaday world. Weiss reminds us that "sport" means "to disport," i.e., to divert and amuse. Hence, sport is that segment of popular culture by which humans divert themselves from labor. As we look to the future, one observation appears certain—humans will play as long as there is time called leisure after work is done.

Sports have become a major research arena for cultural geographers. Two of the most prolific scholars on sports geography are Richard Pillsbury and John F. Rooney Jr., represented herein with articles on stock car racing and golf, respectively. They recently collaborated on one of the most exhaustive treatments on American sports, *The Atlas of American Sport* (1992).

According to Pillsbury, stock car racing is clearly one of the most visible elements of southern popular culture. It has developed not only an extensive following, but also a widespread mythology. In chapter 19, he examines the origins and distribution of stock car racing to determine if the sport has a southern orientation. Based on southern-born drivers and the location of headline events, Pillsbury notes that stock car racing peaked in the region in the 1960s and 1970s. In chapter 20, he emphasizes that the southern tradition has vastly changed in the 1980s and 1990s in personnel, fans, and types of tracks. The drivers are no longer exclusively southern and the "good old boy" fans are slowly being replaced by "city-slickers" from the North, who attend the happenings as much for the theaterlike atmosphere as for the actual races. Pillsbury concludes that as the nationalization of the sport continues, stock car racing, like most traditions in the South, is on the verge of losing its regional distinctiveness.

Much of Rooney's latest work has focused on the distribution of golf course facilities in the United States, especially since the golf boom of the 1960s. In chapter 21, he teams with Robert Adams, a geographer from the University of New Hampshire, on a regionalization of golf course supply and demand. They delimit seven regions that illustrate that the "Northern

Heartland" and "South Atlantic" areas are strongest in golf interest as compared with the "Southern Void" where fascination with the game wanes. They further analyze the best- and worst-served cities, indicating that midwestern metropoles fall in the former category while urban areas on the East and West coasts represent the latter group. In chapter 22, Rooney assesses golf course construction from 1987 to 1993. He concludes that during that period some of the regional inequities have been alleviated; however, substantial deficit areas still exist in California and the Northeast.

19

Carolina Thunder: A Geography of Southern Stock Car Racing

Richard Pillsbury

Early stock car racing was frequently unorganized and often held informally on public highways, pastures, or almost any other flat area large enough for racing. By the late thirties and early forties the sport began to be more structured, with small quarter-mile and half-mile dirt tracks scattered throughout the country. In the Midwest the most famous center was Soldier's Field in Chicago; other early centers were located in Upstate New York and adjacent New England, southern California, and of course the southern piedmont. In the South, racing was poorly developed during this period, and it was not uncommon for many of the early drivers to spend part of the season traveling the northern and midwestern racing circuits. The real turning point for stock car racing in the South seems to have been the opening of the first superspeedway at Darlington, South Carolina, on Labor Day, 1950. Over 30,000 fans turned out at this first major-league stock car race and racing in the South was never the same again.[1]

Today the most important races are controlled and sanctioned by one of two racing bodies: the National Association for Stock Car Auto Racing (NASCAR) and the United States Auto Club (USAC). NASCAR, the older of the two, was formed in 1948 and held its first race the same month in Daytona Beach, Florida. The Grand National Division, the most prestigious division of NASCAR, was created the following year and features what appear to be late-model street cars, or at least autos closely related to them.

Reprinted by permission from the *Journal of Geography* 73 (1974), 39–47.

The number of sanctioned Grand National races expanded rapidly during the early years: nine held in the 1949 season; 36 in 1954; 43 in 1959; reaching a maximum of 62 in 1964. The prize money has also increased, with an estimated purse of $2,601,965 in 1971, not including various types of residuals available to winning drivers from sponsors and other sources. The 1971 NASCAR Record Book, for example, states that the champion K & K Insurance team netted more than $100,000 in 1970 from these residuals.[2] In recent years NASCAR clearly has dominated stock car racing both in terms of prestige and potential prize money.

The United States Auto Club was formed in 1955 when the American Automobile Association, the dominant racing organization to that time, stopped sanctioning auto racing. The activities of USAC are somewhat more diverse than those of NASCAR as a result and the racing portion of the organization includes four main divisions: the Marlboro Championship Trail, Stock car, Sprint car, and Midget. The Championship Trail, or Indianapolis-type racing, has always dominated USAC, and some writers have described the stock car division as the almost forgotten stepchild of the organization.[3] As a result of this apparent lack of interest in stock cars USAC has sponsored a limited number of stock car events, only twenty in 1970, and the prize money has never equaled either that of the Marlboro Championship Trail or NASCAR's Grand National circuit.

Possibly the greatest distinction between the drivers of the two sanctioning bodies has been the NASCAR drivers' concentration on a single type of event, the stock car race. Typically USAC drivers compete in a cross-section of racing events and in recent years increasingly in NASCAR Grand National events because of the large purses. A. J. Foyt, one of America's most famous race drivers, is primarily a USAC driver and is widely known for his three Indianapolis 500 wins. Foyt's interests typically extend beyond USAC driving, however, and he also is a past winner of the Le Mans 24-hour endurance race and in the 1972 Grand National season won the first two major races. In contrast, few NASCAR Grand National favorites would even consider driving in such a variety of races and with only occasional exceptions almost entirely restrict themselves to stock cars in one type of event or another.

Distribution of Stock Car Racing

The distribution of stock car racing today shows a dual pattern. When all tracks are considered, stock car racing clearly is not a regional activity in any sense of the word. Stock car tracks of some type are found scattered throughout the country, and every section of the United States apparently has stock car racing in some form. Even major tracks are fairly widely distributed, the areas of paucity indicated on Figure 19–1 being as much a function of the low population densities in the central United States as any other factor. The distribution of major-league racing, however, shows a much more restricted pattern. If we consider residences of major drivers as a surrogate measure of regional interest in stock car racing, it is evident that while racing may be widely spread, levels of interest are not (Fig. 19–2). Most areas of the country have produced a few favorite drivers, but the top professionals in the sport appear to come from four major regions: the Carolina-Virginia piedmont; a band of cities extending from Wisconsin through central Indiana; southern New England and adjacent Upstate New York; and central and southern California.

All of these areas were early centers of stock car racing and all apparently still have major concentrations of the sport. But are the levels of interest in the various regions of equal importance? An examination of the number and types of tracks, sizes of major race purses, and extraregional fame of local drivers would indicate that this is not the case. Stock car racing per se may be locally important in each of the regions, but only has the South and the southern-dominated NASCAR Grand National division been able to project itself into a national image. Few Americans outside of the local areas involved, for example, can name the stars or even the major races of the southern California or the Upstate New York circuits. In contrast most racing fans have at least heard of such NASCAR stars as Richard Petty and Bobby Allison, and such races as the Daytona 500 and Darlington 500 are nationally telecast.[4] To further emphasize this point it should be indicated that the Grand National circuit is not restricted to the southeastern states, it is just dominated by them. Extraregional drivers have competed in Grand National races from its earliest days with some of these Yankees such as Charley Glotzbach, Pete Hamilton, and Fred Lorenzen becoming widely recognized for their driving ability. Major NASCAR races also have long been held outside of the region, including those at Riverside International Raceway in California, Michigan International Speedway at Irish Hills, and Dover Downs in Delaware. It would appear that there has been sufficient opportunity for other regions to develop a major stock car tradition, but not the interest.

Why the South and more specifically the Carolina-Virginia piedmont should have developed as the major center of top-flight stock car racing in America is not clear. Some authors and many race fans have attributed the growth of great drivers in that region to the importance of moonshining. They suggest that the early drivers learned their trade running "shine" and

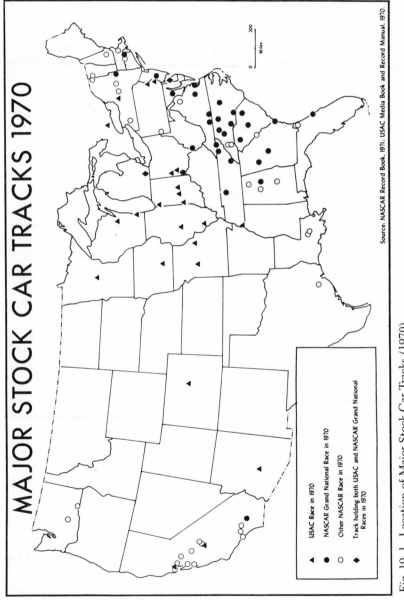

MAJOR STOCK CAR TRACKS 1970

USAC Race in 1970

NASCAR Grand National Race in 1970

Other NASCAR Race in 1970

Track holding both USAC and NASCAR Grand National
Races in 1970

Source: NASCAR Record Book, 1971; USAC Media Book and Record Manual, 1970.

Fig. 19–1. Location of Major Stock Car Tracks (1970)

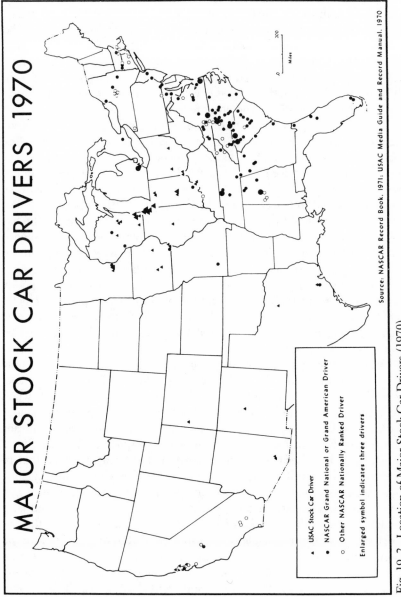

MAJOR STOCK CAR DRIVERS 1970

Source: NASCAR Record Book, 1971; USAC Media Guide and Record Manual, 1970

△ USAC Stock Car Driver

● NASCAR Grand National or Grand American Driver

○ Other NASCAR Nationally Ranked Driver

Enlarged symbol indicates three drivers

Fig. 19–2. Location of Major Stock Car Drivers (1970)

racing on Friday nights.[5] There seems to be little doubt that this was at least occasionally the case in the good old days of dirt tracks, heavy unmodified cars, and barnstorming drivers trying to make a living in a very unorganized sport. But it seems questionable that moonshining has been a significant force in the development of stock car racing as we know it today. In modern racing the cars are not adaptable to moonshine running, the drivers have little time for such hazardous extracurricular activities, and much of the moonshine is traveling not by car, but by truck. If moonshine had been the real underlying growth force for stock car racing in the South, the sport probably would not have developed much past the Super Modified cars that still dominate the other regions of the country.

A more plausible alternative to the moonshine explanation for the recent rapid growth in interest in stock car racing in the South was suggested by Richard Petty who pointed out that "Open-cockpit racing cars never caught on in the South, nor even midget racers. I guess it's just the people in the South were so poor, and those fancy race cars were so exotic that they didn't know what to make of them. People *identify* with stock cars" (italics added).[6] The truth of this view is immediately apparent to anyone who has owned a foreign car in the South. Foreign and sports car sales and service outside of the major cities has been almost nonexistent. Foreign and/or exotic cars seem to have never held much fascination for southerners. Whether this occurred because of a case of acute chauvinism or a poorly developed economy that could not afford many of these expensive vehicles is not entirely clear. One direct result, however, is that stock car racing now enjoys a more devoted grassroots following than any other sport in the South except football.[7]

The present stature of stock car racing in the South is a result of not only positive growth within the region, but also the relative lack of parallel growth in other areas of the country. During the 1930s and 1940s when stock car racing was in its infancy the sport was widely spread throughout the country. But during the critical 1950s and early 1960s when significant growth took place within the South, bringing the sport to legitimacy, little growth occurred elsewhere in the country. It has been suggested that in contrast to the South, where stock cars were the only race cars available, race enthusiasts in other regions became interested during this critical period in a variety of cars, beginning first with foreign sports cars and later branching out to the European Grand Prix cars. The interests of the talented and the wealthy outside the South all too often were diverted to the more exotic specialty race cars, relegating stock car racing to a subsidiary role in their interests. This is not meant to suggest that stock car racing declined in absolute numbers in the North and West during the fifties and sixties, so much as it is intended to indicate that stock car racing in these regions did not grow during the critical period when the sport reached its prime in the South.

The distribution of stock car racing within the South is not uniform by any means. As examination of the distribution of the top ten NASCAR drivers from 1949 to the present indicates not only the relatively concentrated regional distribution of the sport within the region, but also that the distribution has changed through time. In 1949 five of the top ten drivers lived in metropolitan Atlanta, while three were located in the North Carolina piedmont, one in Virginia, and one lone Yankee in the Chicago area (Fig. 19–3). During the 1950s with the decline of the famous Flock brothers from Atlanta, the concentration of drivers shifted northward to center in the Carolinas and Virginia. By 1964 almost all the top drivers had become located in the South with the relative decline of stock car racing outside the region, and in 1969 we find that all ten top Grand National drivers lived in three states: North and South Carolina and Virginia. In essence, what is evident from these distributional maps and Figure 19–4 is that NASCAR Grand National drivers have gone through three phases. During the early period NASCAR was essentially a regional organization, although there were some competitors from outside the area. During the 1960s the overall pattern contracted severely with the decline of stock car racing in general, and by 1964 all of the top drivers either were from the region originally or in a few scattered instances had adopted it as their homes. The final phase, not apparent in Figure 19–3 but quite evident in the map showing the distribution of all Grand National Drivers in 1970, indicates a reversal of the consolidation phase and a general broadening of the impact of Grand National racing. In 1970, 40 percent of the drivers resided outside the old strongholds of the Carolinas, Virginia, Georgia, and Alabama, and this trend becomes increasingly pronounced as each year passes.

The factors that have led to this new widespread interest in Grand National stock car racing are complex, but seem to be associated primarily with increased publicity through telecasting of the races and the ever greater purses of the major events. It is interesting to note that during the early 1950s little news of NASCAR events was published in major regional newspapers, and indeed one or more people needed to be killed before either the *New York Times* or even the *Atlanta Constitution* would carry the results of any major race other than Daytona Speedweek. By the late 1960s more news was carried in both newspapers and magazines and most races were at least reported in the major regional newspapers. According to many writers and drivers, it was the telecasting of major races during the late 1960s that was the turning point in promoting a new national following for

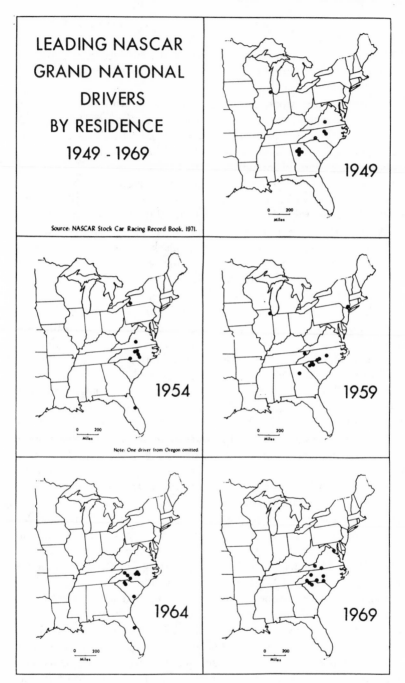

LEADING NASCAR
GRAND NATIONAL
DRIVERS
BY RESIDENCE
1949 - 1969

Source: NASCAR Stock Car Racing Record Book, 1971.

1949

1954

Note: One driver from Oregon omitted.

1959

1964

1969

Fig. 19–3. Leading NASCAR Grand National Drivers by Residence (1949–69)

GRAND NATIONAL DRIVERS, 1970

Note: Map does not include one driver residing in Porterville, California.　　　Source: NASCAR Record Book, 1970.

Fig. 19–4. Location of Grand National Drivers (1970)

the sport. Today many people who have never attended a Grand National race now follow and can quickly spot Petty's number 43 Dodge, Junior Johnson's Chevrolet, and the Wood Brothers' Mercury.

Conclusion

In conclusion, it is clear that the actual pattern of stock car racing little resembles its myth. While most southerners believe that stock car racing is a peculiarly southern institution, it actually has nationally distributed roots and the beginnings of a rebirth of national interest. Basically the pattern of stock car racing has gone through three stages: an initial period of nationally diffused interest before the development of a large following; a formative period in which stock car racing gained a regional identity as other sections lost interest; and a modern period of decentralization. The map of 1970 Grand National driver residence locations indicates that this decentralization process is quickening, which is further amplified by the 1972 and 1973 seasons. During the 1972 season Richard Petty, voted several times as the most popular NASCAR driver, joined with Andy Granatelli, a longtime USAC competitor, to compete as a team. The first two races of that season were won by an outsider, A. J. Foyt, while the first race of the 1973 season was won by Mark Donahue of suburban Philadelphia. Thus, like many regional traditions, stock car racing apparently is losing its southern regional identity with the onslaught of national attention and interest, although slowly.

Notes

1. Richard Petty, *Grand National: The Autobiography of Richard Petty* (Chicago: Regency, 1971), 30.
2. Phil Homer (ed.), *Stock Car Racing Record Book* (Daytona Beach: NASCAR News Bureau, 1970).
3. *USAC Media Guide and Record Manual* (Indianapolis: United States Auto Club, 1970), 35–56.
4. It was a shock to many racing fans in 1972 when Petty teamed with Andy Granatelli and painted his car Petty blue *and* STP red.
5. "Stock-Car Racing Riding High," *Business Week* (August 12, 1950), 23.
6. Ray Blount, "Million-Dollar Sunday Driver," *Sports Illustrated* 35 (1971), 17.
7. Ibid.

20

A Mythology at the Brink: Stock Car Racing in the American South

Richard Pillsbury

Fireball Roberts is gone. The Petty listed on the leader board is more likely to be Kyle than Richard. Junior Johnson and Cale Yarborough are successful businessmen up in North Carolina. The thought of a driver appearing in the family Buick at the Charlotte track to do battle at a Grand National event with the expectation of driving it to church on Sunday is too bizarre to even consider as a historical incident. King Richard still drives, but hasn't won a race for so long even he probably can't remember. Even the Saturday night dirt track races are disappearing, giving way to Sunday extravaganzas on their reincarnated short paved ovals.

There is little room for the antics and lifestyles of the good old boys of yesteryear. Speeds exceeding 200 miles per hour, six-figure racing machines, steely-eyed financial types looking over your shoulder, and television cameras everywhere make it difficult to raise hell anymore. Fellows in three-piece suits have seemingly taken the sport and made it into an industry. And one accepts it because the money is good, competitive cars are expensive, and the fame isn't too bad either. The South is changing and good old-timey southern stock car racing is changing right along with it.

Family Grand National racing teams with brother Bill driving the car on Sundays, brother Ernie acting as crew chief and engine builder, and Dan working in the shop and on the crew have all but passed from the scene—

Reprinted by permission from *Sport Place: An International Journal of Sports Geography* 3 (1989), 3–12.

the Elliotts of Dawsonville, Georgia, notwithstanding. More typical today is the Hendricks Motorsports organization and its recently built 50,000-square-foot car-building facility in Harrisonburg, North Carolina. Hendricks races four or more cars, including three Grand National cars under different sponsors. The Motorsports operation, however, is just a small part of the Hendricks organization, which includes more than fifteen automobile dealerships and a seemingly endless list of other activities. And while the Hendricks operation may be one of the largest in the sport, it is far from unusual. Stock car racing is a big and good business. It is also an important business in this region as it reaches an entire class of consumers.

First, we must understand that stock car racing does not play the same role throughout the region. The center of NASCAR Grand National racing is in North Carolina and surrounding states. The sport initially had an almost national aspect to its distribution, with drivers from throughout the eastern states and races not only in the South, but in the Northeast and Midwest as well. The first 500-mile race sponsored by NASCAR, however, was at Darlington, South Carolina. Over the years the number of midwestern races has declined, the role of the California circuit became less important to the greater scheme of things, and the forays into the Northeast were more pro forma than real.

Simultaneously the circuit has maintained major races in such obscure locations as Martinsburg, Darlington, and other places which are far from the madding crowds with tracks that would be judged inadequate if put forth for a race at any other venue. Broadcasts of the NASCAR races similarly reflect this bias. While national audiences tune in for the ESPN and traditional network television broadcasts, it must be remembered that *Beach Volleyball* and *Green Acres* also gain national audiences as well. The radio network, in contrast, is almost entirely concentrated in the Atlantic coast home areas. Walk into a gas station in the fall in eastern Tennessee, southwestern Virginia, or North Carolina on a Sunday and the play-by-play will not be describing NFL combat, but rather the shoving matches between the Skoal Bandit and Coors/Melling. That these folks take their car racing serious can be seen by the car carrier in the rear of the station with a few worn spare tires still lying on the raised rack.

The rise and continuing important role of stock car racing in southern life has much to do with the region's personality and historic isolation from the mainstream of American cultural life. There has been and continues to be a plethora of professional sporting alternatives in the region. There were few professional sports organizations based in the South until recently, except for the hapless Atlanta teams—frequent poor performers located in a city that is far from universally loved by the rural southerner. This lack of quality sports entertainment is often solved by local fans following their university teams. Many southern men indeed do follow their local university basketball and football teams. However, fewer than 15 percent of most NASCAR region southerners have graduated from college and fewer than 60 percent have graduated from high school. Educational levels in the rural areas, where stock car racing is followed most avidly, are even lower. It is extremely difficult for these folks to identify, much less avidly follow, the "dawgs" or "cocks" when they were disenfranchised from this part of the regional life at birth.

Car racing, on the other hand, has long been the spectator sport of the "good old boys." Richard Petty, Junior Johnson, and Bill Elliott are country boys with little formal schooling and obvious "aw shucks" origins. They represent the success of the disenfranchised good old boy against the system. These men have it all without a college degree, or Ralph Lauren jeans or Perrier water. Fans tell and retell stories of Richard Petty going to the White House in a tow truck. The pressure to get "in touch" with King Richard has led to the expansion of the Petty racing compound in Level Cross, North Carolina, to house a popular museum and daily tours. Bill Elliott's squeaky clean family life and his use of the popular Ford products have inevitably brought him the king's mantle even while Petty still tools around the track remembering past glories. The Elliotts open their shops each year on a Sunday for a one-day tour to more than ten thousand people. No mean trick in tiny, rural Dawsonville, Georgia.

The typical rural southerner identifies with these drivers. In fact, race fans actually do not follow the fortunes of Ford or Buick or Chevrolet in these mortal combats, rather they follow and talk about Elliott and Dale Earnhardt and the king—that's Petty not Presley. The Skoal Bandit, the Coors/Melling team, Kodiak, and many other car and sponsor names may appear on the seemingly endless stream of racing paraphernalia. Everyone knows Richard Petty is the blue and red number 43; Harry Gant is the Skoal Bandit; and Bill Elliott is the Coors/Melling red number 9. The stars in this system are the drivers, not the machines.

The Theater of Motor Sports

The mythology and reality of stock car racing cannot be totally comprehended outside the actual race setting. While all sports have theatrical aspects to their character, in many ways stock car racing gains its primary identity from its stage setting. Tailgate parties and dressing up in the colors of one's favorite team add to the individual's enjoyment of college football games; for stock car fans these are the total event.

Despite organization changes, the actual sporting event—the theater of stock car racing—is much the same today as it has always been. Strictly speaking, southern stock car racing is not a single sport, rather it is composed of three separate stock car racing milieus that attract essentially three unique audiences. While almost all fans have been to all three event types, few regularly attend more than a single type of race. The three basic types include the Winston Cup Grand National circuit, the short paved tracks, and the even shorter dirt tracks of the Sportsmen, Modified, and other "lesser" divisions.

The Talladega 500

Grand National racing is the epitome of the sport, and the Talladega 500 is one of the classic events. The Alabama International Motor Speedway is a 2.66-mile high-speed oval lying almost sunken beneath the red clay of central Alabama. Located a mile south of Interstate 20, the speedway is barely evident to passing expressway motorists and could easily be missed by spectators arriving on the access road, except for the crowds on race days.

Spectators begin arriving in numbers the Thursday before Sunday's race in RVs, pickup campers, and cars to stake out good camping locations for the ensuing sporting weekend. Most early visitors come from out of state, often North and South Carolina, where they regularly arrange their work schedules to take vacation, leave, or extended weekends on these all-important weekends—much like avid deer hunters who become ill on the Friday before opening day.

Most race fans begin the long drive on Sunday morning. The stream of cars along I-20 west out of Atlanta picks up noticeably on racing morning. One is soon able to spot other spectators on the way to the race by their bumper stickers, dress, and cars. They arrive early and stay late. By noon the backup on the Interstate extends for miles. Nearing the track from the east one first encounters the souvenir area with about a dozen trailers gathered alongside the road hawking trinkets depicting the heroes. The large crowds around these booths get into the mood of the day by purchasing T-shirts and hats naming their favorite drivers. A few trailers are devoted to a single driver, while more typically the trailer shops specialize in several drivers. The breadth of the paraphernalia is almost beyond comprehension; the amount of sales is amazing.

Most arriving spectators do not hurry to their seats once settled in the sea of parked autos and trucks. In fact the parking lot becomes the center of the action for the next several hours. Barbecues are set up next to the tailgate, coolers opened, and contents consumed. The sweetish smell of marijuana soon hangs heavy over the parking lot as the blue-collar rednecks meet old and new friends and the "real" devotees get down to some serious beer drinking, eating, and discussion about the ensuing race. Rivalries are dredged up; the technical "equalizer" of the month debated; old stories about previous races attended discussed.

It should not be construed from this description, however, that these spectators are "poor white trash" who just wandered out of the deepest woods of Erskine Caldwell's tobacco road. Their cars are late-model American speed machines. Their pickup trucks are expensive, pampered chariots. Not many '55 Chevy half-tons with gun racks on the rear windows make it to Grand National races these days. The cheapest seats in the poorest grandstands sell for more $20 each and prices rise quickly. Attendance is expensive and most can easily afford it.

As race time nears, fans increasingly make their way to the stands to drink more beer and discuss the passing parade. The parade, and that truly is the only term for it, consists of an armada of scantily clad young women roaming back and forth across the front of the stands ostensibly looking for their seats, although four hours and forty-six passes later they are still looking. Crowd response to these young women becomes increasingly pointed as the heat rises and the beer flows. First wolf calls erupt as the more attractive, less dressed damsels parade down the platform, then Rebel yells follow, and finally more explicit requests to "take it off" are shouted out. The drama culminates some time after the beginning of the race when a young lady accommodates the crowd and parades topless down the front walkway of the stands until the security guards arrive. The ensuing discussion with the security team usually fills the second quarter of the race's tedium.

Oh yes, the race. The track surface is sunk well below ground level at Talladega and other high-speed tracks to protect the spectators from that occasional flying car cartwheeling down the straightaway. The straightaway also means that the cars will be traveling in excess of 220 miles per hour past the stands. The cars are identified primarily by the numbers painted on their tops, the only part one can see from the grandstand. Each pass takes about twelve or thirteen seconds to run the length of the grandstands. The presence of thirty or more cars in a pack makes each pass last about thirty seconds. This goes on, with sufficient yellow caution flags to bunch the pack whenever it starts to lengthen out too much, 188 times or so until the race is over.

The fact that few watch the race is quite understandable. Not many can actually see the race. The only people who have a good view are the few hundred sitting in the skyboxes or similar quarters, which are outfitted with comfortable chairs, bars, bathrooms (a real problem in the grandstands with all that beer flowing), and a multiscreen closed-circuit television system showing the entire race. A handful of people sitting on top of the tallest RVs in the infield also have a good view, as do the few thousand additional people at Talladega sitting in the highest section of the grandstand. Everyone else has come for the excitement of the afternoon, the roar of the crowd, the beer, and the cries to "take it *all* off!"

Lanier Raceway—Dirt Track

The dirt track occupied the opposite end of the stock car spectrum. Lanier Raceway was a typical dirt track located in northern Georgia, interestingly enough across the road from Road Atlanta, a road track used for IMSA and other exotic racing. It was a traditional southern 3/8-mile clay track with a concrete grandstand built into the hillside overlooking it. The opposing side was somewhat atypical as it had been dug out into a series of terraces where families sat on lawn chairs in the back of their pickups and watched the race in style.

Races were run every Saturday night with the gates opening at 4:30 and racing beginning at 7:30. This was the lowest level of sanctioned racing. The drivers arrived as soon as they got off work and loaded up with their pride in tow on two-wheel trailers.

There were no full-time professionals among these drivers, although many spent more time preparing their cars than working on their regular jobs. Several classes of cars were run, ranging from essentially street cars with numbers taped on their sides with duct tape to super modifieds, which probably were not recognized by their mothers.

The track was wet down during the afternoon to make it slick. As race time approached, cars warmed up on the track to road-check their performance and help harden the track surface. The noise was deafening—it was not by accident that these tracks were located far from population concentrations. Racing began with a minimum of fuss as warm-up laps merged into races. The novice classes began first. Scant attention was paid to these racers, except by family and friends. Accidents were too frequent to count, and the slippery clay track, the mechanically unsound cars (some didn't even make it through the warm-up rounds before conking out), and the less experienced drivers all contributed to exciting racing and numerous caution laps. Speeds were low, less than 80 miles per hour mostly, and the safety equipment was designed for speeds twice that.

Dirt track racing was not only the most unsophisticated level of racing, it also attracted the least elite audience. The crowd essentially was composed of individuals and families from the lowest, most isolated social and income brackets. This was primarily a family affair—from the drivers, whose wives and girlfriends shouted advice from the pits during the race; to the track owner, whose daughter was "Miss Lanier Raceway"; to the spectators, who brought wives, young'uns, and friends for an evening of entertainment.

Most of the drivers and spectators were regulars who came every week to cheer on their friends and acquaintances. You would see old-timers who still liked to race; young drivers hoping against hope that they would be noticed by potential sponsors and be able to move up the racing ladder; frustrated men of all ages living out a dream as best they could with their limited resources. The crowd was friendly. The mood was a family one where all were there to have a good time. No one felt the need to put on airs or their Sunday best or acted out scenarios. This was the rural South at its best as one encountered folks that rarely went to town, who felt uncomfortable at the Atlanta suburban shopping malls, but would be found affirming their faith at the country fundamentalist church on Sunday morning.

Lanier Raceway—Paved Short Track

The middle ground of stock car racing is filled with the paved short track. The dirt track is rapidly disappearing from the scene today as track owners upgrade their facilities to meet the rising expectations of their clientele. Lanier Raceway was paved in 1988 and the changes that have taken place are interesting in that they well illustrate the essence of the differences between dirt track and paved short track racing.

First the races themselves were moved from Friday or Saturday night to Sunday afternoons. Many of the dirt track spectators seem to be gone, moving on to some other dirt track in the area to continue their Saturday night tradition. The spectators are obviously more middle class, or at least upper lower class in their cars and dress and lifestyle. More beer appears, along with more of the behavior common to the superspeedways, although these tracks are too close to home for female parades.

The competition is different as well. The cars generally have been upgraded, although many of the drivers are the same. The trailers and stacks of spare tires mirror larger investments by their owners as does the race itself. Most serious drivers and fans are still friends, but somehow the mood is more reserved, more "middle-class festive."

Speeds are also higher, with the new track surface and accidents more spectacular. One recent Sunday racing card averaged an accident on every third lap in every race all day long. Not to worry, the ambulance still was used only once—to hustle a corpulent spectator to the hospital to check on a severe case of heat stroke probably brought on by drinking too much beer and eating too much barbecue.

It is clear that the short paved tracks are the bridge between the good old boys of the past and the corporate entertainers of the future. The stakes have been raised with the paving of the tracks, the cars have been improved, the psychological distance between the competitors and the spectators increased, and the audience upgraded. A little more of the traditional South has been lost. Someday these races may be known as the last stand of the good old boys. Television crews will come in search of the "real" South, writers will talk about going back to their roots in these places, and professors will pontificate about what it all means. Few will know or care about the dirt tracks that came before or the Saturday nights they entailed. None will recognize that these sporting events are not the last vestiges of a past that never was, but the beginnings of a new, sanitized, nationally tuned, regional culture.

Car Races, Spectators, and Mythology

Like many professional sports events today, the modern automobile race is best watched from the convenience of one's own living room. Visibility of the entire track is only possible at the smallest facilities and as a result few spectators spend much of their event time watching the races. Fewer yet are interested in the actual outcome of the race. The road out of Talladega and Road Atlanta and Lanier Raceway is packed with cars long before the checkered flag flutters.

Obviously people attend these sporting events for reasons other than the outcome. People attend for the color, for the excitement, for the opportunity to mingle with others with like interests—much the same reasons that people attend any professional sporting event. People also attend to continue being in touch with the old days and do their part to continue this mythology into the future. Southerners seem to be increasingly aware that their traditional way of life is passing, and more and more are reaching out to hold on to the few remnants that are left.

This passing is best seen in the changing character of the race itself. Dirt tracks, traditional home of the good old boy, are being replaced by the "nicer" short paved tracks. Change is the name of progress. Family and individual racing teams are dropping out of the Grand National series as the costs of competition skyrocket beyond the resources of all but the very wealthy and the well sponsored. All in the name of progress.

There is nothing wrong with progress, but with each forward step there is also a footprint left behind. Each year stock car racing is a little less southern and a little more contrived. Stock car racing has always been thus. Bill France and NASCAR utilized the mythology of moonshining, good old boys, and hype from the very first day to bring this new world into being. The difference is that the boys no longer race for the hometown crowd. They have become media stars.

These changes in many ways represent what is taking place within the southern mythology as a whole. As the NASCAR elite moves ever increasingly into the national arena, the sport becomes more a media package and less an expression of a way of life. As the new sanitized sport promotes teams and drivers more at home in three-piece suits than overalls, the traditional rural southerner is finding less and less to support. It could be validly argued that Bill Elliott is more popular than Dale Earnhardt because he is visually and personally more of a good old boy. But how long can Elliott maintain this "aw shucks" image among the home folks while he jets to races, endlessly increases his television appearances, and becomes more and more removed from the dirty fingernails that work on his car. Identification is the basis of the support of any sport and stock car racing is no different. How does a good old boy working at the local mill identify with a jet pilot, a television star, a millionaire?

The mythology that has always bound stock car racing to the rural southerner is clearly in jeopardy, just as the entire southern mythology itself moves toward the brink. An extrapolation of the current trends in stock car racing clearly brings only one conclusion, the erosion of traditional support with the nationalization of the activity. This certainly is not a new phenomenon and is currently taking place in everything southern from diet to religion. The problem—if there indeed is a problem—is that television sponsorship is predicated on a large on-site audience. The televised sport needs spectators to create the crowd atmosphere in which the electronic spectator can vicariously participate—the sports equivalent of comedic canned laughter. The increasing televisionization of the sport, along with the changes in the drivers and management, inevitably increases stress within the traditional audiences who still haven't adjusted to the other changes taking place in their society.

Several things inevitably must come out of this trend. The traditional audiences at these events will decline in number. In theory, the declining numbers of good old boys should be replaced by the newly arriving extraregional migrants who are today filling southern cities, but these folks neither like nor appreciate the nuances of Grand National racing. Second, the traditional spectators must find a replacement mythology on which to build their regional identity. This is not as difficult as it might seem. The upgrading of the traditional dirt tracks into higher-speed paved circuits has brought a rebirth of good old boy racing with lots of excitement and opportunity for the common man to identify personally with his heroes. This is racing like it used to be without the high prices, poor seating, and stuffed-shirt city people. But will this rebirth of short track racing inevitably bring increased costs of competition, outside sponsorship, outside drivers and cars, and a second disenfranchisement of the traditional southerner?

Conclusions

Southern stock car racing myth, like most of traditional southern life, is at the brink. The promoters, the sponsors, the media executives want to build a national professional sport. The nationalization of the sport is surely in the offing and just as inevitably the "folk" who built the sport mythology will be shouldered aside by the New South. Another regionalism is being lost to that endless influx of carpetbagging corporate Yankees from the Frost Belt who will embrace it and believe that is it their own. The North inevitably will win again. Or will it? Will Grand National racing survive the crisis and retain its audience? Will the traditional southerner bend and continue attending these television spectacles, or will he reach back to his roots and discover that the sport and all of its mythology still exists on those short paved ovals outside of the vision of all that New South imagery created to make the newly arriving outsiders feel at home?

21

American Golf Courses: A Regional Analysis of Supply

Robert L. Adams and John F. Rooney Jr.

More than 20 million Americans played over 400 million rounds of golf during the centennial year of the game in the United States.[1] Golf, once the purview of the privileged few, now enjoys widespread popularity in this country—a fact reflected in the existence of over 12,500 golf facilities.[2] But access to these facilities is very uneven geographically. Golfers in Myrtle Beach and Palm Beach can choose from a tremendous array of courses while the huge populations of New York City and San Francisco are hard pressed to play under any circumstances. Indeed, the demand for golf in many areas has outstripped the supply of facilities so that the availability of courses has often become the principal factor limiting the growth of the game. This article regionalizes the United States based on variations in access to golf facilities, quantifies and explains those variations, and identifies those regions where courses are in critically short supply.

National Patterns of Access

Access to golf facilities is a function of the number of existing courses, the population pressure on those courses, and the public/private mix of facilities. The national pattern of each of these parameters is portrayed in the following sections.

Reprinted by permission from *Sport Place: An International Journal of Sports Geography* 3 (1989), 2–17.

Number of Golf Holes

In 1888 the first permanent golf club in the United States was founded in Yonkers, New York, and it is to that event that the origin of golf in this country is generally traced. Once introduced, golf diffused rapidly, first through the northeastern and north central regions, and then through the remainder of the country.[3] The growth of American golf has been marked by two periods of very rapid expansion. The first boom occurred during the 1920s—the Golden Age of Sport, a time of burgeoning upper-class prosperity. The wealthy, social elite were intrigued by this "new" game and responded by financing the construction of over four thousand golf courses. These courses were heavily concentrated in the northeastern and north central regions and were predominantly private, exclusive facilities.

The second boom in golf facility construction began in the late 1950s and continued until the mid-1970s. Unlike its predecessor, the dimensions of this boom were nationwide and affected a broad spectrum of the population. Enthusiasm for the game was stimulated by increased visibility—first through President Eisenhower's love of the game and then by television, which brought the exploits of Hogan, Snead, Palmer, and Nicklaus into homes across the nation. Golf was embraced by the middle class for the first time. The democratic revolution that swept the game fueled the construction of approximately six thousand golf facilities during the period. Unlike the boom of the 1920s, this wave of construction was dominated by the development of relatively inexpensive public courses, as golf sought to shed its elitist image.

There are now over 190,000 golf holes in the United States. The number of holes, rather than the number of facilities or courses, is used to measure supply because both courses and facilities often have more or less than eighteen holes. The number of golf holes is thus a better measure of a region's carrying capacity, that is, the number of golfers who can be adequately served. The spatial distribution of these golf holes is very uneven (Fig. 21-1). Despite the fact that golf is a warm-weather game, the heaviest concentration of courses lies in a belt extending from the upper Midwest into the Northeast. Although golf here is a seasonal affair, it is obviously attributed great importance. By contrast, most of the South has a considerably lower concentration of courses, with many counties having few or no golf holes at all. An exception to the relatively sparse distribution in the South lies in a region extending from western Virginia southward through the Carolinas into Florida. In the West, the distribution of holes is of a nodal nature, associated with more widely spaced centers of population. Indeed, as one would expect, the national distribution of golf holes gener-

GOLF HOLES
BY COUNTY

Suffolk
N.Y.
Nassau
N.Y.
Montgomery
Pa.

Number of Holes

1600
1400
1000
400
9 54

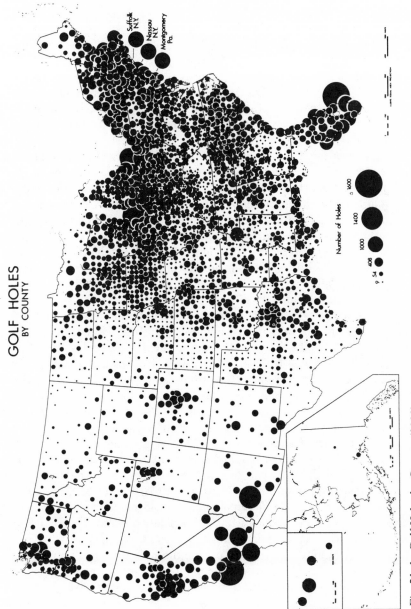

Fig. 21-1. Golf Holes by County (1988)

ally reflects the distribution of population. The correlation, however, is far from perfect.

Golf Holes per Capita by County

The opportunity to play golf is bounded by both the existence of facilities and the playing pressure on them. Many locations are supplied with a large number of courses, but access to them is poor due to heavy population pressure. For instance, the Los Angeles-Long Beach metropolitan area has 1,863 golf holes, yet access, for the average person, ranges from difficult to impossible. A per capita analysis of golf supply provides a truer picture of access to golf facilities (Fig. 21–2).

Broadly speaking, the pattern of per capita access to golf reflects the national distribution of holes. The high concentration of golf holes in the upper Midwest, much of the Northeast, and through portions of the Southeast translates into high per capita access to golf. The sparse distribution of golf holes throughout most of the South translates into generally low per capita availability. The nodal pattern of golf holes in the West creates a patchwork of per capita access. (It should be pointed out, however, that the large size of the counties in this region distorts the areal extent of supply. Both the population and the courses are concentrated in a very small percent of the total area in many of these counties.)

While similarities exist between the areal distributions of holes and per capita access to golf, important differences exist in three regions. A high concentration of golf holes is found both in Megalopolis and on the West Coast, yet both regions are characterized by low per capita availability. In contrast, the Plains region, extending from Kansas to North Dakota, has a moderate to low density of golf holes with extremely high per capita access. Mention of golf seldom evokes images of the Plains, but in terms of per capita availability, this region is the pinnacle of the American game.

A more detailed examination of the per capita access patterns reveals that metropolitan areas often stand out as islands of relatively low availability. The suggested rural/urban bias is confirmed by the fact that people living in nonmetropolitan counties have access to golf at a rate of 117 holes/ 100,000 population, while metropolitan area residents have about half the accessibility, with only 66 holes/100,000 population. Unfortunately nearly 80 percent of the nation's population lives in metropolitan areas.

Significant regional variations do exist in the levels of accessibility among metropolitan areas. The best-served metropolitan areas are strongly clustered either in a band extending from the upper Midwest into New England or in Florida. Naples, Florida is the very best served metropolitan area in

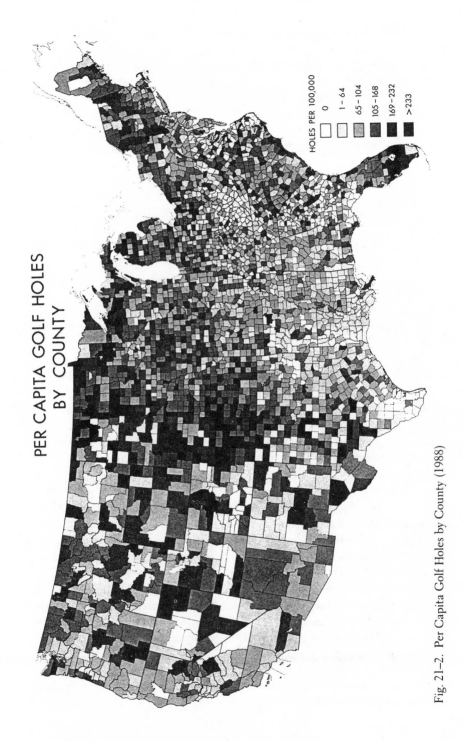

Fig. 21-2. Per Capita Golf Holes by County (1988)

the nation with 599 holes/100,000 population. It should be remembered that the upper Midwest and Florida rank very high in both the total number of holes and the number of holes/100,000 population. The worst-served metropolitan areas are concentrated in Megalopolis, the western Gulf states, and California. The worst-served area is Jersey City, New Jersey, with just three holes/100,000 population. All of these latter regions were previously shown to have generally low per capita access to golf.

Access to Public Golf Facilities

The status of a golf facility, in terms of being public or private, also has a strong bearing on the opportunity to play. A public course is open to anyone willing to pay a green fee; access is limited only by the carrying capacity of the course. Private facilities, open to members only, provide far more restricted opportunities for the population as a whole. The membership of private clubs is usually limited to reduce crowding. Many private clubs have closed memberships or have very long waiting lists as a result. Currently the average wait in New York and Washington, D.C., is nearly five years, and from three to four years in Boston and Chicago.[4] If and when one does gain entrance to a private club, the cost of playing golf usually far exceeds that of a public course—commonly $1,000 to more than $10,000 per year. Membership in private clubs can be very exclusive, with admittance being a function of social status, residential location, or even birthright. Private clubs, therefore, provide the golfer with far more limited opportunities to play than do the more democratic public facilities.

Over 60 percent of golf facilities in the United States are now public, but the ratio of public to private golf facilities varies greatly across the nation. The distribution of the percent of public golf holes by county in many ways mirrors that of total golf holes per capita (Fig. 21–2). Those regions with high per capita access to total holes (portions of the North, the Mountain West, and the South Atlantic) also have a more abundant supply of public golf facilities. Unfortunately for golfers living in Megalopolis and the South, the problem of low per capita access is further exacerbated by the high percentage of private courses in these regions. The major discrepancies between the two distributions (Fig. 21–2) occur on the West Coast and the Plains. Low per capita availability on the West Coast is tempered by a predominance of public facilities. But the Plains, a region of very high per capita access, stands out as a somewhat puzzling discontinuity in the public course dominance of the North.

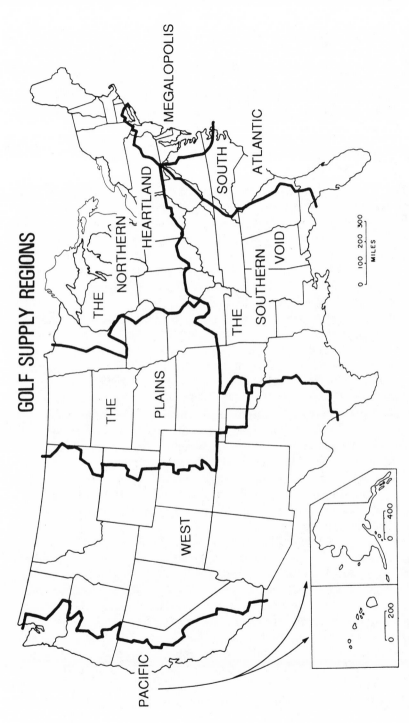

GOLF SUPPLY REGIONS

THE NORTHERN HEARTLAND

MEGALOPOLIS

SOUTH ATLANTIC

SOUTHERN VOID

THE PLAINS

THE

WEST

PACIFIC

0 100 200 300
MILES

0 200

0 400

Fig. 21-3. Golf Supply Regions (1988)

Golf Supply Regions

An examination of the national distribution of golf holes, per capita accessibility, and the ratio of public versus private courses suggests seven distinctive golf supply regions (Table 21–1; Fig. 21–3).

Northern Heartland

The Northern Heartland is the traditional center of American golf. The game was established early and remains firmly rooted in the regional sports culture. Almost 40 percent of the nation's golf holes are now located here. Public golf is available nearly everywhere: in rural areas, small towns, medium-sized metropolitan areas, and throughout the suburban rings surrounding the largest cities. Northern Heartland cities are among the best-served metropolitan areas (e.g., Kankakee, Illinois; Sheboygan, Wisconsin; Utica, New York; and Pittsfield, Massachusetts).

The heavy concentration of golf courses in the Northern Heartland is surprising in view of climatic constraints and the heavily urbanized population. But, as we said before, American golf is a game with northern ties. Though the game was first established around New York City, it quickly spread throughout the Northern Heartland as the sport of the wealthy, social elite. By 1931 over half of all golf facilities were located here. The game became entrenched early in the social and sports fabrics of the region, setting the stage for the demographic revolution in golf during the 1960s and 1970s. That revolution resulted in a huge buildup of public facilities in the Northern Heartland.[5] This relative abundance of golf courses in the region has been preserved by slow population growth over the past three decades. Severe shortages have been confined, as a result, to the region's largest metropolitan areas, such as Chicago and Boston, with their dense populations and high land values.

The strong golf supply characteristic of the Northern Heartland is well illustrated by a cluster of golf-crazed Michigan communities, including Lansing, Grand Rapids, Kalamazoo, Battle Creek, and Jackson. All the counties in this area have in excess of 100 holes/100,000 population with an extremely heavy emphasis on public golf. Play on area courses is very heavy through the relatively short season (seven to eight months). Local course owners claim to host between 30,000 and 50,000 eighteen-hole rounds during a normal season, demonstrating great pressure on facilities even though the areas have some of the highest per capita supply figures in the nation.

It is apparent that the high level of enthusiasm for golf in the Northern

Table 21-1. Regional Access to Golf in the United States

Region	No. of Holes/ 100,000 Population	Percent Public Golf Holes	Metropolitan Counties No. of Holes/ 100,000 Population	Nonmetropolitan Counties No. of Holes/ 100,000 Population	Metropolitan Population Percent of Total 100,000 Population
Northern					
Heartland	96	68	85	147	81
Plains	132	55	90	164	52
South Atlantic	138	55	125	171	74
West	105	63	90	131	70
Southern Void	67	46	62	79	69
Pacific	50	66	47	95	94
Megalopolis	45	48	42	129	97

Source: National Golf Foundation (golf data).
Sales and Marketing Management (population data).

Heartland has both stimulated and been supported by intense course development there. Less obvious is the fact that the golfers of this region have been important catalysts in golf development elsewhere. The resort and retirement golf meccas spread throughout the southern and southwestern portions of the country (Pinehurst, Hilton Head, Phoenix, and Palm Springs for example) are supported, to a very significant degree, by vacationing and transplanted golfers from the Northern Heartland.

Southern Void

The Southern Void is most notable for its extreme paucity of public golf facilities and a generally low ratio of holes per 100,000 population (Table 21–1). The region also contains over one-third of the nation's worst-served metropolitan areas, including Dallas, Atlanta, New Orleans, and Houston. There are few public facilities designed to serve the local residents, particularly in the metropolitan areas and the sparsest populated rural counties. Less than 40 percent of the region's counties contain a public course, and numerous rural counties have no golf facilities. Though private courses raise the regional average, it still pales in comparison to its South Atlantic neighbor, which has twice as many holes per capita. Apparently it takes much more than a positive climatic environment to promote golf course construction.

The Southern Void stands in stark contrast to the Northern Heartland in terms of access to golf facilities. In Michigan and Ohio there is only one county without a golf facility, while 14 percent and 15 percent of the counties in Louisiana and Mississippi, respectively, have no facilities. Furthermore, in Michigan and Ohio nearly all the counties have public courses, but in Louisiana and Mississippi public courses can be found in only about one-third of the counties. To the extent that golf facilities exist in the Southern Void, they are predominantly private. And these private clubs are concentrated in metropolitan areas where they serve the upper class, in resort islands where they serve the transient golfer, or in golf communities where they serve only the residents of the community. In all cases they serve a select, upper-class segment of the population. Golf in the Southern Void is elitist and the exclusivity associated with it is a powerful force limiting the broad-based growth potential of the game there.

Golf is clearly not an integral part of the southern regional sports culture. The Southern Void sports menu has long been dominated by football. Recently basketball has made significant inroads to produce a dual mainstream sports culture.[6] Tennis, swimming, gymnastics, wrestling, and golf have been neglected because of the region's emphasis on team sports. Golf must compete with hunting, fishing, and auto racing at the individual level in this male-oriented sports society. In addition golf here has long had elitist associations that include economic, social, and racial discrimination. These associations, combined with high rates of poverty, have long served to stifle broad-based interest in the game.

The Plains

Per capita access to golf is extremely high in the Plains region, particularly in nonmetropolitan counties which contain nearly one-half of the region's population (Table 21–1). Furthermore, unlike the South Atlantic region where transient golfers exert great pressure on existing facilities, the facilities in the Plains region serve basically the resident population. Almost every county in the Dakotas, Nebraska, and Kansas has a golf course, and virtually all of the play is by locals. The Plains, therefore, ranks number one in terms of access to golf facilities.

The large number of holes per 100,000 population in this region actually does not adequately reflect the high degree of access to the game. Over three-quarters of the golf facilities in the region are of the small, nine-hole variety. These courses are rather evenly distributed over the Plains, serving small to medium-sized population clusters. While the proliferation of nine-hole facilities tends to reduce availability in terms of holes per 100,000 population, the large number and wide distribution of these facilities greatly enhance geographic access to them. Although they are small facilities, they provide abundant opportunities for a dispersed, rural-based population.

Golf developed early in the Plains, especially from the late 1890s into the 1920s. It was a time of great agricultural prosperity that spawned wealthy farmers, merchants, and professionals who often financed the construction of local golf facilities. By 1931 there were approximately one thousand courses in the region, or over 60 percent of today's total. Golf thus became an important part of the social and sports fabrics of the region as it did in the Northern Heartland—a phenomenon that was to sustain interest in the game and promote continued development of facilities. The initial base of facilities was substantially augmented during the 1960s and 1970s when many Plains municipalities took advantage of federal grants to construct courses as part of community recreation projects. Juxtaposed to the construction of a large supply of courses through time has been the stagnant to slow growth of the Plains population since 1930. So the supply of courses here has not been severely diluted by explosive population growth as it has been in many other areas of the country.

Contributing to the abundance of golf facilities in the Plains today is the fact that golf is more than a game. In many small communities the golf club is the focal point of community activity and social life. Small-town and farm residents are united by a sport that serves to bridge most spectrums of the rural-based society. The high per capita availability of golf facilities in the Plains also reflects the elevated sports consciousness of the region, characterized by high participation rates in interscholastic sports and a wide range of adult recreational activities as compared with the rest of the nation. Winter bowlers, curlers, and basketball and racquetball players flock to softball and golf in the summer. The popularity of sport in the region has fostered intensive development of all types of facilities and golf courses are no exception.

The region does have one puzzling golf supply characteristic—a lower percentage of public golf holes than would be expected for a northern, "populist," rural region. The answer likely lies with the fact that many of the present clubs were built during the early decades of the century. They were built by the wealthy elite and were modeled after their private club predecessors in the Northeast. But there is an important distinction between most of the private clubs in the Plains and those that exist elsewhere. They tend to be less expensive and less exclusive, and despite their private status, they serve the needs of a broad spectrum of the local population. The private clubs of the Plains thus do not pose the barriers to participation that they do elsewhere.

South Atlantic

The South Atlantic region has benefited from being in the right place at the right time for golf-oriented development. In recent decades the region has experienced rapid growth in both population and tourism—growth that has been supported by the leisure revolution, younger and wealthier retirees, abundant and cheap air travel, and second home development. This rapid growth coincided with the national boom in golf participation and facility construction that began in the late 1950s. As a result, the South Atlantic region has become America's premier golf mecca for winter vacationers and retirees from the North.

Nonmetropolitan availability of golf facilities is very high (Table 21–1). This availability, to a considerable extent, reflects the proliferation of golf-oriented resorts and retirement communities outside the metropolitan areas, for example in Hot Springs, Virginia; Pinehurst, North Carolina; and Myrtle Beach and Hilton Head, South Carolina. Myrtle Beach is perhaps the epitome of such golf meccas, boasting over forty courses with nineteen more in various stages of construction.

Access to golf in the metropolitan areas of the South Atlantic region is by far the highest of any region. Florida alone contains the nation's top five metropolitan areas in terms of per capita golf supply (Naples, Fort Pierce, Sarasota, West Palm Beach, and Fort Myers). During the past three decades the "instant" metropolitan areas of the region have sprawled outward into rural counties where abundant, low-cost land has made golf course construction economically feasible. Hundreds of metropolitan courses have been built to accommodate and attract the burgeoning population of vacationing and retired golfers since the 1950s. In most cases these courses have been used as tools to enhance the value and attractiveness of resorts and residential developments.[7]

The apparent very high access to golf facilities in the region, however, is deceptive. Per capita access figures based on resident populations fail to account for the hordes of transient golfers that flock to the region. These tourists exert great pressure on existing facilities during the winter and spring months. Severe crowding, six-hour rounds, and unavailable tee times are common. Second, although public course availability is high for the South Atlantic, it is still low in comparison to the Northern Heartland and the West. Much of the recent course development in the region has been in connection with the creation of residential golf communities built around private course cores. Access to such courses is limited to members and their guests. Finally, many of the "public" resort courses in the region are expensive—charging $50 to $100 per round. Thus they are beyond the economic means of a substantial portion of the golfing public.

The West

The West is a sprawling region of low population density interrupted by urban centers. Where there are people, there is golf. There is also a heavy emphasis on public facilities. Rapid population growth in much of the region has been coincidental with the democratic revolution in golf, fostering a proliferation of courses. And the southern half of the region has increasingly become the destination of vacationing golfers and retirees, which has stimulated the development of huge concentrations of courses in Phoenix, Scottsdale, and Tucson. The transient golfer has also been responsible for the creation of many rural resort islands of high golf availability, for example Vail and Sun Valley.

There are some exceptions to the generally high availability of golf facilities in the region. Many large counties are so sparsely settled that they cannot generate enough demand to warrant course construction (Fig. 21–2). Total unfulfilled demand in these instances, however, is not large. Second, population growth in the metropolitan centers of the Southwest has been so rapid that despite a high concentration of courses, crowded conditions often prevail, particularly during the winter-spring tourist season. And although public resort courses abound in many areas, they, like their South Atlantic counterparts, are often too expensive for a large segment of the golfing public.

Megalopolis

This is the most densely populated region in the nation. It is also a region of extremes—great wealth, abject poverty, estates, and tenements. Much of the area has a strong golf tradition associated with the early development of the game in this country. New York City, Philadelphia, and a number of New Jersey cities were early bastions. Unfortunately for aspiring players, golf has been overwhelmed, and in some cases buried, by rampaging population growth and urbanization.

Despite the fact that this region was the hearth of American golf, it is today the worst served of any region. Overall availability is only 45 holes per 100,000 population and availability in metropolitan areas, which contain 97 percent of the region's population, is even lower (Table 21–1). Megalopolis contains a number of the largest and worst-served metropolitan areas in the country, including New York City, Jersey City, Baltimore, and Washington. Golf, quite simply, has not been able to compete with alternative land uses in this region of high population density and extraordinary land values.

To make matters worse, the courses that do exist are predominantly private. Many of the early facilities were built, and are still controlled, by the golfing elite. Even today, it is the private country clubs, with their wealthy memberships, that can best raise the extraordinary capital needed for course construction and maintenance. Public courses exist, but they are in woefully short supply. Overcrowding is the rule on these facilities, with golfers commonly arriving at the courses before dawn to secure tee times for a mid-morning start.

Megalopolis is the epitome of urban golf scarcity. The middle-income residents of Washington, Baltimore, and New York City have almost no opportunity to play the game locally. The central counties of these metropolitan areas are nearly devoid of facilities. The suburban counties would appear to be areas of plenty, but the per capita figures here are highly misleading. Private facilities dominate the suburbs, as exemplified by the quintessential country club landscapes of Westchester and Putnam counties. This is the domain of the wealthy golfing elite. The clubs are extremely expensive, often exclusive, and usually have long waiting lists for membership. They provide golf opportunities to only a small, select segment of the population. Public course availability in the suburbs is very low, even lower than the per capita figures would indicate, for they are besieged by golfers from the entire metropolitan area.

The one apparent anomaly to the scarcity of golf in Megalopolis occurs in the nonmetropolitan counties, where access is at a rate of 129 holes/100,000 population. But it should be noted that there are very few of these counties and, in total, they contain only 3 percent of the region's population. Furthermore they, like the suburbs, are inundated with nonresident play so the effective rate of access is far lower than indicated.

Golf in Megalopolis is geared to the wealthy. Much of the middle class has virtually no access to the game. When the very low rates of access to facilities are applied to the large base population of the region, it is evident that the magnitude of unfulfilled demand here is huge.

The Pacific

The Pacific region is similar to Megalopolis in many respects. Availability of golf facilities is very low, particularly in the metropolitan areas that house 94 percent of the region's population (Table 21–1). California alone contains ten of the worst-served metropolitan areas in the country—Los Angeles, San Francisco, Oakland, Fresno, San Jose, Sacramento, Modesto, Long Beach, Merced, and Anaheim. Again the metropolitan scene is composed of expensive private clubs with long waiting lists and severely overcrowded public facilities. The latent demand for golf here is huge, as it is in Megalopolis.

The region does have a great concentration of courses (Fig. 21–1). Most of these courses have been built since the 1950s, but facility construction has failed to keep pace with the region's rapid population growth. So, despite the addition of new courses, the per capita availability of golf has remained low or even declined in some areas. To make matters worse, some of the fastest-growing metropolitan areas have experienced the demise of existing courses, which have been converted to more lucrative types of land use.

There are also important differences between the Pacific region and Megalopolis. There are many more nonmetropolitan counties in the former and these counties have moderately high access to golf facilities, particularly if they are distant from major urban areas. The Pacific region also has a significantly higher percentage of public courses. While the latter phenomenon may be an expression of a greater willingness to expend public funds on a wide range of public services, it is also related to the region's greater tourist orientation. Many of the region's public courses fall into the resort category and include some of the world's best, e.g., Pebble Beach and Spyglass Hill on the Monterey Peninsula. But a round of golf on these resort courses in California and Hawaii can cost $80-$100. Such facilities do little to accommodate the demands of the middle-class spectrum of local golfers. Rather, the amenity resources of California and Hawaii attract throngs of vacationing golfers who exert great pressure on, and severely dilute, the public course resources of the region.

Problems and Prospects

Golf course construction continues, but at rates greatly reduced from those of the 1960s and 1970s as the result of upward spiraling land and construction costs, heightened environmental concerns, and a generally less favorable economic climate. As of November 1, there were 171 new courses opened during 1988 in the United States (Fig. 21–4). The distribution of these courses is typical of new construction in recent years, and unfortunately, it reinforces, to a considerable extent, preexisting regional inequities

1988 COURSE OPENINGS*

• = ONE GOLF FACILITY

* " THROUGH NOVEMBER 1, 1988 "

Fig. 21–4. Golf Course Openings (1988)

in supply. Over one-half of the 1988 openings occurred in the Northern Heartland and South Atlantic regions, both already relatively well served with facilities. So it is clear that even in these regions of apparent plenty, there is substantial unfulfilled demand for golf. The important role that golf plays in the social and sports structure of the Northern Heartland continues to promote development there. Simultaneously, the South Atlantic region continues to respond to the burgeoning resort and retirement market and rapid population growth. Golf is very important to both regions and both are in the forefront of new course construction.

New development in the Plains and the West was slow, accounting for 4 percent and 10 percent of 1988 openings respectively. While this sluggish construction undoubtedly reflects recent downturns in the agricultural and energy sectors of the regions, it may also indicate that the Plains and the northern half of the West are the only areas where the demand for golf facilities is being adequately met. Per capita availability here is high and population growth has been slow. Such, however, is not the case in the Southwest. Here explosive population growth and a flourishing tourist sector have resulted in supply shortages. This is particularly evident in metropolitan areas during the peak winter-spring season. Unfortunately golf course construction in the Southwest is becoming increasingly difficult. Pressures on fragile natural landscapes and tight water supplies have produced strong opposition from environmentalists and others. Many proposed courses have been blocked. Those that gain approval frequently endure long delays entailing substantial legal and organizational costs. The southwestern golf battle will be long and expensive, and it is doubtful that construction can keep up with the growth of population and tourism.

Megalopolis and the Pacific region, both with extreme shortages of facilities, were the location of only 5 percent and 7 percent of 1988 course additions respectively. The twenty-one new courses will do little to rectify current shortages, for these additions are insufficient to merely keep pace with population growth. The outlook is not bright for these regions. With their huge, dense, highly urbanized populations, they will never be adequately supplied with golf facilities. There are, however, some possibilities that could be explored to ameliorate the situation. Computer reservation networks might be established to ensure maximum use of existing facilities. Golfers could call area service centers to determine where and when tee times are available and make reservations. The construction of multicourse complexes in the rural environs of metropolitan areas should be explored. Other recreational facilities might be included so they could serve as bases for general family recreation. Bus transportation might link these complexes with proximate metropolitan populations. The organizational talents of metropolitan ski clubs have long enhanced access to remote ski areas for throngs of city dwellers. The concept of urban golf "clubs" in conjunction with remote multicourse facilities might be equally successful.

Greater emphasis should be placed on developing surrogates for the regulation golfing experience in Megalopolis and the Pacific region— alternatives with lower acreage requirements. These include short courses, called executive and par-3 facilities, driving ranges, and golf centers. They provide ideal learning environments. And in areas of facility shortage, they allow for continued involvement with golf and have proved to be highly successful economic ventures.

The most encouraging revelation on the map of 1988 golf course openings is an apparent awakening in the Southern Void. Twenty percent of the nation's new courses were built there, with evident concentrations around the poorly served metropolitan areas of Atlanta, Houston, and Dallas. The Southern Void would appear to be a region of both great need and promise—poised for growth. It shares climatic amenities with regions of enormous golf development to the east and west. In contrast though, the Southern Void is not beset with impending water shortages and high land costs. The region would appear to be well positioned to tap the resort and retirement golf market and to remove the shortages that plague local golfers.

There is one type of golf shortage in the United States that knows no regional boundaries—an inadequate supply of moderately priced, public courses in metropolitan areas.[8] The shortage is pervasive and of critical proportions. Everywhere the same two barriers to development exist: the high cost of construction and the exorbitant price of scarce land. Both of these constraints tend to render the creation of a moderately priced, public facility economically unfeasible.

Nevertheless, the problem is approachable. The golf industry needs to retreat from its love affair with "championship" courses designed by high-priced architects. These tracks are long, torturous, highly manicured, and extremely expensive to construct and maintain. The economics of such courses translate into $40 to $80 rounds—beyond the reach of most golfers who suffer from a lack of opportunity to play. The need is not for a proliferation of Pebble Beaches; the need is for some place to play. Paramount among the design objectives for metropolitan public courses should be low construction costs, low maintenance costs, and rapid speed of play. Only then will moderately priced facilities become economically viable.

The second problem, the high cost of scarce land in metropolitan areas, poses more difficulties. Again the situation is not necessarily hopeless. A story might be illuminating—a true one. A few years ago a country club in southern New Hampshire was developing long-range plans for improvement. The estimated costs for the necessary alterations were staggering and were regarded by many as excessive, in view of the limited potential of the current site. The alternative of moving the club to a more favorable site was suggested. The elderly owner of a beautiful, rolling 300-acre farm was approached. He was crestfallen. He loved his farm; he had no living relatives; and for years he had been unsuccessfully exploring alternatives to development—something that would be worthy of the land that he had cared for so meticulously and for which he had such great affection. Unfortunately, just months previous, the developers had finally won. He would have been thrilled if his farm had become a golf course. It would have remained as open space; it would have been beautifully maintained; it would have provided enjoyment to the many who played on it long into the future. It was the legacy for which he had been searching, but the idea had never occurred to him. After all, there was a golf club only half a mile down the road. It was that club that was searching for a new site. Sad story.

Like most sad stories, the one above contains a lesson. When one flies over metropolitan regions, it is striking how many large tracts of open land lie within and proximate to the built-up area. How many of these tracts are held by people with situations and attitudes similar to those of the New Hampshire farmer? To how many has the idea of a golf course never occurred? The possibilities should be explored through comprehensive land surveys. To wait for appropriate parcels to come to the open market is generally futile. Many parcels would never be offered in this way and those that do come to the open market command developers' prices. Systematic surveys and personal contact will not solve all metropolitan golf problems, but many gems might be uncovered that would otherwise remain undiscovered. The effort is certainly warranted, for the demand is huge. And the bottom line reads—no more affordable land in metropolitan areas, no more moderately priced, public golf courses.

Solutions to the critical shortage of reasonably priced, public golf facilities will be difficult to achieve and will require innovative approaches. If solutions are not found, the price will be paid by the middle-class golfer. That huge segment of the golfing population, whose interests were kindled during the 1960s and 1970s, will gradually be excluded from the game. And American golf will inevitably return to whence it came—the domain of the wealthy elite.

Notes

1. The National Golf Foundation was the source of all golf facility data used in this study.

2. A "golf facility" is a site with one or more courses under single ownership.

3. Robert L. A. Adams and John F. Rooney Jr., "The Evolution of American Golf Facilities," *Geographical Review* 75 (October 1985), 419–38.

4. *Golf Digest* (October 1988), 14.

5. Adams and Rooney, 426–31.

6. John F. Rooney Jr., "The Pigskin Cult and Other Sunbelt Sports," *American Demographics* (September 1986), 38–43.

7. Robert L. A. Adams and John F. Rooney Jr., "Condo Canyon: An Examination of Emerging Golf Landscapes in America," *North American Culture* 1 (1984), 65–75.

8. Robert L. A. Adams, "The Crisis in Public Golf Course Development," in *Golf Projections 2000* (Jupiter, Fla.: National Golf Foundation, 1987), 32–41.

22

The Golf Construction Boom,
1987–1993

John F. Rooney Jr.

Over sixteen hundred new golf facilities and additions were opened between 1987 and 1993 (Fig. 22–1). The most important trend is the focus on public access to the game. Over 80 percent of the facilities opened during 1990–93 are public (Fig. 22–2).

Developers and communities have responded to a need that has been intensely emphasized at every national golf gathering since the 1986 Westchester Summit (Graph 22–1). Most would agree that there was a pressing need for additional facilities. The miniboom in golf course construction, however, raises a number of pertinent questions. Were the new courses built in the right locations? How many additional courses can the United States support, now and in the future? What is the minimum carrying capacity for a golf facility (for profitability)? What is the maximum carrying capacity, after which the golf experience begins to deteriorate? Have some markets now reached saturation? How many and what percentage of golf courses are providing an unsatisfactory experience because of poor maintenance, inadequate service, or obsolescence? The answers to these questions are important to the assessment of the resurgence in golf facility construction.

Geographical variation in new golf facility development from 1987 to 1993 is evident (Fig. 22–1). Returning to the earlier query, were these golf

Reprinted by permission from *Sport Place: An International Journal of Sports Geography* 7 (1993), 15–22.

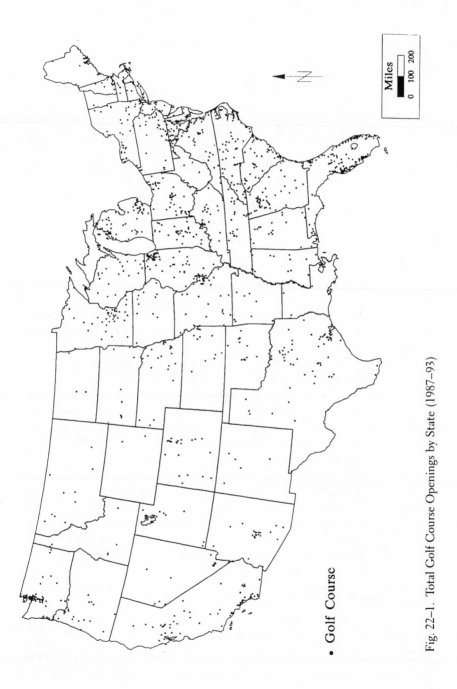

• Golf Course

Fig. 22–1. Total Golf Course Openings by State (1987–93)

Fig. 22–2. New Public Golf Courses (1990–93)

courses built in the right places? We know that variations in golf participation rates are largely a function of access to municipal courses and daily fee golf. That is why participation is so high across the northern United States (Northern Heartland region), where almost every small town has a golf course. Thus we have high rates of participation (15 to 20 percent) in states well supplied with public courses, whereas low rates (5 to 10 percent) are found in states poorly supplied with public courses.

It is vital, therefore, that the new courses are constructed in areas with pent-up demand. Many metropolitan areas, particularly the largest areas, were in short supply of public golf. Construction since 1987 has alleviated some of those critical shortages. For example, Atlanta, Dallas, Houston, and Louisville, all in the Southern Void, have added substantially to their public sector inventory. Moreover, urban areas in the Northern Heartland have likewise increased their number of public courses, especially Chicago, Detroit, Columbus, and Minneapolis-St. Paul.

Resort areas have also flourished. This is particularly true for Florida's east coast, Cape Cod, northern Michigan, the Carolinas, Colorado, and the desert Southwest. Our data demonstrate that most of these resort destinations are geared to northeastern and midwestern golf travelers. As such they can be viewed as an enhancement to supply in those regions.

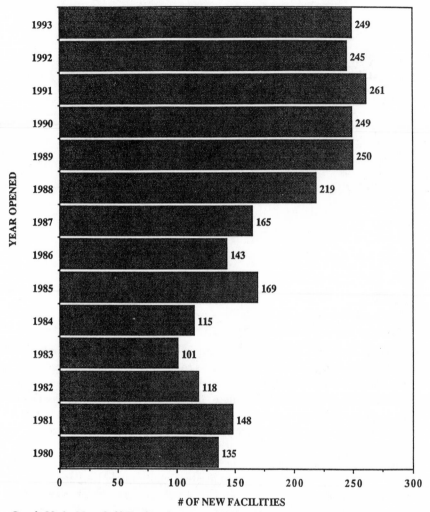

Graph 22–1. New Golf Facility Openings (1980–93)

Let us return to our original question. Were these facilities built in the right places? In most cases, the answer is yes. The construction surge has brought supply in balance with demand in some metropolitan areas: St. Louis, Omaha, Portland, and Indianapolis. Access has improved dramatically around Baltimore, Washington, and Boston.

Severe shortages, however, still remain. Construction in California has barely touched the supply deficit. Los Angeles, for example, has less than

40 percent of the courses that it could theoretically support. San Francisco and San Jose, where demand is extremely high, could support substantial additions to their course base.

Major problems continue to plague a number of eastern and southern markets, particularly in the public and daily fee arena. New York City, Philadelphia, and many of the fast-growing suburban ("edge cities") in New Jersey, Connecticut, Maryland, and Virginia are in desperate need of more golf courses.

Southeastern Sun Belt cities have finally begun to identify with the game. Demand across the South continues to be low as compared to the Northern Heartland. It remains to be seen whether the new urban affinity for golf there will spread to the small towns and rural communities as it has done throughout the North.

In summary, the recent upswing in golf course construction has helped to balance supply and demand. It has solved the public access problem in a number of cities. But in other places it has simply been a case of the rich getting richer: more and better courses in the strongest markets. Major shortfalls remain and it will require creative genius and substantial capital to generate construction in California and the Northeast.

23

Selected Reading VII

Chapters 19, 20, 21, and 22

Bale, John. *Sports Geography*. New York: Spon, 1989.

Boyle, Robert H. *Sport: Mirror of American Life*. Boston: Little, Brown, 1963.

Guttman, A. *A Whole New Ball Game: An Interpretation of American Sports*. Chapel Hill: University of North Carolina Press, 1988.

Hoffmann, Frank, and Bailey, William G. *Sports and Recreation Fads*. Binghamton, N.Y.: Haworth Press, 1991.

Isaacs, Neil. *Jock Culture, USA*. New York: Norton, 1978.

Loy, J. W., and Kenyon, Gerald S. *Sport, Culture, and Society*. London: Macmillan, 1969.

Michener, James. *Sports in America*. New York: Random House, 1976.

Rader, Benjamin S. *American Sports: From the Age of Folk Games to the Age of Spectators*. Englewood Cliffs, N.J.: Prentice-Hall, 1983.

Riess, Steven. *City Games: The Evolution of American Urban Society and the Rise of Sports*. Urbana: University of Illinois Press, 1989.

Rooney, John F., Jr., and Pillsbury, Richard. "Sports Regions," *American Demographics* 14 (1993): 30–39.

———. *Atlas of American Sport*. New York: Macmillan, 1992.

Rooney, John F., Jr. *A Geography of American Sport: From Cabin Creek to Anaheim*. Reading, Mass.: Addison-Wesley, 1974.

Wells, Twombly. *200 Years of Sport in America*. New York: McGraw-Hill, 1976.

Index

About the Contributors

Robert L. Adams is associate professor at the University of New Hampshire. His Ph.D. is from Clark University and research specialties include recreation, tourism, and sport.

Laurence W. Carstensen received his Ph.D. from the University of North Carolina. He is currently associate professor of geography at Virginia Tech, where his specialties include cartography and geographic information systems.

James R. Curtis specializes in urban, cultural, and Latin American geography at California State University–Long Beach where he is assistant professor of geography. His Ph.D. is from the University of California–Los Angeles.

Richard V. Francaviglia is director of the Center for Greater Southwestern Studies at the University of Texas–Arlington. He holds a Ph.D. in historical–cultural geography from the University of Minnesota.

Warren G. Gill is executive director at Harbour Centre, Simon Fraser University in Vancouver, British Columbia. He is an urban/transportation geographer with a Ph.D. from the University of British Columbia.

Beverly Gordon is associate professor in the Department of Environment, Textiles and Design at the University of Wisconsin–Madison and serves as director of the Helen Allen Textile Collection.

John A. Jakle specializes in the vernacular landscapes of America at the University of Illinois–Urbana where he is professor of geography. His Ph.D. is from the University of Indiana.

Albert LeBlanc is professor of music at Michigan State University, where he specializes in popular music.

Richard Pillsbury received his Ph.D. from Pennsylvania State University. He is professor of geography at Georgia State University and specializes in American ethnic geography, foodways, and sport.

John F. Rooney Jr. is emeritus Regents professor of geography at Oklahoma State University, where he continues to specialize in sports geography. His Ph.D. is from Clark University.

Stephen W. Tweedie is associate professor of geography at Oklahoma State University. His specialties include applied geography, recreation and sport, and Eastern Europe. He holds a Ph.D. from Syracuse University.

Barbara A. Weightman is professor of geography at California State University–Fullerton. Her specialty is the geography of religions and belief systems. She holds a Ph.D. from the University of Washington.

Wilbur Zelinsky is emeritus professor of geography at Pennsylvania State University, where he specializes in historical, cultural, and ethnic geography. His Ph.D. is from the University of California–Berkeley.

About the Editor

George O. Carney is professor of geography at Oklahoma State University where he has taught introductory cultural geography since 1969. His other teaching interests include music geography, the history and philosophy of geography, and historic preservation. He holds degrees from Central Missouri State University (B.A. in geography and M.A. in history) and Oklahoma State University (Ph.D. in American social history). Dr. Carney has authored more than sixty-five publications including six books and numerous journal articles, monographs, and book reviews. He has been awarded grants from both public and private agencies including the National Endowment for the Humanities, National Endowment for the Arts, National Park Service, Atlantic-Richfield Foundation, and the Smithsonian Institution. His honors include awards for both teaching and research: *Journal of Geography* Best Content Article, National Council for Geographic Education Distinguished Teaching Award, Oklahoma State University Regents Distinguished Teaching Award, American Association for State and Local History Certificate of Commendation, Association of American Geographers Applied Geography Award, and the George H. Shirk Memorial Award for Historic Preservation in Oklahoma. His popular culture maps have appeared in such diverse outlets as the *Washington Post*, the *Encyclopedia for Southern Culture*, and the Public Broadcasting System (PBS) network.